may anthologies 2002

tenth anniversary edition

edited by Andrew Motion and Nick Cave

Varsity/Cherwell

Varsity Publications Ltd
11–12 Trumpington St
Cambridge CB2 1QA

First published 2002 by Varsity Publications Ltd

This collection © Varsity Publications Ltd 2002

ISBN number 0 902240 33 1

Typeset in Baskerville by Ed Hall
Produced by Origen Production
Printed and bound in ROI

Original concept by Peter Ho Davies, Adrian Woolfson,
Ron Dimant

Permission to reprint "Tiresias", excerpted from Stephen Burt's *Popular Music*,
granted by the publisher, the Center for Literary Publishing.

Permission to reprint "The Newspaper Man" and "Mrs Begum's Son and the
Private Tutor" granted by A P Watt Ltd on behalf of Zadie Smith.

A CIP catalogue record for this book is available from the British Library.

Further copies of this book and other titles in the series can be bought
through Oxford and Cambridge bookshops or direct from Varsity
Publications Ltd.

Editors:	Rachel Aspden (Cambridge)
	Tim Martin (Cambridge)
	Benjamin Hewitt (Oxford)
	Thomas Hill (Oxford)

Editors:
Rachel Aspden (Cambridge)
Tim Martin (Cambridge)
Benjamin Hewitt (Oxford)
Thomas Hill (Oxford)

Executive Editors:
Andrew Motion
Nick Cave

Publisher:
Ed Hall

Subeditors:
Glenda Newton
Rudolf Eliott Lockhart

Cover Photo:
Katie Pelen

Cover Design:
Ed Hall, Katie Pelen

Editorial Committees: Sarah Penn, Sarah Price, Lynn Morris, Sean Forester, Emily Haworth-Booth, Sarah Savitt, Eliza Young, Jeremy Young, Jon Stainsby, Laura Barnett, Elaine Moore

With many thanks to:
Our main sponsors: Bloomsbury, Hodder Headline

also to:
Cambridge College Sponsors: Clare, Jesus, Churchill, King's, Corpus Christi, Clare Hall, Lucy Cavendish, Robinson, Sidney Sussex, Fitzwilliam, Gonville and Caius, Queens'; Oxford College Sponsors: Christ Church, Balliol, Merton, Queen's; the Christopher Tower Fund and Natwest, Cambridge branch

Thanks also to Carole Blake, Tim Harris, Dr Michael Franklin, Diana Tapp, Joti at Natwest, Linda Barnett at Origen, Lionel Parker, Ken Barnett, Rob Sharp, Simon Elliston Ball, and everyone who submitted work

Contents

May Anthologies 2002

A Selection from the Last Ten Years: May Anthologies 1992–2001

May Anthologies 2002

Foreword

All anthologies offer the delight of surprise – of unexpected combinations, strange differences, unpredictable links. This book is no exception – but it gives another kind of reward as well. Because it contains the work of writers who are close to the beginning of their writing lives (and who in many cases are publishing here for the first time), it has a workshop-floor quality. This can mean lack of polish, inelegance, even confusion. But it also means freshness, excitement, risk – and these dominate everything that follows. The range is impressive, the intelligence properly watchful, and the emotional weight substantial. A heartening confirmation, in fact, of what anyone buying this book would want to feel: that new writing in Oxford and Cambridge is thriving.

Andrew Motion

Europa
Nicki Heinen

Tricksy Jupiter had a grin in his eye.

Spanning fields in a wink and wiping the god from his handsome brow
he landed four limbed,
hands to hooves and feet cloven
to the whisper of her summer dress.

His skin bred soft silk poils
as he gambolled among clean stiff poppies.

His back twisted on the ground,
and she in the noon light
caught his gaze as blood clots in the vein.

Was it girl or plaything of dark skies came forward
long hand outstretched and lips flushed,
to the rise and trembling fall of his breaths?

She listened as the heat sighed her name
and the bend of her waist met his.

A swallow circled in the haze
where they lay,
her lashes dusting his pale coat,
her heavy lids closing.

The light shrank.

At evening
cold air and ocean spray woke her,
and her eyes drank in sea,
black waves rolling to the black horizon.

Sometimes, by night,
you can taste her salt tears in the waters.

Wyatt and Me
Jeff Kochan

I want to write about Wyatt. I don't know. I'm not much of a writer but I think maybe writing things down sometimes helps you understand them better. Wyatt is my neighbour. We live down in McNally Flats on 72nd Avenue. My house is number 11 and Wyatt's is number 12, right across the street. I moved into my house last March. I noticed it one day when I was delivering equipment to the old brick factory on the river and didn't think I could afford it, but I'd paid off my truck that summer so I called anyway. It wasn't too much and the relator said it was because the house is old and small and everybody wants new and big these days. I like it though. It's made with bricks from that factory and there's enough room in back for my truck. Besides it's just me and Shelby and she spends most of her time outside anyway.

It was still pretty cold when I moved in so there wasn't much happening outdoors. I notice things like that because my desk is pushed right up against the front window and sometimes when I get tired of reading I like to sit and look at the street. Wyatt's house faces south and gets lots of sun so I guess that's why Shelby started going over there and sitting on the front step. It worried me a little at first because I didn't know who lived there or if they liked cats, but Shelby's real independent so I just let her.

I saw Wyatt for the first time at the beginning of April. I remember when because I'd been really busy with deliveries the last two weeks of March and so I decided to stay home for a few days and just read and maybe relax a bit. I guess it was about ten in the morning and I was sitting and looking out the window because I had been reading poetry and I have to stop to think a lot when I read poetry. That's when I saw Wyatt. He came out from around the back of his house carrying a pair of hedge clippers. Wyatt's house is like mine, except bigger and there's a hedge in front, which is why he had the clippers. Wyatt was wearing an old brown sweater and a baseball cap, so I couldn't see those eyes of his, just a few dark curls sticking out around his ears. I remember I thought how big his hands were. Even from way across the street I could tell.

Wyatt started sort of cutting at the hedge and I remember thinking how funny it was, him trimming his hedge like that when it was only the beginning of April, but that's just Wyatt I guess. Anyway, Wyatt was working at his hedge when all of a sudden he stopped and looked around to the front of his house. That's when I saw Shelby sitting on Wyatt's front step. She must have meowed or something and got Wyatt's attention. I don't know. Maybe it's dumb, but I got a little scared seeing Shelby there and Wyatt with those hedge clippers and

14

those big hands. But I guess they already knew each other because Wyatt walked right on over, put down those clippers and just started petting Shelby. I was pretty impressed. Shelby usually kind of likes to keep to herself, but with Wyatt's hands touching her like that she just sort of laid down and stretched.

I started seeing Wyatt every once in a while after that, usually in the morning if I didn't have any deliveries scheduled or if it was Sunday. He would come out from around his house or I'd look up and he'd already be there with some garden tool in his hand and wearing that old sweater and cap. Usually he'd try cutting at the hedge or he'd push around a bit in the flower beds with a hoe, but I guess maybe he never really knew what he was doing and he always gave up after a few minutes. Sometimes Shelby would be there and then Wyatt would just sit right down and start petting. I liked that, when he petted Shelby. I don't know. I guess there are just some people who even if you've never met them you can't keep from looking at and wondering what they must be like. That was Wyatt. Seeing Shelby making friends with him like that made me feel kind of good, like maybe I knew Wyatt too.

I remember one Sunday morning sometime about the middle of May I was out trying to fix up some of the brickwork on the front of my house and I sort of looked up from what I was doing and glanced over at Wyatt's house. He was there, sitting on his front step drinking from a cup that steamed. I kind of waited, seeing if maybe he saw me, but he just sat there staring at his hedge and flower beds and sipping sometimes from that cup. I tried to go back to work but I couldn't concentrate. I kept trying to think of how I could say hello and I kept looking over to see if maybe he was noticing me, but Wyatt just kept staring. I wished Shelby was over there because then maybe I could walk over and get her and then I could say hello to Wyatt. But Shelby was out back hunting mice in the raspberry bushes. I tried working for a little while longer but my hands started shaking a bit so I quit and went around back to see how Shelby was doing.

A few days later in the evening my doorbell rang. I looked out the front window like I always do because usually it's someone trying to sell you something but I saw that it was Wyatt. I guess I felt kind of nervous right then, thinking maybe Shelby had done something and Wyatt had come to complain or maybe Wyatt knew I watched him sometimes and he was going to give me a piece of his mind. I almost didn't open the door but then I thought that was dumb and anyway he was friends with Shelby so I opened it. I guess I was kind of surprised. Wyatt is quite a bit shorter than I am. He's not really little, just sort of small, and I could tell that he was still probably pretty strong. You'd think it might look kind of strange with those big hands of his and him being small, but it was okay. I guess Wyatt's just about right.

Anyway, the main thing about Wyatt are those eyes of his. Wyatt's got these big eyes that kind of look right into you. They're not scary or anything, just kind of deep I guess, and maybe sort of sad. Sometimes when he looks at you it's hard to look away.

So Wyatt was standing right there on my front step introducing himself. That's when I first knew his name was Wyatt. I told him my name and then didn't know what else to say so I just stood there. Then Wyatt said he was a sculptor and that he had sold a sculpture and he needed to deliver it and he was wondering if he could hire my truck. I said okay and that I was free the morning after tomorrow and he told me the sculpture was big and that we'd need a forklift so I said I'd get one.

After Wyatt left I tried to read for a little while but couldn't concentrate. I didn't sleep very well the next two nights and I kept thinking about how I live across the street from a sculptor.

Wyatt builds his sculptures in a big tall shed behind his house. His back-yard is a real sight. There's a couple of apple trees and some bushes and a big garden that's all weeds and there's steel everywhere, pieces of sheet and plate and lengths of pipe and rod and even a few I-beams and a vessel head. Right in the middle of the garden are three sculptures that are sort of sunk into the dirt and rusting.

I pulled my truck up about eight-thirty and Wyatt was there. We went into the shed and, I don't know, that sculpture was pretty big. It was maybe nine feet high and four feet wide and it was just standing there on a pallet and, well, I guess sometimes I just say things and when I saw Wyatt's sculpture I said I thought it looked like poetry. I felt dumb, like I didn't know anything, but Wyatt said thanks so I guess it was okay. He told me the sculpture was called Sound of Tears and it's funny because when I looked at it again I thought maybe that's what it sort of looked like.

I set the runners up and drove the forklift down off the bed of the truck and into Wyatt's shed. I got the forks in under the sculpture and raised it up a few inches and then started working it out of the shed while Wyatt stood back and watched. I got that sculpture outside and up onto the front part of the bed and then drove the forklift back up the runners and parked it behind the sculpture. Wyatt and me threw some chains around his sculpture just to make sure and then Wyatt locked up the shed while I secured the runners and we got in the truck. I drove real slow.

We took the sculpture up to Temple Hill where a lot of rich people live and I felt kind of funny driving my truck along those streets, but I guess they could see we were carrying a sculpture and that it was okay. Wyatt pointed to a big house with lots of windows and said that's it so I stopped and while he went to ring the doorbell I took the chains off the sculpture and then set up the runners and brought down the forklift. Wyatt came back with a man who was bald and the man told me to put the sculpture on a concrete pad in the middle of his front lawn. The pad was round and looked new and I put Wyatt's sculpture right down in the middle of it, but the man said to move it and that it looked better that way.

The man talked to Wyatt while I drove the forklift back up onto the truck and secured the runners and chains. When I got back I saw Wyatt was holding a cheque for a lot of money and that a woman had come out of the house and was standing next to the man. She asked the man what the sculpture was called and he said Samson's Fears and she said who's Samson and the man told her that she was stupid and didn't know anything. I felt mad, and I wanted to tell the man that he was stupid and that that wasn't the name of the sculpture at all, but I looked at Wyatt and he was just standing there looking down at the ground and I was just the truck driver so I kept quiet.

Back in the truck Wyatt sat there with that cheque in his hand and stared out the window and didn't say anything and I guess maybe he was feeling pretty bad. I tried to think of something to say and then I remembered something I'd heard about how a man can have a lot of dollars and no sense and so I said that. Wyatt smiled and shook his head and said he thought that maybe I was right. Then he put the cheque in his pocket and I thought maybe he was feeling a bit better and so I felt better too. We talked a little bit on the way home and when I dropped him off Wyatt tried to give me some money and I said that's okay we're neighbours and that the forklift owner owed me a favour. Wyatt said okay and that he would see me later. I went to return the forklift and do some deliveries and I remember how I kept smiling all afternoon.

I didn't talk to Wyatt for a few days after that. I was really busy with my truck right then and I wasn't around at all during the day. That first night after dinner I thought maybe I would go over and ring the doorbell and say hello but, I don't know, Wyatt and me still didn't really know each other and I guess I thought just showing up like that for no real reason might look kind of dumb. I remember how a couple of nights later I was sitting at my desk reading and I looked up and saw Wyatt standing in his front window. It sort of surprised me and I looked away and I guess I felt kind of funny knowing that maybe Wyatt was looking at me, but then I thought he was probably just looking at the street so I looked back but he was gone. I don't know. Sometimes I just get really scared and I feel confused and I wish things were different. I didn't fall asleep for a long time that night and the next morning I didn't want to go to work but I had deliveries scheduled for the whole day and besides I own a house now.

The next day was Sunday so I wasn't working but my truck had been running kind of rough that week so I got up early anyway and went out back to do some work on it. I cleaned the air and fuel filters and checked the injector timing and I was loosening up the push rods when I heard someone walking up alongside the truck. I looked up and saw it was Wyatt. He said hi and I said hi back and he said he just wanted to thank me again for helping him with his sculpture and I said it was no problem. Then he asked me what I was doing and I said adjusting the clearance on the exhaust valves. Wyatt said oh and then he just sort of stood there and looked down and kicked a bit at the gravel and, I don't know, I thought maybe he didn't know what I meant so I said did he want to see. He said sure and then he stepped up onto the bumper next to me and watched while I worked and explained what I was doing and a bit about how a diesel engine works. Wyatt asked some questions and I could see

17

he was interested and I felt pretty good and, well, I guess maybe kind of nervous and excited too because Wyatt was right there and I've never really taught something to someone before.

When I was finished with the valves I replaced the rocker cover and Wyatt asked me if I played crib and I said yes but not for a long time. He said that's okay and maybe I could come over for a game later and I said sure after I finished up with the truck and got cleaned up. He said come by in the afternoon.

Wyatt left and I adjusted the idle on the truck and then started the engine and let it warm up so I could recheck the valves. While I was sitting in the cab letting the engine warm I tried real hard to remember how you play crib.

That afternoon I went over to Wyatt's. He was in back and it was a nice day so he had an old card table set up with a crib board and a deck of cards and a jug of real iced tea. Shelby was there too, fooling around in the weeds over where those three sculptures are in the garden. Wyatt said hi and gave me a glass of iced tea and we sat and talked a little bit before we started playing crib. It took me a game before I could remember everything, but after that I did okay. It was pretty good. I don't know. I know some people because of driving my truck but it's a long time since I really just sort of sat like that with someone. I guess I kind of keep to myself and I'm not really much of a talker but Wyatt didn't seem to mind just sitting and playing crib and not talking too much. It was pretty good.

After that Wyatt and me played crib most Sundays and Wyatt showed me how to play gin rummy too. He told me a little bit about being a sculptor and I sometimes told him about something I'd read or a funny story about Shelby or driving a truck and he always laughed at the stories. It's funny because I sometimes feel kind of dumb around people, like I never say the right things or they don't know what I mean, but I didn't really feel that way around Wyatt and that's when I started thinking maybe Wyatt and me were becoming friends.

I remember on the Canada Day long weekend Wyatt and me were playing gin rummy in his backyard and we kind of lost track of time and it got to be time for supper so I asked him if he wanted to come over for some of the stew I'd made that morning. He said sure and while he put away the card table and chairs and things I went home to warm up the stew and make some biscuits which are pretty quick and easy. Wyatt came by and we ate and he said it was really good and that he hadn't had a good meal like that in a long time and, I don't know, I guess it was true because he ate two big bowls and a whole bunch of biscuits and it made me feel pretty good. After supper we did the dishes and then Wyatt went into the living room while I made some coffee.

I brought the coffee and some poppy seed cake into the living room and set them on the coffee table. Wyatt was standing in front of my bookcase looking at my books. I don't know. I think maybe I felt a little nervous just then because it was the first time I'd had someone in my house and no one had ever seen my books. Maybe it's dumb, but I guess I think since I'm only a truck driver and because I never finished school people might get mad or think I'm stupid for trying to read all these books and maybe I'm not real smart but sometimes I get kind of angry and confused and I think maybe those people are just dumb and that I don't understand anything about the way things are. Anyway, I guess that's why I never really tell people about my books.

But I'm pretty sure Wyatt didn't think my books were dumb. He just kept standing there in front of the bookcase and looking at them and then he asked me what I was reading right then. I went over to my desk and I brought him the book about soldiers in World War One and the one about the Alberta pioneers and the Walt Whitman one. Wyatt took the World War One book and looked at it and said he wished he knew more about the First World War and so I said he could borrow it. Wyatt set the book down on the coffee table and then he looked up at the bookcase and took down the big book on gardening. I said that that book had some really nice pictures in it and he nodded and flipped through a few of the pages and then closed the book and laid one of his big hands across the cover and just sort of stared at it for a while. Then he said that his mother liked gardening and, I don't know, the way he said it made me feel kind of scared, like I didn't want to hear any more. But Wyatt put the book back on the shelf and he looked at me with those eyes of his and then he told me his mother was really sick and that she was going to die soon. I don't know. All of a sudden I just felt really scared and I looked at Wyatt and I thought maybe I should put my arms around him and say it was okay, but I guess I wasn't sure if that was all right so I just said that I was sorry and how I had never known my real mother. Then I didn't know what else to say so I said the coffee was getting cold.

We sat done on the sofa and drank our coffee and ate some cake and didn't say anything for a long time. Shelby jumped up onto the sofa between us and Wyatt started scratching her ears. I told Wyatt the story about how I was once driving my truck on a delivery when all of a sudden Shelby jumped up from behind the seat and down into my lap and I was so surprised I almost drove off the road. Wyatt smiled and petted Shelby but I could see he was still thinking about his mother and I thought maybe he wanted to talk about it so I asked him where she was and he said Saint Mary's Hospital. I asked him what was wrong with her and he said that she had become sick last September and hadn't been able to leave the house. Then in January she finally started feeling a bit better so she tried to walk over to a friend's house for a visit and had slipped on the ice and broken her hip. She went into the hospital and they said she would get better but she just kept getting worse until now she was almost gone. I asked Wyatt if maybe there was something I could do and he looked at me again for a long time with those eyes and then he asked me if I would go with him to the hospital the next day. I don't know. I was sort of surprised because I didn't really know why he wanted me to go with him, but I guess I could tell from the way he was looking at me that it was probably pretty important and so I thought well Wyatt's my friend and I said okay. Wyatt said thanks and then I said hey guess what and I went to my desk and came back with the crib board I had just bought that week. Wyatt laughed and we played a couple of games and then we made plans for the next day and he went home.

The next day it was raining and since Wyatt doesn't have a car we went to the hospital in my truck. We got to the hospital and went upstairs to his mother's room and, I don't know, she looked pretty sick. Wyatt went up to her and put a hand on her forehead and she opened her eyes and when she saw him she smiled a little bit. Wyatt asked her how she was feeling and she said fine and then she said tired and Wyatt said he had brought his friend and he introduced me. She couldn't really raise her head so I had to sort of step in close next to Wyatt and I said hello. Wyatt's mother smiled at me and she said hello back. Then I went and stood where I was before and Wyatt's mother told him that she was glad he had a friend because she didn't want him to be all alone when she was gone. Wyatt took one of his mother's small thin hands in his big heavy ones and squeezed it and brought it to his lips and I could see there were tears on his face and I thought I might cry too but, I don't know, I don't think it's a bad thing but I sort of felt happy too because that's when I knew that Wyatt and me were probably really good friends and that maybe he thought I was pretty important. We stood like that for a little while and then a nurse came in and said hi to Wyatt and asked him how he was doing and he said he was okay. The nurse wrote some things down on a chart and then she looked at me and smiled and left. Wyatt and me stayed with his mother a little while longer and then when she fell asleep Wyatt leaned over and gave her a kiss on the forehead and we left.

On the way home Wyatt didn't say anything but when we got back to my place he asked me if I wanted a cup of coffee and I said sure so we walked through the rain over to his place and went inside. It's funny because whenever Wyatt and me played crib or gin rummy it was always outside in his backyard so I had never been in his house before and when we got inside I could see that it wasn't just Wyatt's house it was his mother's house too. It was pretty nice with lots of old furniture and afghans and little statues and things and even a few pictures of Wyatt when he was little.

Wyatt made some coffee and we sat down at the kitchen table and I guess we were still both feeling pretty bad because we didn't say anything we just sat. Then after a while Wyatt looked up at me and I looked at him and he just kept looking at me for a long time with those eyes of his and, I don't know, I couldn't look away and I started feeling a little nervous but Wyatt finally just smiled and put one of his big hands on my arm where it was on the table and he said thanks for going to the hospital with him. I said that it was okay and that we were friends. Wyatt smiled again and then we just sat there like that with his hand on my arm and drinking coffee and thinking about things.

A week later Wyatt's mother died. Wyatt asked me to come to the funeral with him so I did. After that I helped him pack up his mother's clothes and some other things and then some of his mother's friends came and took it all

20

away. After that Wyatt and me went for a walk down by the river and Wyatt told me the names of some of the ducks and song birds around there and then we just sort of sat on the rocks not really talking about anything. I don't know. I guess I've always been pretty good at just keeping my own company and I didn't ever really think about it much, but now that Wyatt and me are friends I sometimes just sort of get to wondering. I guess I sometimes still feel a bit confused by things but I think it just takes time and, I don't know, Wyatt and me, I guess we've got time.

Pretending to be Brando

Laura Kolb

Artie
is not particularly lonely.

Outside it is August, and between buildings
clouds roll together.
Hot, his shirt sticks to him
and to his chair – wet down his back.

Doorchimes. Pretending to be Brando
he is too cool to turn.
In the glass case on the wall he watches her come in:
shorts, a blue T-shirt
with a goldfish on the front,
bangs. Maybe sixteen.

– I want an umbrella, she says,
for under five bucks.
A black one.

He is out of black umbrellas for under five bucks.
He does not like to be out of anything. He tells her
   – we got red umbrellas and blue umbrellas and
   even one with different colored panels,
   we got a regular carnival of umbrellas –

She stares; and something in
Artie feels sick because he can't say
– Jesus Christ, let it go, kid.
Really, I was being very funny in a sort of
talky way and
you could have at least smiled –
But he hands her a red umbrella
takes her five
gives her two back.
She asks (deadpan under those bangs)
– So why this one?

and Artie squints his eyes, leans back and drawls
– 'Cause baby you'd look good in red –
and even though this time she smiles, when she leaves
the door lets in the smell of dust and coming rain.
    He feels cold glass under his arms, cold sweat
    sticking to everything, all summer long.

Tracheotomy

Dave Thorley

That's him, serving his stretch
in the opposite bay: puffing his puff
from a vent in his neck. Flying the flag
of a ladder of smoke, braying his breath
like a tug-boat. That's the man with a cigarette
plumbed into his windpipe, with the sharp end
signalling Morse to the tides of his chest.
Still with the prints on his Adam's apple, still
with the pinch in the throat strings where the man
on the spot had divined the place,
drilled and countersunk the fuselage
of a spent biro. Not for him, posing
with an elbow crooked and a fag
in his fist; not for the taste
of the chopped and roasted; not the chit-chat
of smokers' corner but the flow
of the marbled, cumulous river
through the neck of his snorkel.
I heard a rumour he's learning to whistle.
Just look at that –
slipping a wink and a note to the porters
for a bag of tobacco
and papers and filters.

Interview

Greg Kimura

The boy was supposed to begin the day at six am.

That way he would beat the commuters into the City, his uncle said.

Once he was there he could orient himself, find a place for breakfast and drink coffee and walk around, and kill time until nine-thirty. The area around the university (Morningside Heights or Upper West Side – the boy didn't know which, he'd heard it both ways) had to be full of coffee shops, his uncle said.

"Like that place on *Seinfeld*."

The boy flew in last night for the interview today. His journey began the day before that. It started with the drive to Fairbanks, flying stand-by to Anchorage, Seattle, Salt Lake City, Cincinnati and Atlanta before arriving twenty-seven hours later at LaGuardia Airport. It was his first time in New York City.

The boy stood at the baggage carousel looking for his uncle. He waited until the other passengers left with their bags. The boy went to a bank of telephones and called his number.

The uncle picked up the telephone and said "Hello?"

He told the boy to find a taxi. He didn't have a car.

Besides, the uncle said. This is kind of a surprise.

He thought the boy was supposed to arrive yesterday. When he didn't, the uncle figured the boy had decided not to come.

The boy said he was sorry they'd got their signals crossed, that he did not make stand-by a couple of times. He said that he'd be by soon.

He pulled his duffel bag across the airport floor, out the automatic door and into the congealed air of the underground arrival ramp. He walked up to a woman in a policeman's cap and orange vest. She reached for her shoulder and spoke into the microphone attached to her collar.

A moment later a cab drove up.

She opened the door for the boy. He thanked her and gave the driver an address in Astoria, Queens.

The boy *did* awake at six am to the sound of beeping emanating from his wrist. He pressed the watch button and slowly opened his eyelids.

He watched his chest lift up and down and felt the warm sweat saturating his T-shirt.

Light poked through the edges of the roll-up window shade, illuminating the upper half of the walls. Dust motes speckled across the light, disappearing when they floated into shadow.

He thought he was still watching the diaphanous motes when the knock on the door lifted him from sleep. He hopped from the bed and hurried toward the door.

By the time he turned the knob, the boy decided he would pretend to his uncle that he had been awake.

"Time to get going," the uncle said. "It's eight o'clock. It'll take you at least an hour to get into the city now. I'd go with you myself, but I've got to be at work." He paused and looked at the boy.

The boy swallowed, stifling a yawn in his throat, and he felt the moisture glass over his eyes.

"Well," the uncle said. "I left directions on the counter. You should be fine. You know where on campus you're supposed to go?"

"They sent me a letter with all that stuff. Thanks. I guess I'd better get ready."

The boy didn't have time to shower, so he wet his hair in the sink and patted the sweat from his torso with a terry cloth towel. He cupped his hands and splashed water over his puffed eyelids to wake up.

The boy dressed in a rush but spent extra time tying the tie. It took two tries to get the length right and the dimple in the center of the knot.

It was his first tie, brown polyester with slanted stripes of red, orange and yellow. He bought it at the Fred Meyer in Fairbanks, especially for the interview.

The moment he locked the apartment door and stepped out of the vestibule, he was submerged in heat. He even felt the hotness reflect up from the bright concrete and heat his toes in the dress shoes. He took off the corduroy jacket and folded it over his arm, moving briskly toward the bus stop.

At the bus stop, the boy stood in line with the others. He shifted from foot to foot and switched the sport coat from one sweaty forearm to the other, then back again. He kicked shards of green glass off the kerb.

Finally, the bus pulled up. He followed the others up the steps and watched the coins bounce through the metal innards the clear plastic fare box. The air in the bus was cool. It chilled the sweat on his skin and in his clothes.

He started shivering, a low-grade shiver, but once it got going, he could not stop it.

The boy sat down next to a window and reached into his front pocket for his uncle's directions. The paper was damp.

The bus followed a road that was lined on both sides by barred-over storefronts. He read the signs: ____ Dollar Store, ____ Deli, ____ Bodega – LOTTERY TICKETS HERE.

26

The bus drove over the bridge.

The same signs lined the road on the other side of the river, but the colour of the people on the street changed from brown to black.

A skinny black man with a green, red and yellow-knitted cap and a Walkman entered the bus the first stop after the bridge. He moved into the seat beside the boy, bobbing his head in rhythm and staring ahead through sunglasses.

The boy listened to the tinny music coming from the man's headphones and tried not to look at him out of the corner of his eye. He had never seen a real black person before, only on television.

The boy stared out the window. Then he looked at the directions in his lap. *Bus follows 125 St until it gets to Broadway. Stay on until Bway. Get off at Bway and 116 St.*

The boy leant his forehead against the bus window and thought about his uncle.

Every summer that he could remember growing up, they would go to fish camp on the Yukon River.

They would catch salmon after salmon in the fish wheel.

The boy never tired of watching the fish wheel turn around and around in the river's current, the weir dipping in and out of the water.

Sometimes the weir came out of the water with a fish.

As the weir rose in the air, the fish would fall into the sluice. Then it would slide down the sluice into the fish box and flap around until it died.

Most of the time, though, the weir would rise empty.

The boy and the uncle would sit on the bank and make bets that the next time, or the next time after that, it would come up with a fish.

Over the long winter, the boy would daydream of fish camp in class. He would imagine laying on a sandbar warmed by the long summer sun, watching the weir rise from the water and betting with his uncle, and feeling all right.

The boy had not been to fish camp for two summers now. He stopped going after his uncle got divorced.

After that, the uncle gave up fishing.

He spent most of his spare time hanging out at the village tavern. He told the people sitting at the bar "Alaska doesn't feel the same. Things here have changed." They nodded and sipped their beers.

"Alaska is too small a place for a man to live in anymore," his uncle told someone who told his mother.

She told the boy she didn't trust his uncle when he got in these moods, and to watch out.

"All we need is another drunk Injun in the family," she said.

The uncle was a baggage handler at the Fairbanks Airport at the time. He said he was going to ask to transfer to New York City. No one believed he was serious about leaving until he was gone.

After he left, that was it. No one took the boy to fish camp anymore.

The bus turned left onto Broadway.

The boy moved forward in his seat. He readied himself to press the tape to ring the bell for the next stop. The bus was still moving when the black man stood up and began walking to the front.

The boy looked around the bus. Six other people were standing, making their way to the front or the rear door.

They clutched the backs of chairs and the handrails overhead and leaned against the braking and turning of the bus. Their exaggerated movements reminded the boy of astronauts holding on to keep from floating away.

The bell dinged twice.

The boy missed his chance to be the one to press the tape. He sat in the seat and watched the bus empty. He waited until he was the last person. Then he rose and walked out of the bus.

The boy crossed Broadway and stood outside the entrance gate to the university.

He began sweating immediately, but he put the corduroy jacket back on. He thought it was right to wear it to the interview.

The boy had already memorised what the letter said, *9:30 a.m., _____ Hall, room 211*, but he read it again before folding it and slipping it in the inside breast pocket of the jacket.

He looked up at the curlicued metal gate and through it, to the university grounds. Then he stepped through.

The white stone of the campus spread around him. He moved straight ahead, but people passed by and crossed in front of him. He slowed his pace, then sped up, to avoid bumping into them.

When the boy reached the green stretch of grass at the center of campus, he stopped and turned all the way around.

On one side stood a staircase as wide as the square of grass. It led up to a huge grey brick building with stout white columns. The columns supported a pyramid-style roof. Out of the middle of the roof rose a white, saucer-like rotunda.

On the other side stood what the boy guessed was a library. It was a squat concrete building that looked like a cube cut in half and covered with rows of windows. Above the windows was a stone veneer wrapped around the building.

The boy read the names carved into the veneer: *Democritus, Demosthenes, Diogenes Laertes...*

The boy looked at his watch. It read 9:25 am.

"Perfect timing," he thought.

He stared into the faces of the people walking by him. A young man in a T-shirt and shorts approached the boy, walking across the grass.

The boy thought his features were Asian, maybe even Injun. The young man looked like a student to the boy.

When the young man was close enough, the boy said, "Excuse me."

He asked the young man if he knew where _____ Hall was.

The young man pointed to a building next to the library. The boy thanked him.

As he started walking to _____ Hall, the boy realised the young man never said a word. He never even looked at him.

Room 211 was a classroom, filled with twenty other prospective students and their parents.

The boy took one of the few remaining seats. It was in the front row.

The boy stared around the room.

He was the only person wearing a jacket or tie. One girl wore shorts and a T-shirt that said 'Choate.' Her legs were crossed and she was chewing gum. She dangled a thick-soled black sandal on the toes of one foot.

Another boy wore jeans and a polo shirt with a crest on the breast pocket. Under the crest was a word or a name that was too small for the boy to read.

Kids and parents leant over their desks and spoke to each other in voices he thought were a little louder than necessary.

The boy took off his jacket, draping it over the back of his chair and listened.

"Yes, we're doing the City today...Tomorrow we have an appointment at Trinity in the morning and Wesleyan in the afternoon...The lacrosse coach called and wants him to go there. I think it's fine but his father wants him to keep his options open...Next week we're looking at schools in Western Mass...My dad says that Columbia is okay for law school but he wants me to do my undergraduate at Yale or Brown..."

A man and woman walked into the classroom and stood at the chalkboard.

They surveyed the room, the young people and their parents, and took papers out of their briefcases. It took a minute for the conversations to cease.

The couple introduced themselves. They told the group: "This informational session will last approximately forty-five minutes and save your questions until the end, please."

But before they began, they said, they wanted to know where everybody was from.

The boy thought they wanted to know where people lived, but as they went up and down the rows, the prospective students listed off the names of their schools.

When it came to the boy's turn he said, "Minto High School".

The woman asked him where that was.

"Fairbanks, Alaska," he said.

"Is anyone here from somewhere further away than Alaska?" the woman asked. She raised her chin and scanned the room.

"No? I think we have a winner."

She smiled at the boy and he smiled back.

It was the next person's turn. The girl in the desk behind him shouted out her school's name. The boy's head was cocked to the side to listen and she shouted directly in his ear.

The boy cringed and covered his ear with his hand, before he realised what he did. A few people laughed.

The boy laughed uncomfortably, too.

The informational session began.

The man and the woman took turns speaking. They paused occasionally to consult their notes.

They said the university had originally been called King's College but changed its name after the Revolutionary War. They listed its undergraduate enrolment and said it was the smallest of all the Ivy League schools.

They talked about the benefits of going to college in New York City, as opposed to another city or the country.

The boy already knew most of the information they cited. He had read the bulletin and brochures the university sent him.

At the end of the presentation, the man asked if there were any questions.

A flurry of arms shot in the air.

Which is more important, grades or SAT scores? Where does the crew team practice? Do you have single-room dormitories? What are your study abroad opportunities? Can we choose our advisor, or is the advisor assigned to the student?

After a while, the man looked at his watch and said, "Time for one more question. The campus tour will begin in five minutes."

After that the class broke up.

The boy waited until most people filed out before he went to the chalk-board. The man and woman scribbled in their notebooks and spoke to each other under their breath.

"Excuse me," the boy said. "I have an interview here today.

Is that here or somewhere else?"

The woman looked up.

"Oh, no," she said.

"This is an informational session and campus tour only. We don't do personal interviews on campus."

The boy's throat tightened. He held out the letter from the admissions office. The woman looked at it and handed it back to the boy.

"Yes, that's the general letter for the informational session and campus tour. You see, we don't do personal interviews here. They are done at the student's school or home community. Alumni usually do the interviews."

"Interviews take place after the application for admission has been processed," the man added.

"That's in November for early admission and December or January for standard admission."

The boy was silent. He thought his voice might break if he spoke, so he waited a moment for the feeling to pass.

"I thought I had an interview," he said, almost whispering.

"I don't even know if there are any alumni where I'm from."

"Wait a minute," the woman said. "You're from Alaska, right? We have an alumni group in Anchorage."

"Anchorage is four hundred miles away from where I'm from." He throat tightened again and heard his voice rise. He tried to control it back down.

"I mean, I said I'm from Fairbanks but I'm really from a village outside of Fairbanks. Anchorage is a long way away."

"Can't I just interview while I'm here?"

"Son," the man said. "I don't think you understand. It doesn't work that way. If we gave you a personal interview, we'd have to give everyone else here a personal interview."

"Now, you'd better hurry up. The campus tour is almost ready to start...you don't want to miss that."

The boy looked at the woman. She pursed her lips and shook her head as if to say "Sorry."

She smiled at the boy again.

Then she looked back down at the table and the notepad. Finding her place, she resumed scribbling.

The boy walked past the tour group crowded by the door of _____ Hall, ignoring the stares of the prospective students and their parents.

His face felt red and it was wet with sweat.

The boy didn't say anything.

He didn't have to. No one spoke to him.

He returned to the grassy area in the center of campus to get his bearing and then walked toward the gate opposite the one he passed through earlier.

The boy thought that if he could only get off campus, he would feel better.

The sun was higher in the sky now and he felt it against his scalp. Sweat started beading-up under his hair, but he didn't care.

He passed beyond the gate. The university was behind him.

He crossed one street that was busy and another that was not. The boy would have kept going straight, but he came up to a concrete abutment.

He peered over the abutment. A park sat four or five stories below.

It looked like a big park, but he couldn't tell for sure. It was filled with broad trees. Not the scrawny spruce and alder brush that grew along the Yukon, but real, tall trees with big green leaves. The branches were so thick with them he couldn't see what lay below them.

The boy looked for a way to get down.

The entrance to the park was a block away. From the entrance, you climbed a long, alternating staircase – like the type you see in old mansions on TV – to get down.

The boy passed through the entrance.

He hummed to himself as he walked down the stairs. He started counting steps, but lost track.

The park was filled with people. They were all black, except for the boy. Some people walked along the blacktop paths that crossed the park. Others sat on benches under the shade of the trees, fanning themselves.

The boy stopped and watched the people. He listened to the rustle of a breeze passing through the leaves.

He had never heard such a sound.

"So many leaves," he thought. "It sounds like a river."

The boy chose a path and walked until he found an empty bench. He sat down.

The bench faced a basketball court that was fenced in on all sides. A class of first-or second-graders was lined-up behind the basket facing him.

The basket was broken.

Hanging from the bent rim was a dark green garbage bag.

The garbage bag was held to the rim by its plastic yellow cinch tie.

The garbage bag had something in it, but it only looked half-full.

The children shouted and squealed, jumping in excitement.

One child, a young boy, was blindfolded.

The teacher spun the young boy around by his shoulders as the children counted: "One. Two. Three. Four. Five."

The young boy swayed to-and-fro for balance. The teacher squared him in the right direction and gave him a broken piece of two-by-four.

The young boy felt the piece of lumber in his hands. He held it by its narrow sides like a baseball bat and struck out in front of him. He swung so hard to momentum almost made him trip.

The teacher moved the garbage bag back and forth like a pendulum. It evaded the young boy's swings. The children shouted in unison, "One! Two!"

The boy missed for the third time. He took off the blindfold and frowned. The children became silent.

He handed the blindfold and the two-by-four to the next child and went to the back of the line.

The children started shouting, again.

The face of the young boy at the end of the line began to relax. He joined in the cheering, too, when the next child swung and missed.

The boy watched the game. Sometimes a child grazed the bag, but no one hit it directly. If a child got close, the teacher pushed the bag out of the way. She had to be careful. A few of the batters almost hit her.

By the time the game made it through half of the line of children, the boy felt sick from the heat.

He stood up, wobbled and stretched. He walked away from the court, towards a quiet corner of the park.

The trees at the edge of the park were bigger than the rest. They were the biggest he'd ever seen, with bark that was thick and rippled.

The bark reminded him of the type of dry mud you sometimes found on sandbars in the Yukon River. The wind blew jagged creases in the mud that made it look like old people's skin. It was so dry and hard, it would cut your feet if you walked across it barefoot.

The leaves rustled in the breeze.

The boy took off his jacket. There was no bench around so he crossed his legs and sat on the edge of the path.

The boy closed his eyes.

Another, louder breeze blew through the leaves and he felt the sweat cool against his face.

He listened to the sound and imagined he was at fish camp.

Sitting on the river bank, the boy and the uncle watched the weir rise up and down, turning over and over in the current. He saw the trapped salmon rising from the water, just like the uncle predicted.

"See," the uncle said. "Never bet against an old Injun."

The boy smiled. The same old joke, every year.

He remembered the squeeze of the uncle's hand on his shoulder.

He remembered feeling the laughing that would start out from giggling, and grow until they could not stop.

The feeling of the laughing, the boy and the uncle, together.

Laughing so hard, his guts hurt.

Bathers at Asnières
Olivia Cole

Move in too close and this world could fall
apart – sit far enough away and let weekenders
float by, adding girls and wives to the stolen
Monday leisure of basking men and boys.

Let you and I remain convinced of the chase
and flirt of two punts, their slow dance, and
close call, of book and newspaper being read,
let the leather of boots seem hard enough, from here,

for walking. Forget the hand and eye of the puppeteer
who, sketch book and models abandoned somewhere
near Asnières, found the true false suppleness
of a girl in a pool, convinced that like a ballerina she

can stretch and fly, the ease and arrogance of weightlessness
letting him cast by once more from the other side
of the decade, world and river: re-finding a boy's
hat as red, and pencilling out the discarded clothes of lovers.

Green
Irene Hahn

For some reason, the scent of cooking rice was strongest not in the kitchen, but in Ahjima's bedroom. She and her husband had slept in separate rooms for as long as I could remember, she upstairs, he downstairs, and as a child I wondered if this was because she had wanted to cook in her room and he had said no. I spent long hours searching for a wok or a rice cooker of some sort in Ahjima's bedroom, but I never found it.

She had a large Korean bureau pushed against the wall, of a black, alabaster-like surface etched with mother-of-pearl cut from abalone shells, the twisting flight patterns of cranes and peacocks meandering their way across its surface. I used to touch it in a sort of stupor, much as a magpie might be attracted to a shiny quarter, wondering if the swirling pastel color of the abalone would waver, mercury-like, before my touch. Ahjima had brought the bureau from Korea – if you approached the bureau close enough to touch the cold surface of the large mirror upon it, you could catch the faint perfume of dried roses, although I never saw where they were. I think that maybe they were shoved in a drawer, but at this point I'd leave before looking. The room was always silent, too silent for me to want to stay, although once I walked in and she had left the radio on, which was playing Mozart into the afternoon.

"*Do you want to sleep here, in my room?*" she wanted to know the day I arrived. I shook my head, thinking of the tiny buzz of the fluorescent ceiling light and the bluish relief it threw over everything it touched. "*All right,*" she said, "*I'll let you stay in Soon Ja's old room.*" She led me past the living room and into a tiny space partitioned off from the rest of the house with a folding screen. The scent of rice clung to her clothes and shifted as she moved. "*Please let me you know if you aren't warm enough,*" she said, laying out a thick magenta blanket. "*I know you Americans aren't used to sleeping on the floor, but this is what we do in Korea. I hope you don't mind.*" She smiled and patted my arm. "Okay?" She giggled at hearing herself. "Okay". It was one of the only English words she knew.

"Okay," I said, blushing.

"Okay." Ahjima turned to leave, pulling the accordion screen shut behind her. "Okay."

There wasn't much left to show that it had once been Soon Ja's room, except for a tiny radio and tape player that Ahjima had set on a Korean radio station. I switched it on briefly; a woman was listing this week's sale items for the Sun Mee Supermarket in the high-pitched warble that female media personalities always seemed to adopt on Korean radio and TV channels, a balance of cutesy and deferent that I could never replicate although easily parody. Soon Ja had left two tapes with the playlists written in her precise, round print, and I put one into the tape deck. Running water. Flutes. "River Dreams," the playlist read, along with a few unintelligible Chinese characters in parentheses.

"What are you doing?" I used to ask her.

"Finding my inner zen." She would get up and put a piece of clear blue plastic over her desk lamp to make the room go oceanic, then dance around me, slowly contorting her body into curvy motions, twisting her wrists while holding her arms still.

"Dance with me, sistah!"

"No."

"Then turn up the music," she'd say.

• • • • •

"You know, I'm glad you're here," Jerry told me the evening I arrived, looking at me curiously. "Mr Kim is nice but all he ever talks about are 'the old days' with Mr Sohn, so I've been dying from younger-people withdrawal." She had been Ahjima's first boarder after Soon Ja went to college and Ahjima decided she hated having an empty house. Now she and Mr Kim were Ahjima's only boarders besides myself, living in an L-shaped attachment to the house where three of Ahjima's six children used to have their rooms. "How long are you staying?"

"Just until I can find a place of my own. My job doesn't start for a few weeks, so I have some time."

"Too bad." Jerry scrunched up her nose. "Ahjima tells me you're a family friend."

"Her youngest daughter and I went to school together until I moved to Vermont. We've kept in touch pretty well."

"So you're from Vermont."

"Well, I worked in advertising in New York City for a few years before this, so I guess that makes me a New Yorker by association."

"You don't look New York Korean." Jerry stood in the shade of the front porch; she had just had laser surgery to remove several dark freckles from her face and was forbidden from going out in the sun for at least two weeks, until the red spots healed white. She fished around in her jeans for a cigarette and lit it, inhaled, exhaled. The pale smoke blew into my face.

Soon Ja and I used to joke that one day I would go back to Los Angeles and find her turned into a hoochie, our flippant label for the slim, petite Korean girls in body-hugging black, highlighted hair, and dark lipstick who banded together in Koreatown Plaza, the shopping mall at the heart of Koreatown. We used to meet there every Saturday and pool our allowances to buy a jumbo bowl of noodles from the food court, back when my family lived in Los Angeles. When we were feeling nice we called the enemy "fobbish" instead – fresh off the boat, or, in Konglish-speak, "fresh off the *biengee*" (airplane).

36

"F.O.B.," we would whisper to each other without moving our lips, watching girls in black pick at their food while we noisily chewed mouthfuls of *tak guksu*, the Korean version of chicken noodle soup. Still, I couldn't help saying, "Oh my God," the day I finally came out to visit Soon Ja and realized it had happened for real.

"What?" she said, raising a plucked eyebrow.

"Nothing. You look beautiful". I meant it, too, and for a moment had felt a twinge of jealousy.

"Oh," I said to Jerry. I couldn't think of anything smart to say, so all I said was, "Oh."

"Want a puff?"

"No thanks; I don't smoke." Jerry nodded and flicked a piece of red-streaked hair off her shoulder, revealing a thin line of sequins sewn into the sleeve. I suddenly wondered if any of those girls in Koreatown Plaza had heard me back then, and were lying in wait with a few choice remarks of their own now that I was in Los Angeles. I sure as hell hoped Jerry wasn't one of them.

"How old are you again?"

I told her.

"No kidding? I'd have guessed younger. Lots younger." Jerry inhaled, exhaled.

"Why?"

"No real reason. Just intuition." She smiled brightly and ground out her cigarette beneath a black stiletto heel.

• • • • •

Imagine the United States as a blue blob on the map of the world, a little yellow dot where Koreatown hugs the California coastline, and then a tiny green speck in the middle of the yellow dot. That tiny green speck was me. All sixty-five inches of me, a floral print shirt in a world of Armani, the Korean words I had only heard at home now trailing me in public spaces. So I planted myself in Ahjima's house and spent the next morning drawing the roses in the front yard, just as I had every time I'd visited Soon Ja at her house during my childhood. It was always a different kind of rose when I came; Ahjima would tire of her garden and then uproot it all, planting new strains, different colors. These would be interspersed with plants and shrubs she remembered from her childhood, including a persimmon tree swelling with green fruit, which grew so heavy that they would drop to the ground with the slightest rustle of wind. This year, she had taken a liking to yellow. Yellow roses, yellow forsythias with petals curling around a smattering of red freckles.

I outlined a tiny version of myself in a corner of the sketch and started coloring in my shirt to match the yellow of the forsythias, except that I pressed too hard and the tip of my watercolor pencil snapped. No sharpener, so I filled the rest of my shirt in with pink instead, and found myself staring at what appeared to be a piece of Sandra-shaped bubble gum that had splat on the page.

"What are you doing?" A small boy peered at me over the white picket fence Sohn Ahjuhshee had erected around their yard, sometime between the last time I'd been here and now. Once, many years ago, Soon Ja and I had played with a girl who lived in that house; she had been just about our age. I remember her laughing at me because I didn't speak Korean as well as she, and because I had gotten the grammar wrong when I tried to say, "I didn't see the flower there," after I accidentally knocked a flower pot over while we played kickball in Ahjima's driveway. She had a harrumphing sort of laugh for such a little girl, somewhat like a horse.

"Drawing," I told him in Korean. "*Gurim guryuh.*"

"You have a funny accent," he said, this time in English, then went inside. From above the driveway, I saw a wrinkled face glaring down at me through a curtainless window. It might have been that girl's aunt, whom I had seen only once before, reprimanding Sung Hee for knocking over the flower pot while I chewed a fingernail and looked away.

Hoping to elude the old woman's stare, I moved to the cool overhang of Ahjima's back porch. From the steps, I could see the Hollywood sign on a distant hillside, bright even amid the haze of a Los Angeles afternoon. The thin matchsticks of date palm trees and their poofs of serrated fronds lay in bars across the sign, just enough that I had to twist my head this way and that to make out the true shapes of all the letters. I turned to a fresh page and started penciling in the outlines of the houses on our street, their tiny lawns sloping down into the road, flanked with yucca and tall cacti with thick, fleshy stems.

"Hello." It was Mr Kim, who came outside and stood next to me, his hands crossed behind his back. "Something good?"

"Not really." Surprised at hearing an older Korean speaking almost accentless English, I decided against mentioning it, and held up my Hollywood picture instead. "It'll look better after I paint it for real." He smiled.

"Well, all right. Would you like to take a walk? Good for the heart and the mind."

Mr Kim had retired just last year from his job inspecting agricultural shipments at LAX and spent most of his days at Ahjima's now, except for early morning walks in Esperanza Park, and late afternoon walks through Koreatown. He would tell Ahjima he was going out to buy bread and then walk ten blocks to a certain Latino grocery store where they sold a jumbo loaf for just eighty-nine cents, although there were other places along the way that could have sold him a loaf for just a bit more money. He called the store his treasure trove; Ahjima's freezer was full of bread that they couldn't eat right away. Sometimes he would buy pieces of sliced avocado or mango or giant grapes from the vendors who lay the cut fruit out on their carts along the street, and leaned over the glistening surfaces shooing away flies. It made me miss the way that vendors in New York hovered over metal carts overflowing with hot dogs and pretzels in the winter, the steam shooting out momentarily as they reached in to pull out a fresh hot dog.

Mr Kim walked very fast, much faster than I'd expected, although he had a loping gate that gave the impression that he was moving quite slowly. Sometimes he would get far ahead of me, inmersed in his own thoughts, until the screech of car tires or the shout of children playing in the street awoke him from his reverie and he stopped to wait until I caught up. From a distance he appeared to float past other idlers on the street, buoyed by some invisible wind that cushioned his feet alone. As he walked, he spoke in a slightly dreamy tone that evaporated the din of oncoming traffic.

"I walked to school barefoot once in the dead of winter, all of two miles," he said. "My teacher gave us a lecture on discipline the day before, and how mental strength can overcome even the greatest of physical discomforts. So he gave us a challenge, to walk to school without any shoes on. I was the only one who succeeded, and he made an example of me before the entire school." He smiled. "He was a Japanese man. We only had Japanese teachers back then, during the Occupation."

"*Where were you?*" Ahjima wanted to know when we had returned. "*Dinner is ready and I've been calling you two for fifteen minutes.*"

"*We just went for a little walk,*" Mr Kim told her.

"*Just a little walk.*" Ahjima sighed. "*I suppose you talked about a lot of things.*" And, turning to me: "*Sandra, because I can't speak English, you'll have to talk to Jerry very much and then she can tell me everything that's been going on in your life.*" She smiled. "*At least I can feed you, no? Here.*" She put a plate of spicy pickled cabbage in front of me and watched my expression closely. I blushed and looked at Jerry, who was busily cutting a large piece of *kimchi* into quarters.

"I don't like *kimchi* very much. It's too hot." She blinked.

"What are you telling me for? Sorry; did I miss something?"

"I can't really speak Korean even though I understand it all, so do you think you could translate for me?"

"Okay, I get it. *It's too hot for her,*" Jerry told Ahjima in Korean.

"*Still the same as she ever was,*" she said, then smiled. On the one visit to California I made in high school, Ahjima had watched, amazed, as I quickly transferred all the *kimchi* from my plate to Soon Ja's.

"*What's the matter with you?*" she said.

"*She's a hamburger girl,*" Soon Ja explained for me, since by that time I had already forgotten the Korean words I needed to tell Ahjima myself. "*She likes American food. Steak and potatoes. That sort of thing.*"

"*Granola,*" I blurted out, thinking of the backpacking trip through the White Mountains I had taken the summer before. Soon Ja froze. "*I don't think there's a word for that,*" she whispered.

Ahjima began picking the kimchi off my plate. "*Well, no matter. There are plenty of other things to eat,*" Sohn Ahjushee said to his wife, scanning each morsel with his eyes before plunging it in his mouth. He had never been able to do anything without looking extremely preoccupied, and although his face had a pale doughiness now that I didn't remember from before, the nervous energy of his movements was still there.

"*Have some kalbi*," Ahjima said, piling Korean barbecued ribs on my plate. "*Chap chae. Dubu. Bindae duk. You must like those better?*" I had forgotten how much Koreans eat and watched with wide eyes as the piles of noodles and tofu and yellow bean pancakes grew into an explosion of food. That night, I had a stomachache that seemed to go on for days.

"*Maybe it's the room that's making you sick,*" Ahjima fretted. "*Maybe it isn't comfortable enough? Too cold, maybe? There are a lot of windows in that room. I'm sure some cold air comes in through the slats at night.*" A warm wind stirred the lace curtains in front of the windows and I hurried to pull them together, hoping they'd be drawn enough so that passers-by wouldn't be able to look in. I used to wonder if those curtains would dissolve beneath the hot air of day, all those tiny designs that powdered the windows in a fan of sugar white. Black bars lay just outside the windows; I had never decided whether they made me feel more or less safe. I used to count them over and over when staying overnight at Soon Ja's when I couldn't get to sleep, and try to guess how many inches it was from the windowsill to those cruel points. Long ago, when I could still speak Korean reasonably fluently, I asked Ahjima why those bars were there, and she had patted my hand and smiled. "*There are lots of strange people who live around here,*" she said. "*Poor people. Black people. Brown people. They would rather rob you than find a job.*" She shook her head. "*Watch out for those people who live in the apartment behind us,*" she said. "*Spanish speakers. Drug dealers.*" She exhaled softly. "*Right, Yohboh?*" Mr Sohn only grunted as he passed and waved a newspaper in her direction. I saw Soon Ja standing behind her mother, shaking her head vigorously.

"*She's never really spoken to the neighbors enough to judge; she doesn't speak enough English to do that. She just says stuff when my dad's in earshot because she's trying to convince him that we should go back without actually saying it to him straight,*" Soon Ja told me later. "*She's still upset about 4-29.*"

"Oh no, it's a good room," I said, thinking uneasily of the sleepless nights I always suffered from in unfamiliar rooms. "*Guenchena,*" I told her, stumbling on the syllables. "It's okay," Ahjima blanched.

"*Guenchena-yo,*" she corrected me. "*The respectful form is guenchena-yo. Here, Sandra, help me move your things to Woo Hyuk's room. It's a little bigger there; perhaps you'll be more comfortable.*" Woo Hyuk's UCLA Bruins teddy bear stared me to sleep that night, its bright yellow T-shirt still visible in the dark.

• • • • •

Sometimes, at night, I would awaken to hear the whir of helicopters landing on the roof of the Section 8 apartment complex just a half block away. In the mornings they would always be gone, and a different set of laundry would be drying from the clothesline strung between two balconies on the uppermost floor. Jerry could hear the copters, too, although not as loudly; Woo Hyuk's room was right against the south face of the house and I had a clear view of the

40

apartment from my window. "*Drugs,*" Ahjima said darkly. "*Are the helicopters keeping you up, Sandra?*" She furrowed her brow.

"No, I'm fine," I said. Jerry translated for me, and Ahjima nodded, looking at me with two lines creasing either side of her cheek.

"*Please have some cream cheese,*" Ahjima said, pushing a tub toward me. "Cuhream chees-uh bagel; *that's more American than what I've been giving Jerry for breakfast, right?*" Jerry giggled.

"Yes, it is," she said, "although don't expect a real New York bagel, Sandy. I expect you can sniff out a real bagel from a fake one, you being a New Yorker and all." I put my hands to my cheeks. "Oh, come on, Sandy. You know it's a joke. Lord I need a smoke."

"*What is it?*" Ahjima asked, looking at me confusedly. "*Why is she doing that?*"

"*Nothing. That's how Americans react to jokes,*" Jerry told her.

Soon Ja used to sit in the kitchen in the mornings and open plastic tubs of cream cheese for her mother, who would dip her silver knife into the smooth white surface and spread it thickly on bagel after bagel, carefully cutting a circle out of the center when a slab of cream cheese covered the hole. She wrapped each bagel individually in saran wrap and would then walk two blocks to her tiny convenience store, which mostly sold bagels and packets of gum and cigarettes, a few weekly magazines, detergent and baby powder, individual packets of Hostess cakes and spiced Korean dried squid. Her store didn't do nearly as well as her husband's next door, though, with his crystal vases and gold watches, mahogany pen gift sets, and jars of gummy bears and butterscotch behind the counter for the children while their parents browsed. Still, it gave Ahjima something to do, until her store was looted during the LA riots. Her husband's was spared. Soon Ja told me on the phone that they never figured out who had looted the store, but the newspapers had been filled with enough photos of African-Americans to convince Ahjima that she knew what had really happened, even if it wasn't true. "And it's not," Soon Ja had said, "because Eddie – you remember him, the kid who wanted to be a filmmaker? – filmed what he saw that day, and I've seen the tape." But if she had been fond of gardening before, it was after *Sah-Ee-Goo* that Ahjima started gardening with a vengeance, until dirt darkened the whorls in her fingertips, even when clean, getting to her skin even through her leather gloves. She told Soon Ja, in so many words, that the store could go to hell. She put philodendrons in Woo Hyuk's room, potted tall pink kosmos in Soon Ja's room, dark red chrysanthemums on Duk Gil's bookshelves that Duk Gil would quietly move to her mother's room whenever she came home for Christmas.

Sometime in the past ten years, Ahjima had added a small pot of three slender bamboo stalks that now sat in the center of her living room table. A church friend had told her that if you cut a bamboo stalk into pieces and plant them, those cylinders will eventually take root on their own, slender tendrils silently rupturing green walls, unseen beneath six inches of colored gravel. Sometimes I would come into the living room and see her carefully filling the pot with water until it was almost overflowing. She exclaimed over the plants' tiny leaves or the smoothness of the stalk, darker patches of green blooming beneath the white ring marking each layer of growth. "*It's terrible Soon Ja's samchun never appreciated this*," she snapped. "*So beautiful – just like Korea.*" Soon Ja's *samchun* – her uncle – used to have thickets of bamboo in his Cerritos backyard, up against the fence, but he cut them all down for reasons he never made clear. Without the bamboo, his backyard looked bigger for sure, but it also allowed one to catch glimpses of cars and the outside world through the wooden fence. "*Too noisy,*" Ahjima scolded.

My mother had several Korean watercolors of bamboo hanging up upstairs in our house in Vermont. The black, deft strokes of the calligraphy brush formed my vision of bamboo for many years – a bony plant growing in thickets, not in the bushy canopy of our New England maples and oaks. Bamboo – the word itself even sounded ghost-like, "bam" for being hit on the head with a magic reed, "boo" for the surprise that followed. Seeing them in Ahjima's living room, however, I was disappointed. I could have pocketed those stalks and walked off with them – they were so tiny, and the porcelain they sat in was so fragile.

Sometimes after a fit of sleeplessness I dreamed restless dreams about Ahjima taking root in a gravel-strewn pot sitting on a dining room table, separated from the earth by a sliver of porcelain, her memories sprouting greenly under an American sun. Cut off from her motherland but still able to root in the ground, wherever she may go, given a little water and a little piece of earth. But in the mornings I would awaken to Ahjima's voice, fretting out loud over new color schemes, new combinations of plants from the old world and the new.

Without fail, Ahjima spends the mornings outside, trimming the dead leaves from lemon trees, snipping wilting irises, snapping off the laden stems of red geraniums, ducking under the waxy yellow petals of cacti to spread fertilizer on the dry California soil. There is a row of aloe by the porch, and every day Ahjima picks out stray seeds that have blown in between each aloe's arms. She squats so close to the earth that sometimes her straw sunhat seems to swallow up her body and kiss the soil, the large rose-tinted ribbon around her hat almost brushing the ground. Ahjima always pulls her sleeves up to her elbows as she tidies her garden. Her arms have become freckled and wrinkled just below the line of her shirt-sleeve, although her skin above the elbow keeps the alabaster smoothness and white spotlessness she was so proud of when she was young. In the evenings, too, I can hear the hissing of the hose through the window, as Ahjima's shadow slips across the sunset.

One evening, while Jerry was at her boyfriend's, Sohn Ahjushee, Mr Kim, and I went for a walk. Ahjima had told us the day before that she couldn't come because she was too tired, the day before that she had waved us away saying she had to water her plants, and on this particular day we became careless and forgot to ask her to come with us. As we walked out the door, she washed her hands briskly as she prepared to do the laundry and said, very distinctly, "*Fine, go and have fun while I sit here and do chores.*"

"*I think my wife is getting a little jealous,*" Sohn Ahjushee remarked as we left the house. "*When you get old, Sandy, people tend to become a little selfish.*" But he didn't retrace his steps to ask if she'd like to join us.

Mr Kim talked about the Korean War that day, and evoked a Seoul of burning houses and falling bombs, his hands painting shapes from his past in the evening air. "I worked for the railroad for a few months during the Korean War," he said, "and there were always people coming to me, begging to be let onto the boxcars that would carry them far away from Seoul and into the Korean countryside, where they would be safe. So I would attach as many boxcars on the train as I could find and fill them all with people, send them all far away from that sad place. I remember there was a group of nuns who came to me one day, along with a priest, and they begged to be let on the train. They looked so pitiful, I couldn't refuse...just before they boarded, the priest came to me and took my arm, and he said, 'You are like God to us. I pray that you will survive this war and live happily for all your days.' I cannot forget his face; he was so grateful to me..." Mr Kim's voice broke a little bit, and I saw his eyes grow misty, then clear as we passed a twisted pine tree, whose gnarled bark flowed toward the earth like water frozen in brittle, wavy columns. "Such a beautiful tree," he said quietly. "It's a real shame how much they've cut it – you can see that it used to be much bigger. It's almost cut in half now."

"Good evening," I heard one of the neighbors say, still watering his lawn in the near-darkness, the smoke from his pipe drifting toward us. In the distance, the buildings of the Los Angeles skyline faded into the dusk, their names and street numbers glinting. Hundreds of flowers breathed their fragrance into the air – hibiscus, roses spilling between the slats of white fences, low-lying leaves just grazing the crumbling cement sidewalk. Sohn Ahjushee's voice. "*I hope Ahjima is not too upset.*"

"Yes," said Mr Kim. We walked without speaking for a moment.

"How is the apartment search going, Sandra?" Mr Kim asked.

"Fine," I said, although it really wasn't.

She wasn't there when we got back. Sohn Ahjushee waited outside, watering Ahjima's flowers, the hissing of the hose seeping dully through the window. I sat in Woo Hyuk's room studying his collections of Korean coins and watched the hands of the clock drift past 8:30pm, when one of Ahjima's favorite Korean soap operas went on; past 8:45pm. Just as *Our House* would have ended at 9, I heard Sohn Ahjushee say, "*There you are! Where were you? We were worried.*"

"*Oh, really? Worried, were you?*" They argued for half an hour that night outside my window, Ahjima's shrill voice cutting into the hiss of the hose. "*Do you think I can just do it on my own? I have arthritis in these fingers and it hurts just to water these flowers. And you run off and have fun while I sit here alone? To talk behind my back when you know that I can't speak to her as I'd like?*"

"*Mr Kim came along too.*"

"*Even worse. Well, I can have fun too. Why, I took my own walk while you three were out. You think I'm not strong enough to walk, don't you? Well, that's not true.*" She paused, only to begin again. "*This is ridiculous. Who in their right mind waters flowers at nine in the evening? Stop watering those flowers; I'm going to have to do it again anyway, you always water them so sloppily.*" I saw the silhouette of Sohn Ahjushee's head passing in front of the window as he slipped around to the front yard, heard the front door open and close, caught the shuffle of Sohn Ahjushee putting on his bedroom slippers and padding to his room.

In the morning, I lay quietly in bed, listening to Ahjima tear out the flowers outside my room, the root clumps leaping up beneath her hands in clouds of dirt. When all was finally still and I ventured to peek out the window, I saw a small lemon tree that hadn't been there before, its branches already bowed with fruit, the soil around it dark with its first watering.

"*Sandra,*" Ahjima whispered to me later that day, "*if only you could speak more Korean! There are so many things I want to tell you that I used to tell Soon Ja, about men and about life, but I can't.*" She smiled at me secretively, but I only laughed and excused myself, fleeing outdoors with my sketchbook and sitting down on the warm sidewalk.

I heard the scrape of plastic slippers against concrete; Ahjima had followed me. "*Sandra, I wanted to ask you, did you hear us yesterday?*" I blushed, then nodded yes. "*It's not good for you to hear such things,*" Ahjima said, "*and I haven't forgotten about those helicopters. Perhaps Woo Hyuk's room isn't in the best place for you?*"

"Oh no, I like it," I hurried to assure her, but she had already blown away. I came in for dinner that evening to find all of my belongings carefully arranged in a room downstairs, Sandra's eldest brother Woo Shin's room. It was quite dark and cold as there were no windows; Woo Shin used to joke that maybe this was what being in jail felt like. He had left a stack of pictures of his family next to his bed, and I flipped through them that night, reading all of his captions and looking for any shots he might have left of Soon Ja in her new Texas digs. "A Minneapolis skyline, 4pm, junior year summer with Dave and Rick." "Disney World with cousins, for the umpteenth time." The last photo was of him and his mother; Woo Shin was holding a black-and-white watercolor in one hand and pointing to it with the other, although he might have been pointing to Ahjima. "A ghost flower adrift in strokes of calligraphy," he had written on the back.

A week after hearing the Sohns dueling outside Woo Hyuk's room, I came into the living room to get one of the mangoes Ahjima kept in a fruit bowl there, and saw Jerry sitting on the couch by the window. She was peeking through the slats of the blinds at Sohn Ahjushee, who was sprinkling water over Ahjima's pink tea roses, a small frown creasing the corners of his mouth. "*Look at him watering those plants! It is a nice gesture, but I'll have to do it again later anyway,*" Ahjima said into her ear, floating silently to her side. Jerry smiled while applying ointment to the tender spots on her face where her freckles used to be, and they sat together, listening to the running water. "*He is so lazy! That is what we were fighting about the other day,*" she said, leaning toward Jerry, a secretive smile stretching her mouth, stretching my brain, snapping it just enough to let in a splash of cold panic merely from watching them. "*Look at these joints in my fingers, so swollen and painful – he never helps me. He just wants to play.*" Her tinkling laugh shook the surface of the spring water she held in a small measuring cup.

"*Oh, all men are like that,*" Jerry said, clucking sympathetically. She snapped open a tiny mirror she kept in her pocket and checked her face, dabbing at the ointment with a tissue.

"*Yes, of course,*" sighed Ahjima, getting up. She steadied the bowl of bamboo with her free hand and began pouring drops of water into it, leaning with her eyes almost touching the porcelain to check the depth. I resumed my search for a ripe mango.

"*Don't you think so, Sandra?*" she called. She was coming toward me.

"Oh, no!" I said. For a moment I thought about saying, "*Mee-yan-ha-da*" – I'm sorry – but instead walked to the couch and turned on the television to *Upstairs, Downstairs.* Ahjima sat and watched with me for a few minutes, laughing forcefully when I laughed although she didn't understand any of the words. "*It's very funny, isn't it!*" she exclaimed. I nodded, my cheeks flaming. "*Well, you can amuse yourself. I'll be in the kitchen,*" she said, getting up and floating out in the red Korean demi-slippers she always wore.

"I didn't even know we get that show," Jerry said.

"We do." I turned the television off, went into Woo Shin's room, and closed the door.

It became a bad habit of mine to run away like that, to dig a space where I could hide until someone else sought out an activity all of us could do together. The following Saturday, Sohn Ahjushee announced he wished to drive us all to Echo Park, where he had discovered a lake full of lotus blossoms. Jerry couldn't come because she needed to keep the sun off of her freckles, so it was me, the Sohns, and Mr Kim who went, careening unsteadily along the highway in Sohn Ahjuhshee's ancient white Cadillac. "Mrs Sohn will enjoy these," he assured us as we drove over, Ahjima clutching tightly to the handle located just above the passenger seat window, the diamond butterfly clip in her hair winking in the morning sunlight. "*These car rides always make me ill,*" Ahjima complained. But her sighs faded as we neared the lake, and the large green leaves of the lotus flowers came into view. "*Oh! How lovely,*" she exclaimed, leaning forward to peer at the velvety pink blossoms as we sped closer. "*They seem even larger here than they were in Korea. Lovely. How I love flowers. How wonderful!*" And then, turning to her husband: "*Did you explain to Sandra what the meaning of the lotus flower is? It would be good for them to know.*"

"In the Buddhist religion, the lotus is the purest flower," said Sohn Ahjushee. "No matter how dirty the water is that it grows in, it always comes up and opens as shining and beautiful as it would on an isolated mountain top where everything is clear." Walking along the periphery of the lake, we encountered several of the Sohns' old friends in floppy hats and fishing gear, photographing the flowers with cameras on tripods. "*Take some nice pictures,*" Ahjima smiled to the photographers as we left. And then, almost fretfully: "*If only I could reach out and pick one! I'd like to take one home with me...maybe we need a lotus pond, Yohboh.*"

"*Lovely,*" Ahjima murmured to herself when we returned to her house, cutting flowers and placing them in tall vases. "*Lovely,*" she said, carrying them inside and placing them in different rooms. She came downstairs with a tall gladiola and walked into Woo Shin's room, looked for somewhere to put it.

"*It's not sunny enough in here,*" she said out loud, trying first his bookcase, then his bureau. "*They need to breathe. They need light.*" I watched her face crease into agitated lines. "*Sandra,*" she said, "*do you get enough light in here?*"

"Yes," I said softly. Ahjima nudged the vase several inches to the left. A splash of water sloshed out of the top and started trickling down the sides. Ahjima's face crumpled.

"*I don't think you do,*" she said. "*At least, I know I wouldn't.*" She picked up the vase and trudged upstairs. "*But where can I put you?*" I heard her say. "*Where is there any space left? Not Mr Kim's room, not Jerry's...*" For the rest of the day, Ahjima left a trail of worry as she floated about the house, giving me guilty glances whenever we passed one another. "*We've already tried Soon Ja's. Already Woo Shin's.*" I heard her putting plates away in the kitchen, the clatter of porcelain hitting porcelain. "*Already Woo Hyuk's.*"

"Maybe she's trying to tell you something, Sandy," Jerry said that evening, sipping at her daily post-dinner cup of coffee on the porch. Every once in awhile she peered with narrowed eyes at the horizon, as if half-expecting the sun to come back and burn her face with a stray ray. "Damn this city. There are never any stars here." We looked up together at the dull night sky, glowing slightly yellow from the city lights.

"There should be at least one more room, in the annex," I said. "I'm surprised she hasn't moved me there yet – I mean, I know for sure she had six kids. Doesn't that mean there's at least one more room?"

"Which rooms has she put you in so far?"

"Soon Ja's, Woo Hyuk's, and Woo Shin's."

"Well, I have Jae Jin's room and Mr Kim has – oh no, wait. I know what it is."

"What?"

"The Mister and the Missus sleep in separate rooms because of his snoring, remember? Mr Sohn sleeps in the eldest daughter's room. Duk Gil, the one who had already gone to college by the time you met Soon Ja. So there's nowhere left to put you."

"Ohhhhh..." We sat without looking at each other for a very long time. Jerry's cigarette glowed red into the evening, burning brighter, then fading. On, off. Ashes falling. I could hear Jerry breathing very deeply, until she inhaled too much and started to cough.

"How's the apartment search going?" Jerry said in between wheezes.

"It's okay," I said.

"For real?"

"No," I said. "But it'll have to be okay very soon."

"Yeah." A slight wind blew a heavy fragrance in our direction.

"Mmmmm, what is that?"

"I think it's those new flowers Ahjima planted this afternoon, the little white ones."

"She has a way with plants, doesn't she?"

"You bet."

When there was nothing left to say, Jerry held out her cigarette. "I know you don't smoke, but anyway – do you want a puff?" I shrugged.

"Sure, what the hell."

"Okay." Pretty soon I was coughing worse than she was.

Aqua Alta

Hannah Langworth

And they went back after twenty years,
Friday-tired, boxed in for a few hours
fidget, squabble and peace. Stansted disappears
fell away from white wings. Water-loud showers
greet them with a painting. They peer
at it through moving windows, known, but now as
faint as watermarks. Then the damp palaces roll
out like a wave, and their feet feel wet and cold.

Well-slept, they walk though wet and pigeon goo,
plastic bags round good boots because, "you said
it wouldn't flood!" All the places that they knew,
and mostly can't remember, follow them. He'd
be reading the Blue Guide, she'd look at shoes
and still know everything. They'd drink wine, tread
duck boards to hidden altars, the rainy beach,
write postcards to the girls, one each to each.

Aloft. Nervous at the rush-off. Bound in book,
hears the shudders chink as the blue light
fills the window like a plastic glass. Looks.
Good weather. Up and up and right,
her box of high water drops and hooks
from that old place. Silver-white,
it's an old chandelier, wrapped like plane breakfast,
a few lumps of light and water, some dust.

Stillbirth

Susan Gordon

He's left you
with more
and less
than what you had before.
You press your lips to the cup he used,
to recreate his kiss;
You lay your forehead to the door
and remember him
leaving.
> There's ruined Carthage in your head,
> The smell of him still in the bed –
> The morning makes you sick.
You leave all last year's debris
scattered around the room
and sit at the window, staring
at a bird out on the lawn –
crying, tearing
at what was nearly born –
like an almost-mother
clutching
at an empty womb.

August

Stephanie Cross

The new bed arrived on Saturday, the hottest day so far. Afterwards, they sat in the kitchen drinking wine from the fridge, hoping a breeze would clear the air. They talked about the weather and how long it could last, how London in August could still surprise with its strength and vigour of heat.

They sat like that for some time, with the sound of sirens coming in off the street and the yells of children, but then he rubbed his eyes and said there was no toothpaste, and that he would go and get some. There were other things they needed – tomatoes, cereal, margarine – and while she leaned on the counter and made a list, he watched (she could feel him) the back of her neck.

"We should get ice cream," he said. "Summer's not summer without."

Soap, she wrote, before she forgot, and then paused to consider.

"You get some – treat yourself. I'm on a diet."

She was not overweight – he thought she was perfect, that she was fine as she was – but in the past months she had gained a few pounds, and now she wore twelves, not a ten.

He laughed at her.

"Didn't you know? Diets don't work at weekends. Besides, today is special. Now, what do you want: strawberry, toffee, vanilla?"

She turned round and held out the list, looking up to meet his eyes. For months at first she had wondered if they were more properly blue or green.

"You choose," she said, and kissed him.

"Bring me something different. Bring me a surprise."

· · · · ·

The bedroom was yellow, as it had been in May, when they had first moved into the flat. Since then they had changed most of the rooms, put a new floor in the kitchen, repainted the lounge and the hall. They had bought rugs, blue and red, from market stalls, and dark fleshy plants in silver pots which they took turns to water and feed. But the bedroom had suited them both and in truth they were bored of the work by then.

They had bought the new bed on the previous weekend, from a warehouse at the end of the central line. It had been a day at the start of the heat and, sitting next to each other on the tube, she had noticed the veins on his hands, raised but still subterranean, like the carriages over ground. To pass the time, she had listed the things that their flat remained without.

"Dinner plates. You know, proper big ones, not just the ordinary size. Champagne glasses. Flutes. And soup bowls too – we ought to have some of those."

To all this he had nodded and smiled, and refrained from asking when they would use them, or pointing out they never ate soup.

Then she had said, "We need new sheets. We must have new sheets for the bed. What about blue, to set off the walls?"

Her enthusiasm, he found, was hard to resist. When she came up with a plan, or saw a film she liked, her eyes smiled in a particular way. This, in fact, had been one reason he loved her, although he did not think he had said. But sometimes her ideas surprised him, and he felt she was yet an unknown.

"Maybe," he said. "One thing at a time."

She pressed her lips together and looked out of the window. Lately there had been little on which they had agreed.

To start with, it had been easy enough. Walking on the street, his arm round her waist, they would see something displayed – a vase perhaps, or a print. They would buy it at once, rarely differing in taste, and only when they got back to the flat consider its utility or where it would go. In the spring, when the shops had sales, they had often walked from the station carrying bubble wrapped parcels and brown paper bags.

Then he had begun to worry about money, and the fact the flat would be cluttered.

"There's no point in collecting things," he said, "They only stand around and get dirty. We don't have much space as it is."

On this matter she had seen his point of view, but his caution slightly grated. They had been spontaneous at first, almost dangerously so – or at least it had seemed to her. They would invent excuses from work and take off for the day, sometimes even for two; travelling to the coast, or wasting time in the city, pleased at whatever occurred. On other days they would not leave the bedroom and, when their bodies were weary and ached, they would talk, turning over their lives. But now things at first unnoticed were forming little resentments. For example. The way he did not rinse his cup in the morning, and she would need a soap-pad to scrub it clean. The way there were holes in his socks.

Deciding on a bed was not quite the simple matter that either of them had supposed. Before they left the flat they had measured the room: he called out the figures while she wrote them in biro, on the pad they kept by the phone. This, like much else, had been bought in the excitement of newness and with the aim of doing things right, but in three months there had been few calls, and none that required a note.

In the end, their purchase took the best part of a morning and when they had finished they were tired and cross. She could not avoid the thought he was ridiculous, bouncing on mattresses to test the give of the springs, and he had been annoyed by her manner, and her customer's voice. In fact, the place had disturbed her, with its beds in grids of sleep. But they had wandered out on to the pavement, into the crowds, and the heat and the light had soothed them.

"We're like a proper couple now," she said as they walked.

He looked round at her, puzzled. She had applied her mascara a little too thickly, and her bottom lashes had copied themselves on to the pale skin of her cheek.

"Of course we are," he said; and then, "Why, weren't we before?"

She reached for his hand and gave it a squeeze, her nails briefly drained white.

"Yes. But it's like we've said it now. We've told everyone in the shop.'

To her, it has not seemed a fact before: their togetherness had always been tacit. The flat they lived in was after all only rented; the television that they watched at night, hired for six months at a time. Until then, even their sleeping arrangements had been comfortably temporary – two single mattresses pushed together, the join visible through the sheets. But the new bed was different. It was, she thought, an agreement. They would take it with them wherever they moved; position it in rooms they had yet to see. They would make love in it, oversleep in it and, when they were ill, they would lie down in it and rest. Each time they packed their things in boxes and travelled on and into the city, they would leave behind the impression of castors: shadows, stamped there on the floor.

On the previous night, after the old mattresses had been consigned to a skip, they had slept on cushions pulled from the sofa.

"Did you ever do this when you were little?" he had asked her, amused. "Camp in the house, I mean."

She laughed.

"Of course. But I could never get to sleep. Sooner or later, I'd always sneak back to bed."

She rolled over to help her remember.

"I'd take picnics too. Being awake in the night makes you hungry."

He smiled.

"But not tonight?"

"No, not tonight."

It had been his turn to cook. They had eaten chicken and rice and steamed vegetables, and afterwards chocolate mousse.

He was silent for a while and she thought he was asleep. Then he started up on his elbow.

"What is it?"

He was pulling the cushion that was under his head, trying to turn it round or something else she couldn't make out.

"Coffee."

"Hmm?"

In the dark her brain was slow.

"We must have dropped some coffee on the sofa. I keep smelling it. It's keeping me awake."

She smiled at the thought.

"Placebo effect."

"Ha ha," he said, and continued fidgeting.

She wondered which one of them had spilt the drink.

After a while he was satisfied and laid back down. Then he sighed.

"Happy now?"

"Very."

He spoke it with an effort, like pushing off a dream.

After dinner he had gone to the study to read the papers he'd set aside. He worked as a lawyer, but did not want to, and talked of giving it up to write. When she came in at eleven his head was on the desk and his hair growing hot in the lamp. Around him, his books were heaped into piles, shaggy with post-its at relevant points. One arm rested on the page he'd been reading, and she thought it looked like he'd tried to reach out for the words, to hold them, to stay awake.

It amazed her he could sleep like this, with the light in his eyes and his stomach bent at an angle. For her, sleep was something that had to be coaxed, and often escaped entirely. She needed the dark, and quiet, and at least to lie down.

In May, when they had travelled to America, he had slept for the length of both flights. She had not even dozed.

"He doesn't like flying," she'd told the hostess, "he prefers it if he's asleep."

As far as she was aware this was not in fact true; but it had been something to say. Returning to England they took an afternoon flight and arrived in London at dawn. To him the journey was familiar; a family friend in New York, but to her it was something new. She had insisted on sitting by the window though he'd told her there was nothing to see, that after ten minutes she would be bored and end up by watching the film. But instead she had seen from the windows how darkness was held between days, and, as they had flown across it, night had seemed then a quantifiable space. But beside her he had slept soundly, and only opened his eyes at Heathrow.

Curled on the cushions, she had wanted to tell him of this – to speak, in fact, about anything, in order to hear his voice. His breathing, however, was like a reproach: he was tired and not to be troubled. Instead she had thought about their weight pushing down on to the fabric and crushing the soft velour.

She did not know how much they weighed together, the two of them combined. Earlier in the day, when she had stripped the mattresses, before they had gone to the tip, she had noticed the dents their bodies had made: two 'c' shapes, one in another. Looking at the beds, becalmed and bare, in the mess of their unwashed clothes, she had imagined a time when one c would reverse and she would sleep with her face to the wall. Then, in the sunlight, it had been like a sum, a calculation of months and weeks, but in the dark she was afraid and shivered into his spine, and hid her face at the base of his neck.

• • • • •

At three he was back, sweat smoothing his T-shirt to fit to the lines of his shoulders.

"Look," he said, showing her the grooves the bags had cut in his palms.

"Poor baby," she said. "What did you get?"

She probed into the packets and cans.

"Patience," he said, tapping her gently, and reaching in himself.

The cold of the ice cream had made condensation in the bags and when he brought out his hands they were wet.

"Here," he said. "I thought these were good. I got one for us each."

He held out a lolly; not a grown-up ice cream, but the kind with smudgy jokes on the stick.

"Did I chose right? Is this a surprise?"

"This," she said, "Is perfect. I haven't had one of these for years."

The paper wrapping was soggy and tore easily, and gave its own pulpy taste to the whole. For a while they ate in silence, thin, milky ribbons snaking on to their wrists, then he said, "The road's melting too."

"Hmm?"

"Outside. The tarmac is melting. It's all over the place."

They finished their ice creams and went to look, not bothering to lock the door.

Blisters, shiny and fat, were appearing in the surface of the road and there was a thick, dead scent in the air. Concerned drivers lent from their windows, steering slowly around the mess. "Hotter than the Med!" a man called as he passed. She smiled and half waved her hand.

They remembered, before they went back in, to check each other's shoes. The carpets in the flat were pretty and impractical and already wore signs of their tenancy. It was not an easy operation, balancing on alternate legs, and in the narrow hall they stood shakily, and held each other for support.

Inside, in the shade, their eyes complained at the dimness and unpacking the shopping was awkward. He admired the fact that she had an order for this, as for other such things. Baked beans, tinned fruit and fish were put at the back of the cupboard nearest the floor – these were the things they used least. In front were jams, jars of coffee, anything that was glass and could break or fall. Above the work-surface, in the wall cupboards, were the cereals and pasta and bread. And on the high shelves above these were things they rarely touched: flour, plain and self-raising; decorations and candles for cakes. He could not remember when these had been needed.

By the time the bags were empty, they were both hot and flushed. The ice creams had done little to cool them, and her tongue felt slimy and thick. She had half begun to imagine that the heat was a fever, or a virus, which had some-how got into their blood.

"I'm tired," she said.

He put an arm round, lifted a few strands of hair from her face.

"Rest. It's too hot for anything else"

They walked together to the bedroom.

Then they saw the new bed, stilled wrapped in plastic, and filling the room with an oily smell. If they wanted to rest, they would first have to make it, and struggle some more in the heat.

It was August, and September was two weeks away.

She sat on the bed and put her head in her hands and cried quietly for a time.

While it lasted he placed a hand on her thigh, and when she'd finished, he brought her a tissue. Then, because there was no need to talk and nothing else to be done, they kicked off their shoes and lay down, and the polythene stuck to their skin.

To a Girl I Saw Once Washing Her Car

Jennifer Donnelly

I watched a girl clean her car
It's angry eye blue and
She stoops to clean her car,
Polishing her own reflection in the stern metal.
She's washing her face and cleaning her car.
Her hands dip deep in the bucket
As the contract, suds run from between her fingers as she's cleaning her car
The sponge expands, shrinks; she mauls it.
And she pounds it over her blue car.

Her top, riding up
Shows a slim strip of pale over her shorts
Her back: a dimple.
And those shorts
A red band across her thighs.
She's humming between her teeth as she cleans her car.
Her hair bundled up at the back.
Knotted up in a yellow silk tangle.

What should I do?
I only watch that back.
Her sinews flexing
Heel to waist stretching
Shoulder to waist
Leaning.
Her bare white belly brushing the car as she cleans.

And I wonder
As her belly brushes the angry eye blue car that she cleans
If her skin shrinks from the cold, the hard.
And if her flesh withdraws into goose bumps.
She is wet and dripping
Up to the elbows.
And that skin, like a pale peach, shines.
Just as soft, just as downy.

I speculate
That if I should nibble her
My lips would grow wet
And would she taste the same?
I cannot imagine that warm skin yielding
Not when she's stretching over her car
Methodically smoothing wax
Onto its steel blue coldness.
Those wide flat hands
And shining flanks
Too strong for me.

I walk away, a feather wisp
Streaming with her reflection
Pooling with the water,
Under her feet.

They called it "The International" and "Old Betsey" and even "The Empress Dowager."

Christopher Simons

Narrative:

When they were almost overrun
on 7 July, the converts found
the rusting muzzle of a gun
nuzzling the foundry's ash-strewn ground.

The Italian one-pounder, their workhorse,
had fourteen shells left; the munitions man
from HMS Orlando *had gone hoarse*
calling for pewter vessels to melt down
to make more shot. The evening meal was rice,
with jam, and tea, and horse.

Mitchell, a US gunner, scraped
the rust from the discovered gun,
said to date from that '60s scrape,
the Anglo-French expedition.

In fact it was a common Chinese cannon.
Dumb luck – the Russians' useless shells were shaped
to fit the bore; spare wheels from the Italian
made it a trundling, sooty mouth that gaped
out through a gap at Fu-hsiang's Kansu horsemen
and coughed out "Tientsin."

Commentary:

At this stage, even Captain Poole
didn't turn down a proffered pull
from the beseiged's most helpful tool:
poolfuls of fine French Monopole.

Not even bulletproof Boxers
or the Red Lanterns' aerial blades
could have so impressed the Dowager
or the Hanlin barricades.

Bainbridge wrote of "us foreign devils who thus
apparently constructed a new weapon
out of our combined inner consciousness
and loosed a dragon on the Son of Heaven."
To Backhouse, the Empress herself confessed
it had disturbed her tiffin.

A Short Fairy Story

Nick Gill

She was beautiful when I first knew her, and she was eight. You see, this is where the problems begin: people get in trouble these days for calling children beautiful. But she was. I have certified witnesses who will testify to this. I suppose that was part of it all: I knew her when she was a child, and when she'd grown up, and she was beautiful in both stages. I never saw that brace-wearing, knee-splinted, acned chrysalis she withdrew into for the six or seven years we all wish we didn't have to go through. Maybe it would have been just a touch different if I had.

Anyway, being eight. Everyone can remember being that age when your best friend is the most important thing in the world, can't they? You wake up, and run off to find him (or, if you happen to be a girl, her – you don't get cross-gender best friends at age eight), and you spend all day playing soldiers, or hitting inno-cent brambles with sticks and discussing which, if it came down to a fight, would be the last of the X-Men left standing (it was always Wolverine, right?). And then your mum (or maybe his mum, depending on whose house you were at) would call you in for tea; and then you'd watch TV, and you'd go to sleep and you'd do it all again the next day. And your days would be made up of nettle-stings, bumble bees and great imaginary worlds masquerading as the row of fir trees at the end of the garden. Everyone remembers that, right?

Well, I don't. That doesn't mean it didn't happen, of course; but I don't think it did. I don't remember a lot of being small, though. There were lots of bright, stainless steel instruments, lots of white coats peering curiously, and many occurrences of the word 'phase', but that's about it. I had lots of friends; I know for a fact that I had lots of friends, but I also know that no one else could see them. As you can imagine, this made interaction with normal people slightly tricky.

She didn't have any friends either. I'm sorry if this is going on a little too much for you, but this is pretty important; to me, at any rate. It's what they call 'backstory' in films (and I do wish they didn't), and it's normally relevant; I'm not sure if this is, to be honest, but it might be, and I don't want to run the risk of missing something out that I'll wish I'd put in, because I don't think I'll be able to go back and do it again.

Friends. Right. She didn't really have any either. I think our parents must have met in a waiting room to someone or other (who had letters after his name, stainless steel instruments, a white coat, and a familiarity with the word 'phase', probably). She was sitting opposite me, in a chair that was far too big for her.

She was...OK, this just isn't going to work. We've all fallen in love and written appalling poetry in an attempt to pin down the fragile beauty we've seen before our simple, unworthy mortal eyes, and we all found out pretty quickly that what we'd written was just that: appalling. What we, none of us, realised was that it wasn't because we were bad poets; granted, we were bad poets, but that wasn't why we couldn't do it. The reason we couldn't do it was because beauty isn't meant to be appreciated by scribbling down words about it; the same words we use to order our pizzas, lie to our bank managers and joke with our friends. It's meant to be appreciated with the eyes and the heart and that bit at the top of your stomach that goes all tingly when you see this work of perfection before you. And you can't write that down.

So, she was beautiful. She was like a champagne glass being filled with liquid sunlight by a thousand angels, if that's any help. She was small for her age, and she waggled her fingers at me when I glanced over at her. I blushed, because I didn't know what girls were at that stage; to be honest, I'm not sure I do now. And suddenly, like that, we'd known each other for ages. I don't know if this happens quite a lot with children, but from that moment we just talked and played as if we'd known each other for all our eight-year lifetimes.

This isn't going to be one of those 'we fell in love then, and we're still in love now' stories, by the way. Oh, I suppose you knew that already. Yes, that's right, she did leave. And you know, I couldn't tell you when. Childhood's funny like that. We talk about our 'childhood' like we talk about 'Thursday'; like it's just one little chunk of time. Just like I couldn't tell you what time it started getting dark yesterday, I couldn't tell you when she left. But leave she did, because I can remember her not being there.

And then, of course, the Hormone Goblin came along and danced his wild way through my bloodstream, bringing oil to my hair, hair to strange parts of my body, and strange parts of my body to places they'd never been before. It was an odd time, but mine was no different to anyone else's; it was screwed up, of course, but then puberty is a screwed up time, and a time for screwing things up; both happened to me, in roughly equal measure. And then that too was gone; and, again, I couldn't tell you when. But, gradually, the tide of grease went out and my voice settled into a fairly incomprehensible mumble and, like everyone else, I started the business of finding something to fill my days. I settled on accountancy, because it seemed to require only that I knew how to use one computer program and that I be able to count. Six months of training, and I was there.

This is where she came back in. And, just like that, she was back, and we'd known each other forever again. And, as you might recall, puberty isn't an exclusively male pastime. She'd grown breasts and legs and fashion sense and lipstick and who knows what else. And, it seemed, she wanted to share all of these things with me. Particularly the fashion sense. We went shopping, and it transpired that I was 'dumbing myself down'; I think I probably mumbled something about services to mankind, but she shushed me and put an orange silk doublet into her basket.

I didn't know anyone actually made orange silk doublets.

She bought all these things for me, and wouldn't even hear of my paying for anything. "They're presents" she said. We spent most of a day, with me trying on whatever she gave me, and her paying for them. I suggested we go to the BMW garage, but she didn't fall for it. While I was trying on a pair of purple flared corduroy trousers, I asked her where she went when she left. "To play with the fairies," she said. I stopped, with the trousers half way up my legs and looked at her. She giggled at me then, and passed a pea-green cummerbund through the changing room curtain. "Perfect," she said.

We went back to my house then. She walked in as if she knew it already, dropped the staggering number of bags she was carrying, and collapsed onto them with a sigh; there seemed to be enough room for two on all the clothes, so I joined her, and she wrapped her arms around me with another sigh. Suddenly, she pressed her lips to mine briefly, then looked me in the eyes with a serious expression.

"These are presents for you" she said. "I want you to understand that". I explained that I was familiar with the concept of gift-giving. She bit my nose and said "No. These are presents. Is it all right for you? I mean, do you mind having them?" I didn't. She smiled, and pressed her lips against mine for a longer period of time; and then we were making love, on all the bags of newly bought clothes. You don't need to know any of the details, I don't think, but I feel I should say this: you remember when you still had ideals, and you thought that things could be perfect? Remember how you thought sex could be – sort of a cross between *9½weeks* and *Ghost*? It was like that.

I woke up in bed with a beautiful young woman next to me. She was already awake and was watching me.

"I have another present for you," she said. I told her that I'd have to give her something before she was allowed to get me anything else. "I think you've given me quite enough already," she giggled, then looked serious again.

"You might flip," she said. I didn't reply. She flicked a quick smile at me, and reached for my bedside table; when she rolled back to me, she was holding a jewellery box. "Open it".

Whatever I'd been expecting, this wasn't it. A tooth on gold chain is an unusual morning-after present under most circumstances.

"You don't remember, do you?," she said, biting her lip.

"I…" I began, and then stopped, because I did remember. When our teeth had been coming through, we'd both lost our lower right canines at the same time, completely painlessly. We'd both run to show and tell each other, and we were so excited and giggly that we gave each other our teeth and promised to look after them forever.

Look, it made sense at the time.

I looked down at that little white lump, and didn't quite know what to say. I heard her say "You don't still have mine, do you," and I couldn't quite tell if it was a question. I didn't say anything.

When I looked up, I half expected to see her in tears, but she was beaming. "Good job too," she said. "Two people looking after teeth is just too weird". And then she giggled again, took the chain and hung it round my neck. And then, feeling sleepy again, I closed my eyes.

That was some time ago. It quickly became Monday again, as it so often does, but she wouldn't let me get out of bed and go to work. Her arguments were quite persuasive, and to be honest, I'd never really enjoyed being an accountant anyway; so she went off to work instead. I can't really find the energy to leave the house, so I just stay in, trying on different combinations of new clothes. When she comes back, we kiss, and then we kiss some more, and then we make love. There was an old saying that lovers can live on kisses and cool water, but I'd never really thought it was true until now. After the sex, we sleep for a while, and then she goes to work again. I don't know what she does, but it must be a well-paid job, because every day she comes back home with something made of feathers, or something frilly or sparkly or shiny and she puts it somewhere so that it fits in perfectly in the house. I can stay in all day now, and not get tired of looking at all the shiny, sparkly, frilly, feathery things that make up the world.

Two Months Later…

Amy Flanders

A small brown hand,
the knuckles dimpled,
a plastic bandage on the index finger,
overturns a stone
and surprises a multi-legged creature,
grey against the sandy soil.
The hand grasps a convenient twig
and, gently,
flips the discovery upside down.
"Do small things feel they might fall up,
the way we do on swings?"

It has no discernible head or tail,
this armored specimen,
only legs and a segmented shell.
Two green eyes take note
of the way those legs infold
and the way that shell curves around
to protect the invisible heart.
The hand with the stick carefully
rolls the bug in concentric circles.
"Can you get dizzy
if you don't know you're moving?"

The ball of legs and shell contracts further.
Schroedinger said
we can't observe a system without changing it.
The observer infolds limbs, too,
and sits, spine curved around stomach,
arms around shins,
chin on knees,
one hand still holding a stick.
"Do scars show on shells like on skin?"

The creature senses stillness
and unfurls. It scuttles off,

following what must be the head,
or maybe it moves backwards.
The green eyes watch the many legs
ripple as they carry the shell
and the unseen heart
to another stone, unturned.
"How does it know which way is home?"

Kids' Stories
Phil Shaw

Remember those stories we wrote as kids
with one line endings where we *ran out of legs*,
always filled with rockets and visiting *daddy*
in places without post, the sense unsteady

as we hastened for language amid the excitement
but still capable of meaning, and to represent
so clearly the things we wanted to say
before we grew up and the dreams died away.

I still have them. They're stored in an *Adidas* box
with adolescent photos, against the flux
of the falling years. They put me to shame
by being so sincere. I remember their names

but never read them. They speak of a strain
too shocking beneath all those growing pains.

Jeany
Josie Long

She has this clumsiness about her that is not sexy. She drops things at delicate moments. She spills drink down herself in restaurants and she chews loudly and for a long time. She can't undress quickly and she giggles at the wrong times. When she answers the phone she always speaks in the same confused tone for a few seconds until she gets accustomed to it, even with me.

I don't like the way she dresses. She wears these skirts just below the knee that flare out and don't cling to her hips like they should. Last weekend she turned up in a green velvet hat like a bucket and wouldn't take it off when we got inside the restaurant. It was damp from the rain and you could almost see the steam rising off her head as she talked and talked and talked and covered her old-lady cardigan in white wine.

She counts on her fingers in shops with this deliberate face like a caveman, screwing up her forehead. She counts out her money and then re-counts it on her fingers, straining to concentrate. Queues form behind her as she does it, miles away. And I have to stand next to her, politely looking at the closest shelves, reading and re-reading the aspirins and plasters until she's ready. When we walk she does that hand-swinging thing that kids do, and then she'll look up at me and crack up as if it's the funniest thing, and I'll smile a bit until she looks away feeling flushed and awkward.

She's always late without fail. Even if she turns up early she can manage to be late. Once she missed the only coach to visit her mother in Exmouth, even though I made sure she got there an hour early. She just watched it drive away. She told me later she thought she'd got onto it, started daydreaming about the journey and only realised that she wasn't actually on the coach when the person next to her wouldn't answer her. But it's odd because she won't ever lie in bed with me in the mornings. She can't just lie there. She has to get up and busy herself with the things that should be done in the mornings, knocking the cups and plates around as she makes tea that's all stewed by the time I get it and stares critically at the toast she's eating. I try to wake up but I can't, and if I ever do, and walk into the kitchen to kiss her neck she freezes up guiltily as if the kitchen and the morning are her private things.

I sometimes hear her singing in the shower when I'm sleeping. There's nothing wrong with her voice as such, but she always stops in the middle of songs then carries on, parodying and criticising herself. She comes back to bed in about three towels, crushing my legs by accident as she clambers over me and wakes me.

She wore the hospital bracelet for three weeks afterwards. She would wind it round her arm with a glazed look on her face, while I would work around her, tidying the dinner things and doing the dishes.

We are shopping today and she is happy. I don't know why but she can't stop beaming and squeezing my hand. We are shopping for shoes, which she loves and I hate. She has told me twice already the precise type of shoe she needs (black with white toes and laces, a small heel, some sort of pattern). We have looked and looked. We have really pissed some shop staff off. She has developed this little routine over the course of this afternoon where she finds a shoe that has one or sometimes (but very rarely) two of her specifications and reassures me that this is the last time, it really is, this time it really is the last one. She puts one, then both, then the other on and walks about awkwardly asking me over and over. A couple of times she has gone so far as to get out her purse, but managed to unconvince herself at the last minute (mainly "because of your face. You were pulling a face") just as I was beginning to feel calm again.

So we are shopping, she is dragging me around and she is happy and even though if I could build some kind of shoe-pile-fire I would do it, and make a special place on it for that cow from Russell and Bromley, I am so relieved, and then this woman starts to talk to her outside this little gift shop and manages to make her cry. It was so sudden I didn't register it until she was all crumpled up in front of the whole Westgate centre. I took her outside and smoothed her hair until she stopped. I wanted to say something. I did that breathing in thing four times but nothing would come. I just waited until she stopped.

Later when we walked home (without any new shoes) she asked me if I'd lost interest. I didn't say anything. In the evening she sat in front of the sofa in a duvet. We had both been crying (for our own reasons). I sat down next to her and we kissed for a while. It was soft and awkward. I put on Van Morrison who she had never really liked, and for that moment it felt like the whole world was perfect except for me.

She stepped out of the taxi utterly oblivious to paying and pulled at the waist of her skirt, waiting and squinting at me. She held out her hand until I took it and we walked into the party together, three hours after I'd told them we'd arrive.

She has this way at parties. People are drawn to her strange little outfits and they fuss around her offering her wine out of cartons and bits of vegetable. She talks, tilting her head side to side her eyes darting about under her straight black fringe and her hands making these little pointed gestures like birds pecking as they move. She tells the same anecdotes that I've heard fourteen times, doing that impression of her mad mother, spilling wine over her shirt. I'm usually quiet. Some idiot interested in cars will find me by a piano and try to argue with me as everyone else gets drunker and does things.

She changes at the thinning-out stage of the night when people start sitting down on the stairs and talking earnestly. I will have lost my car-friend, finally, to go and look for her and she won't be anywhere. This party was the same. It was 2am and I wanted just to leave after I'd been stuck for an hour and a half in a conversation about what children's television programmes people used to watch, politely and quietly acquiescing about *The A-Team*, but all the time worrying about her, knowing how she'd be, trying to see where she was.

I found her in a utilities room by the washing machine. She had drunk a few bottles of wine and was curled up, her knees bent under her horrible skirt. I tried to pick her up but she wouldn't let me. Her face was all smudged. She wriggled away every time I tried to get a hold of her, looking down away from me. The room smelt vaguely of detergent and the washing machine was whirring to itself. It was grubby and I was tired. I tried again and dragged her up so she was leaning on my chest. She started to cry again and I sighed, clenching my teeth and trying not to get angry.

Walking back it had been raining and the air was stinging and cold. She wouldn't hold my arm or walk with me. She tottered about three steps behind me and every time I'd wait for her she'd find some new excuse to stop, looking up at the stars or pulling at her shoes, until I was so sick of it and her and I just wanted to get back and sleep and not have this again and for one time just not have this at all or have to think about everything. Then she says to me as I'm walking off, pushing my fists into my pockets with the cold, "If you don't care any more just fuck off then, don't come fucking back. If you're not interested any more..." She always swears when she's drunk and I hate it.

"Why do you always have to do this?" I say walking back my voice rising, "Why do you have to behave like this? What's wrong with you?" She says nothing and I'm desperately trying to fill the silence after the anger has disappeared with the shouting and I can just see her face again. "But why do you always have to bring it back up? Can't you see that you're not helping it by being like this?" I look at her and I'm close enough to touch her but I feel like I can't. A car rushes past just short of my right shoulder and I spin round and yelp in this stupid high-pitched voice. "Let's go home please" she says.

That night I watched her sleeping for the first time in so long. She sleeps at awkward angles and very lightly, waking up at my touch but tonight she's in this thick drunk sleep. And I remembered those two nights in hospital where I'd stayed with her until she'd dropped off and wanted so much to hold her hands because I couldn't sleep I felt so sick and sad, but knowing how exhausted she was and that if I woke her she'd be the same mess she had been again. I remember most that I hadn't taken it seriously, I'd practically laughed at her when she talked about the pains. I was busy with something. I can't remember what I was busy with but I was busy with something and trying to block out her fluttering about as I always did when I was busy. The next thing she was crying out and had fallen off her chair, and by the time we had got to the hospital they had to put her straight into intensive care while I stood in the corridor, waiting, punching the walls and tearing down the "give up smoking" posters with my hands.

She always thought I hadn't wanted the baby. I had been shocked and I was scared and the night she told me I had freaked out and left, but I always wanted it. Sometimes when we woke up together I would lie with her and feel her stomach as it got bigger and tell her about our baby just so I could say "our baby" and she'd tell me how I could never take it fishing and I'd pretend to sulk and say she would only dress it up like an ugly old woman; and then we would kiss and it would be soft and feel good. I never really let on how much I wanted it.

I remember how beautiful you looked, that it radiated out of you. You looked perfect. But afterwards you still were, because you always were. I never lost interest in you. When you woke up the next morning I wanted to say something. I wanted so badly to say something but it wouldn't come. I wanted more than anything to say something.

Maintaining Your Clockwork Friend
Dave Thorley

If only I had known, I should have become a watchmaker.
– Albert Einstein.

Take a thumb to the key in the base of his spine
and trill through a couple of turns; tune
up the strings down the shafts of his limbs,
through the hook and the eye and the tackle and block.

Tighten his gemstone jeweller's screws –
use a telescope lens and a thousandth
point blade – and polish his cogs
on a handkerchief. Take the tweezers

and slot them hand into glove, cog into cog.
Tick through his motion. Flick over
one of his miniature pistons; check that his gears
and his steel-wound strings sputter in sequence.

Let his joints off the ratchet; draw out
a series of semaphore signals. Make sure
of your angles: The scope of a goose-step stride
is roughly proportional to the spread

of the stretch of the third and fourth fingers.
The heart chimes at the frequency of footsteps.
Titanium's best for a lifetime's last. Come:
shake hands.

A Spider in Trinity College Chapel
Kelly Grovier

Tiny abseiler, dangling
From the marble index
Finger of Sir Isaac Newton,

How many hands calibrate
The hours of this,
Your dust-bejewelled dial?

The evening sun, spinning
Through the mullioned-mosaic
Of Medieval glass above you

Glistens on the unglazed
Angles of your fragile rose
Window, as if the air itself

Somehow were being
Sewn together and time
Were nothing more than silk

Quilts God used to bind
The struggling souls
On whom He comes to pray.

To the Bed

Sean Forester

On Goethe's last words

Cradle of newborns, intimate of lovers
last one to touch the dying, you are there
in childbirth with the pain and energy
riffling through her body. While we grasp
breath, cry, cough, and kick, you form
our first connection to this earth.

You hold the embrace: as if searching,
he moves his fingers across her body
as she tries to absorb all of him
into her hair, her blood, her breath.
But you are left behind in the abandon
when all that is embodied breaks free.

Bed, tell me of those dying: when everything
is stripped away, darkness floods in
– from the abyss above the firmament,
and the unfathomed space below –
to comfort or destroy us, or all is filled
with light, more light. Can you hold us then?

KY

Greg Kimura

I flip a couple of twenties on the table and tell him I want a case of beer – cheap beer – a bottle of Malibu and a bottle of vodka.

"Gonna be a small party," I say. "Couple of dudes I just graduated with."

"And some girls."

We're in the break room. It's almost 12:30.

I'm speaking low, just loud enough for K-Y to hear. The dispatcher Coles is in his office next door and the sliding window to the break room is half-way open.

I don't want him hearing I'm underage and trying to score. He'll give me the come-to-Jesus talk.

Coles's wife has taken to going to the Mormon church and, lately, he's been getting all holier-than-thou.

K-Y sits there and stares at me. He breathes noisily through his mouth.

He sniffs, but he doesn't make a move for the money. So I slide it closer.

The table is filthy, of course. The ashtray is overflowing. It always has been, as long as I've worked here. People have taken to tapping their ashes on the floor and putting out their butts on the Formica top.

Freaking slobs.

The table is strewn with old newspapers and magazines. A stack of dog-eared skin mags like *Big Knockers* and *Snatch* – names you only see on the top shelf at the Indian corner market – sits in the centre.

No one really looks at them. Then again, no one throws them away, either. Heck, not even Coles.

"Shit, boy," K-Y says. "at ain't enough alcohol for a party. That's barely enough for whatcha might call a cocktail hour."

Oh, boy, I think. Here we go.

K-Y's only a couple of years older than me, but he's going to tell me "How much more I could put down when I was yore age." Then he'll tell me "How they raise 'em soft up here in Alaska, compared to back home."

Then – all wistful like, shaking his head like it's a damn shame – he'll say "how I can drink beer pert near all night and never really get a serious drunk on."

God. I've heard it all before.

See, this is my second summer working the warehouse.

It's K-Y's first.

He moved up here at the beginning of the season from a town called Paducah, Kentucky.

K-Y's real name is Joe. Or maybe it's Joseph. Anyway, he pretends and wants people to call him K-Y.

It's supposed to be short for Kentucky. Which it is, I guess. Apparently, he hasn't heard that K-Y's also, like, gay Vaseline, or something.

Or maybe has? I don't know.

Dude got a lot of laughs for that in the crew room at first. Now no one seems to care.

In any case, K-Y's not what you'd call the sharpest tool in the shed.

Whenever he tells people where he's from, he always gets specific and says, "Paducah, Kentucky".

He says it with a straight face, "Paducah, Kentucky", like he was saying "Hollywood, California", or some other place that someone might have actually heard of.

Yeah, right.

As if people up here give a shit about the different parts of Kentucky. Or anywhere else, for that matter.

To people from Alaska, everywhere else is 'South'. It's all 'The Lower 48', where you were before, and we don't want to hear about it.

Like they say, Alaska's not a place you come to, it's a place you end up in. It's where you go when you were run out of somewhere else, and ran out of country to run to.

I mean, if it was so great in 'Paducah, Kentucky', what the hell is he doing in Anchorage?

What's he doing up here *after* the price of oil bottomed out?

Didn't they get the news in 'Paducah, Kentucky', or what?

Anyway, K-Y's cousin Perry got him the job.

Perry's a journeyman-driver and a Teamster. The manager owed him a favour, or something, and Perry knows someone down at the Local.

Basically, K-Y was 'in-like-Flynn'.

Meanwhile people actually from here are still looking for jobs – any jobs – that will pay the bills.

It's a decent gig here at the warehouse, but I've caught short-timer's disease.

See, I'm leaving for the University of Fairbanks at the end of the summer, where I'm planning on majoring in business administration, or something. Probably pledge a fraternity, too. Study hard, play hard – that's my motto.

When I leave, that means K-Y will get my job.

And because he's Union and I'm not – because I'm too young – he'll end up making more than me.

And he'll get vacation after his first six months.

Paid.

K-Y still hasn't looked at the bills.

He's smiling at me across the table now, like he's got something on me. K-Y likes to play like he knows the ropes.

Actually, the dude is a total moron.

First week on the job, he ran the forklift straight into a port-to-port and punched a hole in it. You should've seen the look on his face, all wide-eyed like a girl. Stupid moron still had the forklift in gear until I pulled him off.

I was the one who showed him how to patch it and caulk it real quick before Coles or anyone else saw what happened.

Sometimes during lunch break, he sits in his Camaro and lights up a bowl. Fires it up like he doesn't even care.

Loser. Talk about a total lack of self-respect.

I mean, I know he does it because I can smell it on him. And I caught him once.

But, you know, I don't say anything. I usually just say after lunch that I'll be on forklift for the rest of the day.

I like to pull rank on him like that.

I can do it because I have seniority.

He doesn't like it but, heck, what can he do? He knows I know what he's doing. Besides, he knows it's the right thing to do, anyway.

It's just I can't *believe* they're going to pay him more money than me after I leave.

Not that I really care.

What I mean is, screw this place.

After I go off to Fairbanks, you'll never see me around here again.

Another thing about K-Y is that he likes to talk.

I mean, dude'll talk your ear off.

I listen because he's still pretty new in Alaska and only has Perry and Perry's wife to talk to. From what I can tell, he doesn't really have any friends besides work.

And all his jawing kind of scares the other guys around the warehouse away.

K-Y tells me about everything.

Like what a drag it is living at his cousin's place. And how fucked up it is in Alaska compared to back home. And how to go down on a woman.

Stuff like that. You know what I'm talking about?

The only thing he *won't* talk to you about is sports.

I mean, what kind of person doesn't like sports? At least some sports?

He'll go on and on with all the reasons he doesn't, though.

"They get paid too much" or "It's all fixed" or "It's mostly spades, anyway."

Spades? You got to be kidding me.

I mean, what, is this, like, the Fifties or something?

What a prick.

I guess they didn't get the message on Civil Rights in Paducah, Kentucky, either.

Memo to K-Y: You don't call black people spades. Not even behind their backs. It's, like, not right.

Well, at least he didn't call 'em the 'N'-word.

God. Like I said.

Dude drives me crazy.

K-Y is plenty quiet now. He knows he's got me by the short and curlies.

He leans back in his chair and puts his hands behind his head, stretching. Then he lights up a cigarette and stands and walks to the machine to get a Mountain Dew.

He's smirking out of the corner of his mouth when he sits back down.

Jesus, I think. He's going to milk this one.

I can tell what he's going to say before he even says it, but I have to listen. He's buying the booze for me, after all.

"Beer, huh?" he says. He takes a long drag, shaking his head back and forth.

"It's for yore own good, ya know, but I ain't gonna buy ya no fuckin' beer. Beer'll give ya a belly."

He leans back in his chair and pats his stomach.

"Beer's for pussies," he says.

"Now Kentucky straight?" he says, leaning forward and placing his elbows on the table.

"That's another story.

"That's a man's drink.

"Kentucky straight'll put hair on yer chest."

"Listen, K-Y," I say. "I don't want any fucking whiskey, all right?

"I want two cases of sale beer, a bottle of rum, and a bottle of vodka. You can buy something for yourself with what's left over. I don't care. That's all I want.

"But don't you be bringing me back any fucking whiskey. All right?"

You know, I don't like to swear around work because everyone here does. If you don't watch it, it'll rub off on you.

Last summer I told my mom to "pass the fucking salt" and she freaked. I apologised all over the place.

Couldn't help it. It just slipped out.

That's 'cause of the element I work with at the warehouse, and I sure don't want to be like them.

But, you know, sometimes you just have to speak the lingo. When in Rome, and so forth.

And, besides, I got to make my point to K-Y.

"No Kentucky straight? Fair 'nuff," K-Y says.

"How about some of them there Bartles and James wine coolers for ya and yore little college faggots? Or maybe some-a that rose-ay box wine, and shit?"

I look at him, pretending hard.

"You got jokes, K-Y," I say.

"Are all you inbreds from Paducah, Kentucky this funny? Or is it just you?

"You want I should make a list and pin it to your fucking shirt?

"I want two cases of beer – whatever's on sale, I don't care – a bottle of fucking Malibu and a bottle of cheap fucking vodka.

"That's it, Goddamn it.

"Take what's left over and buy something for yourself. Get something that comes in a bottle, for once, instead of a jug."

"Fuck you, motherfucker," K-Y says, grabbing the money.

"Yore *my* bitch now. I gotcher ducats. Y'all'l drink whatever I buy.

"And y'all'l like it, too. Asshole."

Oh, great. It's hopeless.

I knew I should've asked one of the other guys on shift to buy for me, not K-Y.

I should've known this would be another thing he'd use to drive me crazy.

"Hey, you two. Pipe down."

It's Coles.

He's slid the glass window all the way open and is sticking his head into the crew room.

"Some of us are trying to get some work done here," he says.

"Sorry, Coles," K-Y and I say together.

"It's 12:35."

That's Coles's new Mormon way of telling us to get the fuck back to work.

It's after work.

I'm standing at the passenger door of K-Y's pick-up, rummaging through the grocery bag, lifting the bottles and reading the labels.

Rum.

Vodka.

...Jim Beam.

"K-Y," I say.

"What is this?" I hold up the bottle.

"That, son, is some of the finest yalla likker y'all'l *ever* put your mouth to."

K-Y is trying to be smooth about it, but he can tell I'm pissed. He's getting ready to tell me the difference between "yellow liquor" and "white liquor" like he has a million times before in the crew room, but I cut him off.

78

"I'll give you something to put your mouth to, Jethro," I say.

"Hey, now. They wasn't no beer on sale, anyway, so I got you some Jimmy B," he says.

"Sour mash. Kentucky straight. The best."

I squint at him. I feel my face turn hot.

"*They wasn't no fucking beer on sale*, huh?" I repeat. "Nice fucking grammar, K-Y, you Colonel-Sanders-Kentucky-Fried-Deliverance motherfucker, you.

"Nice fucking grammar."

I don't know what else to say, I'm so mad. So I take the easy shot. The shotgun approach.

"Trust me," he says. "Yore gonna like it.

"Here. Crack her open.

"We'll have us a slug right now. It's good."

"I'm not going to *crack her open* and I'm not going to *have a slug*," I say and drop it back into the bag.

"Jesus H Christ, K-Y. My parents aren't leaving until after dinner tonight. If I come home from work smelling like your goddamn pappy they'll never leave for the weekend."

"You see," I say. "It's actually pretty simple.

"My parent's don't leave, I don't have a party.

"I don't have a party, I don't need the booze.

"I don't have a party, I don't get laid.

"End of story."

"Take this shit," I say, dropping the bag on the hood of the truck with a clang. "Here. Just take it. I don't want it.

"Can't stand the stuff, anyway."

"Now, don't be mad," K-Y says, looking genuinely sorry.

"Brought back yore change." K-Y reaches into his breast pocket.

"You know what?" I say.

"Keep it.

"Just keep it."

I pick up the bag, turn and start walking to my Camaro.

"Put it in the bank," I say.

"Or, better yet, take it and buy yourself a fucking clue."

"Hold up, partner," K-Y says, shuffling toward me.

"Wait.

"Ah'll make it up to you.

"Tell ya what.

"Ah'll get us some nice sweet sticky-bud. Ah'll bring it by and we can all get toasted. 'Kay?"

I stop and turn around.

"Whoa, partner, yourself" I say.

"One: I don't do that stuff. Weed is for losers. And two: there's no way in hell you're coming by my place.

"God, we see enough of each other at work."

"Aw, come on, now," K-Y says.

"Ah'll show you how to *really* party."

I realise now that this is what the hassle has been about all along.

K-Y is trying to weasel his way into my party.

Shit.

Sometimes, for a guy going off to college – a good college like U of F – it takes me a while to figure out what's going on.

So I change my tone.

I want to let him down, but I don't want to make him feel like like an asshole.

"Sorry, K-Y," I say. I start walking again.

"There's going to be some women there tonight and if things go as planned, the couples are going to pair-off pretty early."

"Even better," K-Y says.

"Ah'll show these gals of yores what it's like to make love to a real Southern man."

"That so, K-Y?" I say. "You let me know when you spot one."

"A real Southern man, that is. You got that?"

"Fuck you," K-Y says.

I turn around, walk to my car and unlock the door. K-Y doesn't flinch.

He just doesn't get it.

You see, these girls I've invited, they're all like me.

They're going away to college at the end of the summer.

The last thing they want to deal with is a loser who drives a pick-up truck and has no prospects other than working in a crummy warehouse.

I mean, K-Y is the kind of guy who gives himself haircuts.

No kidding. Swear to God.

I've literally seen him cut that mop of his in front of the mirror in the warehouse bathroom. I couldn't hardly believe it. Dude used the orange-handled scissors we have for cutting box twine.

Only thing missing was the bowl.

"K-Y," I say. "You're not coming to my party and that's final."

I open the door of my Camaro, slide into the seat and slowly roll down the window.

"And another thing, K-Y," I say.

"Yeah?" he says.

"About buying me the alcohol," I say. I start the engine.

"Uh-huh? What?" he says.

"Thanks for nothing, you Civil-War-losing cocksucker," I say.

Then I start the engine and peel out of the parking lot.

So the party started out pretty cool.

But it faded pretty fast, too. Girl I ended up with only went to third base.

"No, no," she said, pushing me off.

"I'm not...I mean, don't. Oh. ...Please don't.

"Oh, stop. I mean it.

"Please. Please.

"Leave my panties on."

Anyway, I'm telling you. She, like, had these big titties. She only let me stick my finger in, but, oh, did I work it good.

Just thinking about it now gets me going. I could just imagine how it could've been.

But it's the same old story. Prickteasers.

Anyway, we ended up making out and talking for most of the night. Mainly about what we'll study in school and how we won't change. Stuff like that.

It's all bullshit, but what can you do?

After she went home, I cleaned up the house as good as I could and put the empties in the boot of the Camaro. I was too pumped to go to sleep, so I opened K-Y's bottle of Jim Beam and took a couple of sips.

I shivered when it went down. Then I chugged it 'til my eyes watered over.

The next thing I know, it's morning.

I woke up because the phone was ringing by my head. I didn't know what time it was, but it must have been late because the sun was pretty high.

When I moved, my head felt like it was going to cave in. I had that steely taste in the back of my mouth and laid back down until it passed. The machine picked up. The volume was turned down so I couldn't tell who called. I hoped it wasn't my parents saying they were coming home early.

Then I closed my eyes and passed back out.

Now it's Monday again and crazy in the warehouse. I'm running from place to place, humping crates and forking pallets onto the trailers by myself.

K-Y isn't here to help me yet and the drivers are getting impatient.

"Light a fire under it," a driver says. The drivers all know *I'm* the responsible guy in the warehouse. But it's one of those days.

I'm way behind. Everyone's late. Nobody's happy.

C'est la fucking *vie.*

Drivers get pissed if they're not set up to run in the morning. At some point – I don't know exactly when – they get penalised if they're late on-site. Then they have to pay out of their own pockets.

The Union's fighting it, but I don't expect they'll get very far anytime soon, what with management being a bunch of assholes like they are.

So, in the meantime, everyone's taking it out on me.

At 10 o'clock break, I go to the crew room and slide the window open. I lean over into Coles's office.

He's on the phone, of course, pretending like it's real important and he can't stop.

He holds up a finger for me to wait.

Goddamn, Coles, I think.

Shit's falling apart in the warehouse and he's ordering more toilet paper for the bathroom, or some such bullshit.

Finally, he hangs up the phone and takes a deep breath, like he's got the weight of the world on his shoulders and he just shrugged.

He messes with some papers on his desk and then decides it's time to deal with me.

"Now, son. What's on your mind," he says.

Son, I think. That's rich.

He always was an asshole. Now he's talking like a Mormon asshole.

"What's on my mind, Coles?" I say.

"Oh, I don't know."

"I'm on the shit list of half of the drivers this morning. Which I'm sure you've heard about already.

"I'm only halfway down the manifest because K-Y's not here.

"Why don't you go into that Rolodex of yours and find me his number?" I say.

"I want to be the one who wakes that Southern-fried bastard up today," I say, touching the tip of my nose with my index finger and then pointing at him.

Coles looks past me out the window.

His mind's on something, but I can't tell if it's my swearing, or the fuck-you gesture or something else that's put a bug up his ass.

"K-Y, huh," he says.

Coles tosses his pencil down on the desk and frowns.

"K-Y won't coming back here any time soon," he says

I feel the gravel in my throat, as if all the saliva just got sucked out and the pulse beats in my head.

I have that sudden funny dream-like feel about things.

Everything in Coles's office, including Coles himself, grows a fuzzy edge around it.

"Wha–. What are you talking about," I say.

I can't get anything else out.

"K-Y called in sometime over the weekend. Left a message on the message machine," Coles says.

"Sorry. I forgot to tell you."

Coles doesn't look at me when he speaks. He looks at the cork message board above his desk and at the yellow Post-It notes stuck to it. He's picked the pencil back up and is sniffing it.

"Yeah," he says. "That's right.

"Said he was calling from Whitehorse. Yukon Territories.

"Said he'd had enough of Alaska and was heading back home.

"Said he was sorry.

"Said he hoped I got this message in time to call in someone to help you out today."

A Hollow Knock

Yuriy Humber

with blind dry
buttons of eyes

nothing was left him
but touch

"The Rain", Zbigniew Herbert

When the young man
came back home
he had on his forehead
a little glistening scar
A splinter of glass
still lodged securely
like a clear pane
to help him observe

Doctors said he needed to open
his mind as much as his eyes
to re-comprehend space previously familiar

Descending
into the garden he
apprehended the metal shed
on whose door
he could see his initials
R E captured
in navy-blue spray-
paint
      within
hung a birdcage

Inside the house an aunt noted
how slim and very quiet
he was
tracing the cage

with resigned fingers
in parallel lines
The dry skin of his face was
compressed in concentration
straining to make him believe
it is true –
he lived
here
now he must remain
where
all greets him with
a sad paradox

He winced
discovering the family scene
through the kitchen window
then stared past them
trying
to imprint the surroundings into his eyes
to accept his return

Birds

Hannah Forbes Black

Their small closed faces like days of the week
or like nothing at all
save a single face, repeated

A sudden abundance of birds
and of bird shit

Remembering you, or what pertains to it
I begin as ever framed in the light
allowed by the doorway and end
in sheaves of wheat and paper, in lust, in penance

The screeching, the long-scattered

The feeling of wanting to leave this minute
is brief
and you'll thank me when you learn to endure it

little Machiavel, ruler of pigeons,
giver of bread
they think you are providence

Like Tigers

Skye Wheeler

You slept with your giants in the other room
I lay with Insomnia, her face like a clock, she
Waited and waited with her pretty back to me
So I would know not to blame her for my infidelity.

We were still drunk in the morning, oats swollen
For porridge, thick on themselves. In your dream
You reached above your head and around their necks,
I liked your London-lit skin. How you felt like text.

"Lucifer wept in the Tate." We went to see Pollock,
I went for the bra I had showing through my top
Making me capable of what you would never do
Sickened, it was as if you could see my guts and oats
Between you and the paint, "I see through you,

Sleepless."

I'm almost there you said. I can almost see the leap,
The faith I will need to do this. We said what we meant.
It took a while.
It ran along lines. (Just remember
in the wild space of your mind you
Survived, lived and lived like tigers.)

Salvador

Hannah Forbes Black

I wake in the night to the old understanding that the conditions of the world, like those of a foreign planet, are not amenable to human life. All the window can offer's an indifferent orange dark; an indifferent, uninterpretable noise floats up from the streets below.

The lift slides through floor after floor; the numbers on the digital display succumb to the same rapid decline. I'm going to lie down in Salvador's bed and forget there's such a thing as up or down.

Outside, the caretaker's dog is running the widest arc its tether allows, back and forth barked hoarse at the local cats. They're out in force tonight prowling their unnatural habitat, engaged in the usual bitter territorial spat – although the subtle divisions of ownership and license their neighbouring states undergo are for the most part invisible, from time to time made manifest in bloody skirmishes. The fine line differentiating district and district is mutable, sieving the dark through minute gradations of feline politics – I can make nothing of it except a vague hostility.

I open Salvador's front door with my own key (triumph of love over insurance). The geography of the house isn't yet familiar to me in all its transformations – at night, for example, it can feel like a home known in childhood, the horrors of its shadows still faintly tangible.

These furtive late-night visits are forced upon us not only by my insomnia but also by Salvador's landlady, a woman stranded somewhere between sixty and a letter from the queen, whose old age is queered by a vigorous sense of purpose. Salvador met her on one of her regular outings – she was shaking a collecting tin outside Asda, holding forth on the patterns of politics and disaster that forced her children from her home.

"The government will tell me nothing about either of my boys," she told Salvador, back then, in response to an accidental flash of eye contact. She in her turn will tell Salvador nothing of their location, of their purpose, of their names.

The supermarket's revolving door produces a man who tells Salvador, in a stage whisper, "Don't listen, she's crazy. She's talking shite."

But Salvador's already wrong-footed by the old woman's strange gaze, and besides he doesn't know what shite means, he's not from here at all. That's how come he ends up taking a room, out of pity and curiosity, and how he ends up striving to keep us at a distance, on the inscrutable grounds that it's best not to aggravate the old woman's solitude. I try not to argue: reason from men is blood out of stones.

I'm sitting with Salvador in his kitchen. We're both naked, which pleases me – that's a kind of innocence, isn't it? He's holding a pack of cards.

"You divide," he's saying, "these cards into four lots of seven, and the rest go here." Here is where he gestures with his hand. "You put the lots of seven in a row on the left and you pick the first pile up. If you have any kings – look, I have the king of clubs – you put them in a row here. If you have any aces you do the same over here, but I don't so I won't. Then if you can you arrange the rest into...alternating..."

"...Sequences?"

"Yes, like your solitaire. Do you understand? Look, the four of hearts, the three of clubs, the two of diamonds. You put the leftover cards here like this –"

"Why did you bother putting them in lots of seven? It all ends in the same thing."

"It makes it harder."

"Why do you want to make it harder?"

"It's a game," says Salvador. "Do you want to learn?" I am mute, learning.

"So you pick up the other cards, the ones we haven't used yet, and you put them in four lots of six, face up –"

I throw down the card I'm holding, only incidentally the ten of spades. "I don't like this game."

"We can learn another."

At which point a voice arrives from upstairs, calling "Salvador, Salvador", plaintively, as if expecting in fulfillment of the misnomer to be saved. Sadly for the owner of this voice, Salvador gives, automatically, the only answer he can – "yes?" – which is sad for me too, who has the whole thing showing, breasts and vague improper triangle of hair and all.

"What did you do that for?" I hiss.

Salvador smiles sweetly, nakedly, and does something eloquent and foreign with his shoulders. He opens the larder door and I step inside to hide.

"Salvador," says the voice, "who was here with you?"

"Nobody," says Salvador. "I was playing a patience game."

Now is the time to reflect on these voices – that one is English and the other Not from Round These Parts, a measured and foreign voice. In an adopted language, nothing is invested, hazarded, or everything is hazard, pure chance and happy accident. What comes out of Salvador's mouth has nothing to do with Salvador.

"Has the post arrived?" asks the voice.

"Yes," says my baby.

I'm reading the serving suggestion on a cereal box. It begins *why not*, and ends badly, like all things with their beginnings thus.

"Were there any letters with the address handwritten on? With foreign stamps?"

"I'm not sure," says my baby. "I don't think so."

"Why don't they write?"

To this my baby gives no reply.

"You'd understand if you had children of your own," says the voice darkly.

I'm doing naked silent comedy with larder props. It would be funnier with mirrors, or an audience. When Salvador opens the door I'm holding a carrot. The room behind him is empty.

"Who was that?"

"My landlady. Don't worry. She is gone now. She is mad."

"Didn't she mind you not having any clothes on?"

"She didn't say anything about it."

Perhaps the mad disdain the small insanities of the sane, having access to a refined, to a more perfect version.

"She is old," adds Salvador, with the air of a lawyer offering a conclusive proof.

Does that help? I look around me with the wild strange feeling of alienation that the long aftermath of sex sometimes brings. The urgent distraction of lust comes and goes, fixed elsewhere, after all, a luxury like cigarettes, the desire for which might turn as if by accident to a craving and a need and a lingering death.

In any case I kiss Salvador on the mouth.

Salvador's taste for playing cards comes to my knowledge early on – specifically, his love of patience games. It may be that Salvador's childhood was characterised by loneliness, resulting in an adult desire to wallow in it – what do I know? Not even, come at last to think of it, basic detail such as number of siblings and precise place of birth, information that lies so close at hand (specifically, within the often negligible distance between his mouth and my ear, an invalid space further weakened in the nocturnal, postcoital fudge surrounding most of our conversations) that I've forgotten to inquire after it.

Sometimes I like watching him play, not to learn but to watch the movement of his hands and the migratory order he conjures, although the motivation behind each small act remains opaque. As a child, *which I was*, I used to press king and queen together, face to face, for the vague sexual thrill: same suit was legit, but, say, king of clubs and queen of hearts was extra-marital, and therefore charged with a dizzying, pre-pubescent eroticism. Otherwise I might well wonder at the durability of the cards' weak satire of power: a system nursed through its various modifications by bored soldiers, bored kitchen staff, bored hotel porters – a warning of the protean forms that boredom can take – a symbolic graffiti of boredom.

Is *this* what seduces Salvador? You think of old women at the bridge table, intent on the mock war bloodless in their hands, a codified violence that prepares

90

for God knows what future battles, in the twilight of and the suburbs of human life.

Sometimes I hate watching him play, in principled resentment of pastimes. Absorption in a game is psychic time away, OK, from me, which seems to pre-figure the end: where's you? In these moments, Salvador fixated on his cards, there's only the one sour version of events.

"Salvador," I ask him, my voice gone small, "how many brothers and sisters do you have?"

He wrenches his eyes from the cards to me with a look of justified malice, a surgeon disturbed halfway through a delicate operation. "What?"

"Do you have any brothers and sisters?"

"Why?"

"I'm interested."

"Two sisters. I am interested in the game. Why can't you be interested in the game?"

She cries often, Salvador's landlady, her tears in the morning undifferenti-ated from her tears in the evening, the whole tedious process of grief more like a steady leak of vitality, a mechanical error, than a symptom of sadness. I have an idea, in any case, that real misery stops showing, exhausts, eventually, the limited available means of expression. When I explain this to Salvador, in the strange accented English his strange accented English inflicts on me, he's unmoved.

"That's not, maybe, the case. It's not for you and me to say."

"What's wrong with her?"

"She misses someone. Maybe it's someone she's invented, but you can miss an invention also."

We sit in my reproachful silence, in mutual estrangement from our mother tongues.

In a country far away enough that the long strands of rumour and print and compassion that make up a life don't reach, somewhere I have no say, the land-lady's sons are allegedly engaged in some half-hearted, half-arsed, half-brained and interminable struggle.

"Legitimate expectations," she explains, "for example that buildings remain standing, go missing overnight. There's been some guilt, some sorrow, some beautiful pieces of journalism, no national assets of particular impor-tance. I think there's a colonial link – isn't there always? And this idea that you can't just leave people to die. Says who? People die just as efficiently in com-pany."

"Which country is this?"

"I don't remember, sweetheart."

"In the absence of hard information, it's difficult – with respect – to follow what you're saying."

"Why do you want hard information? So you can ignore something with a name?"

"I would be happy if you stopped this argument," opines Salvador. Thinking this a pleasantly idiomatic turn of phrase, he's taken to offering his happiness and the conditions for it to all and sundry.

"We're not arguing, baby," in my best approximation of reassurance. "We're just talking."

But we're no longer even doing that – the old woman's staring out of the kitchen window, and it's some time, some silence, before she tells me, "They were beautiful children. They grew to be handsome men," to no effect, no change or movement of my mood.

"I resent the demands she makes on my care for the world," I tell Salvador, "which is already limited, perhaps by some failure of personhood or perhaps just because we're only allotted a certain amount of empathy, the majority of which gets used up in these kind of situations, boyfriend-girlfriend situations, parent-child situations – you know, I find it hard to care what happens to someone else's grown-up children."

"*Personhood?*" says Salvador.

"And in any case, are there any children? There's no evidence to suggest that her sons exist, that this war exists. Why am I even thinking like this? She's managed to suck me into her fruitloop paranoid interpretation of the universe. Soon I'll believe her. My powers of disbelief are probably as limited as my capacity for fellow-feeling."

"*Fruitloop?*"

"Who am I, anyway, not to believe her? What's the difference between this conflict and another? There's always something wrong in the world – you only have to turn on the news – have you noticed, by the way, how she switches off if any good news comes on? If I can't feel for this, what can I feel for? Have I become numb? Have I stood outside my life for too long?"

"*Conflict?*" says Salvador. "*Numb?*"

He's been teaching her his games. She takes to one especially – day and night the sound of cards being dealt out or flipped over, a papery slap as each finds its place, is audible through the thin walls of her home. Wandering into the kitchen just before dawn for a glass of water, I find her motionless in her chair, cards spread out on the table before her. Her head's tilted back and she stares at the ceiling as if it will unlock the frozen game, her hands palm up among the cards waiting for the secret code of the end to fall into them.

"It doesn't come good," she complains to Salvador.

"It's true that some games play themselves out," he says, his usual placid self, "but I think that it makes it more fun, not to know before you start." Later, though, I catch him staring at the same unturned page of his grammar book for minutes on end, muttering something about women in his mother tongue.

This new pleasure's invigorated her; she's left off writing long letters to the Pope, the Prime Minister, the UN Secretary General; her long speeches on the subject of the horrors inflicted on her sons have contracted, grown less and less frequent.

I find one of her games abandoned on the living room floor, cards still in place, and puzzle over it for a moment. "All the sense it makes you have to make up yourself. How do you stand it?"

Salvador shrugs. "The cat has my tongue." If you pick it up, his book falls open at Famous British Sayings.

In the further terrains they have to leave the sleek vehicles they're used to – those are too brash, too pumped-up with noise and light. They go on foot instead, but this makes the world seem too close. They hang out on the edges of where they're supposed to be, awaiting orders, avoiding the centre, fascinated by it. They set up camp, break camp, move half a mile down the river. There's no sign of the enemy – instead, rumours that the enemy has, anyway, altered, that the guerrillas are now on the side of the government and that the apparently innocent left-leaning splinter group (spearheaded by that tree-hugging, peace-loving guy who's been shown twice on CNN shaking hands with Mandela) has gone politically AWOL, swung full throttle into radical militancy. There are jokes about how much of a cock-up the entire operation has been, since day one however many years ago, which make the boys laugh when they're not lying awake at night imagining what it's like to die, or what it's like to carry on living like this.

The old woman's got a thing at the moment for buying flowers – the whole house stinks of them.

"Don't throw any out," advises Salvador. "She'll get angry. They're to celebrate the baby."

"What?" Percussively, and *ff.*

"The baby," Salvador repeats, who has not yet grasped the English tendency for selective, rhetorical deafness.

"What do you mean? What do you mean?"

"She's pregnant," he explains patiently.

"You're joking. You are, you're joking."

"No."

"Isn't she a bit too old for that sort of thing? Isn't she, anyway, supposed to be consumed by grief?"

"I think it's a good thing."

"You would – that's how you see the world – you think the world tends towards goodness. O God – has she" – and this has only just occurred to me – "*slept with someone?*"

"I suppose she must have."

"She can't be pregnant. It's not biologically possible."

93

"Wait until you see her." Salvador returns to his diligent perusal of the OED (three new words a day, is the scheme), as if nothing untoward has passed from his knowledge to mine.

Which is how three days later I find myself pressganged into accompanying the old woman to her first antenatal check-up.

"Why can't you do it?" I ask Salvador.

"I'm not a woman," he says, affronted.

"Doesn't she have any friends?"

"No. Don't be stupid. You'll enjoy it. Women's things."

An hour later I'm waiting for the womanly thing in question to emerge from her appointment.

"When are you due?" asks the woman sitting next to me, an identical same-sized child on either side.

"Never. I'm not pregnant."

Perhaps the words come out wrong. "God knows I was only asking," she says. "God knows I'm glad I had mine." She absents herself to the other side of the room. Her moonfaced children follow her, the one shadowing the other, then the other the one, as if their real life were a blanket shared between two, yanked back and forth over the course of a night.

The old woman reappears accompanied by a doctor.

"This is my daughter," she says, pointing at me.

"No I'm not."

"Very funny."

I give in. "What is it?"

"The doctor wants a word."

The doctor hustles me into his room and tells me the old woman's secret.

She's some way past fertility: this is a phantom pregnancy, but the world is in any case full of phantoms (ever followed up on any of those small-hours exchanges with half-seen strangers, the ones you meet waiting for the night bus who loom, glowing fag-end to the fore, out of outer darkness to complain about the cold and then recede back into the shadows, to no especial response save your instant, reflexive forgetfulness?) and if she wishes to why should she not bear another?

"These are the accounts," she says, back at Salvador's, "of my campaign to end my children's suffering."

She shows me a shelf full of hardback A4 notebooks, with page after page of figures, mostly in deficit. "This donation was from that lovely BBC newsreader," she explains, pointing to one column, "who I met at a party."

"Are your sons professional soldiers?"

"I suppose so. They did badly at school. What else could they have done? Why do you talk so much about choice?"

"I wasn't. Do you never feel like giving up?"

"Never! People are very encouraging. Here, in this scrapbook – this is a letter from the Prince of Wales."

"You've worked so hard…"

" 'For so little', you're wanting to say. It doesn't worry me that people think I'm wasting my time."

"I didn't –"

"No need to make excuses. No, it doesn't bother me at all. I look at other people's lives and I think, what do they really have? What does Salvador have, besides his cards? What do you have, besides Salvador?"

What I'd wanted to ask was, *Are these phantom children too?* but I bite down on my tongue. I don't know yet how to tell her the secrets of her state, or if it's in my power to prevent her from labouring to deliver a wombful of air.

The footsoldiers of the enemy, even if they are human, seem to spend all night awake. Their whispers and the small sounds of their movements, almost beneath sound, perhaps beneath sound, surround the barracks at night. Even the journalists, their visits less and less frequent, no longer ask who they are, or why you're here.

When Salvador tells me he's going away, we're halfway through a joint game of patience.

"Home? We're not done yet."

"You know what I meant."

I put my cards down. I feel myself small in the whole wide world. I think about my breath, how it works, when in and when out. Still I'm scanning the cards, seeing where this ace could go, to uncover the six of clubs.

"You've known for a long time this would happen," Salvador's saying. "For a long time. Since always."

Home looms at his back, coming closer, lifting off the map, recoloured in real shades, the contours of its landscape acquiring depth, height, substance. What I want to know is, can he believe in it yet? Am I still the realer to him, out of the two – and who will remember to tell me, after this uneasy interim, when the handover of power from me to it's complete?

"I didn't want this to happen in this way, but I never thought I could make my whole life here."

"Not much happens as people want," I say, not really in reply. We don't look at each other.

I can see the near future: sad songs, the abuse of alcohol, and an intimate knowledge of the curricula of late-night TV. And then to start and end again.

"I don't feel at home here," he says. "I work shitty hours in a shitty restaurant. I'm wasting myself."

I hold up my hands for him to stop – reminded suddenly of Salvador's landlady in her sometime spasms of maternal ESP, her hand help up in a gesture of prevention, hissing "Keep still!" at the least disturbance. I keep still. I try to listen to Salvador's anxious silence, to decode it.

"I'm sorry," he says, finally. He begins to cry, embarrassed by it and pressing his hands to his face.

"And if she lies down to have her child, what then?" I ask him, or anyone. "And what if her sons are real, and don't come home?"

I move a card, then another, and another. He dries his tears with his sleeve. We fall back, because why not, into the half-finished game.

Restricted View

Olivia Cole

Cast yourself into a chair, excuse your limbs,
feet, shoes, as they find a path around and
over the legs of those who sit in a row,

gathered to wait for the writer who takes
the stage with assured caution, *tiny nervous
practised* steps, to speak, between thought

and the lighting of a cigarette, unconsciously
of the writer's unconscious fear – unable to do
anything but let slip through the blue, a flitter

of anxiety, as he tells of how, "the life's" "not the
romantic cutting off of one's ear" and tenderly
strokes his own – still there – visible through

the pregnant pauses that load the swirling air.

Peter on his Dead Uncle
Matthew Sperling

Only with you gone did we realise the grave
presence of you, what weight absence would show
punctuating void space. Only with you
gone, standing now at your grave

reading the sign explaining why the grass
is never cut (*close mowing is avoided
to protect the woodmice, pheasants, foxes, toads & numerous
butterfield...*), only now, seeing the voided

place at my aunt's side
where you would have stood at your own funeral
with an umbrella & a black coat & a bad
joke...Oh, paragon of the manly & clubbable, fat

uncle who I never liked much, now that you're gone
why do I feel I should have known you more
than this? And I...

                    I remember the last time I ever
saw you – pock-marked, wasted – & remember
something Lucian Freud said (or Derek Jarman?)
about *the sad geography of human limitation,*

& look at the cold, toady skin of my own hands,
(my own flesh failing like something out of Rembrandt,
like that swollen, tuberous clown's-nose),
&, ignoring the noise

of the passing cars, leave the flowers, but add
a footprint in the mud: a difficult elegy,
a difficult gesture to a man killed
by cancer – which had to be difficult,

since I didn't know how I felt."

Shell

Sean Forester

Grooved inside, a foretelling colour
of pre-dawn sky, its white edge opaque
when held to the light. But I am drawn down
with the first spiral inward: my eyes reach
round these corners, my body curls
into this seashell, and my mind descends
to the safety there, like the man who coiled
elbows round knees, waiting for the train
to rend muscle and ligament and bone.

So the papers said. To stop corrosion,
workers cover the Golden Gate with paint.
Before they finish, wind and wet start
to coat the cables with rust. Over the years,
hundreds have jumped off the bridge.
In this shell, could I hear, distantly as they did,
voices of the ocean? Or are breakers and
gulls' cries drowned in doppler-affected
engine noise of traffic crashing past?

They faced inwards towards the city's stern
vertical skyline, the petrol tankers
and sailing yachts; looked down, from the edge
of the rail, on the body of the bay reflecting
like quicksilver, saw the shelter of a prison
turned tourist attraction on Alcatraz,
because they could not or would not
throw themselves at the inhuman distance
of the ever-changing, still-constant sea.

Phototropism
Stephanie Frank

October: elms like balding redheads. In the valley the white steeple stands out against the colorless sky. She is a sophomore, this year, and knows that the word has three o's and means 'foolish.'

But Sarah does not feel foolish, nor does she feel as young as she can tell she seems to her mother's joy-pained eyes. Sarah is proud, actually; she feels as though she has grown up in the last year, she feels grown-up. She does not spend hours on the phone with her friends any more, and she never decides what to wear the next day before she goes to bed. She is quieter, slower to laugh. When she does, she laughs richly, low in her stomach. She keeps track of important things she learns about the world; not a list, but something close to it. She is desperate not to forget what seem like hard-won truths.

Sarah does not have trouble getting along with her mother like the girls at school have trouble getting along with theirs. She likes her mother, even admires her, the tidiness of her small features, the lean uprightness that is a kind of elegance, the quiet firmness that intuits goodness. The two of them do not talk much, but they eat breakfast and dinner together, catch each other's eyes and hold them in smile-crinkles over the watery circles of glass-bottoms. These glances seem somehow significant; the way Sarah imagines it, they are secret handshakes that induct both of them into the corner of the world they share.

Sarah has tried to map this region. Sometimes, she tries to imagine herself sucking at her mother's breast, held that close. It happened, once: she has seen a photo. She showed it to her old best friend Nora, wanting her to understand this strange and wonderful closeness where there were no secrets between her and her mother but many secrets between them and everyone else. Nora missed the point – "Is that really you?", she asked, incredulous at the tiny wrinkled face, the already-old eyes. Nora and Nora's mom talk a lot, but Sarah understands that, in a different way, not very much is said.

There is more conversation when Shamus is at the table, but it is not intimate. It is the conversation of acquaintance, town meetings and neighbors and weather, always the weather. Sometimes also the farm animals, on which Shamus dutifully reports as one might a senile grandfather or a despised aunt. Sarah always feels invisible when Shamus talks about the animals; his apologetic tone is, Sarah thinks, intended to convey his understanding that Sarah's mother does not care about the animals, except insofar as they are connected to Sarah's father as grass to soil. Maybe even more than that: Sarah has noticed the awkward chivalry with which Shamus approaches her mother, and she wonders if Shamus also means to mark his feeling that a woman such as her mother – delicate but poised, and more striking with the wisdom of age – should not have to care about farm animals.

In any case, tonight Shamus, quiet, steady Shamus, cannot help but mention the oldest of the dairy cows, pregnant long after anyone would have thought it possible, and without any apparent mate. The birth was difficult, he says haltingly. The calf was dead, and they had to use a chain to save the mother. "I tell you," Shamus says after a pause, "I reckon that is what the end of the world looks like." Checking Sarah's mother's face for a response, Shamus adds under his breath, "Creatures giving birth to corpses."

Sarah wants to hear more about the cow, but she knows better. She waits for her mother to scold Shamus – she will use a quiet, kind voice, Sarah thinks, not the sharp one she would have used with the old Sarah, child-Sarah. But her mother just lowers her head and, after a silence, says she can't imagine how birthing with a chain is done and how anyone could possibly think that would be a help to the mother. "To anyone at all," she said. Sarah is beginning to understand that the way her mother says these sorts of things – as though she were introducing grandly the silence which follows – relates to her father, or rather, his absence.

The dairy cows were Sarah's father's. After the cows had stopped bearing milk, her father delayed slaughtering them so long that they were no longer good for meat, and then it seemed only humane to keep them on. Sarah thinks, sometimes, that she can remember his voice announcing – calmly, steady now – this decision at the dinner table. Her mother, who suspects that her husband planned to keep the cows all along and despises this softness as much as she loves him for having it, denies that this is possible – she was too young – but Sarah knows better. Her memory stretches back as far as the whirl of the rafters above and ahead as she learned to crawl along the living room floor.

She has known for a long time that her mother thinks of the cows as a nuisance, even a trial. She remembers an opening into a conversation that her mother seemed to be having with herself a long time ago.

"We'd better keep them, in case you father comes back."

She was looking out from the kitchen window into the scrubby field, where the old cows moved gingerly, arthritically. Sarah was just tall enough not to need to stand on a chair at the sink when she helped her mother (no help at all, of course) with the dishes. Her mother's hands, idle in the dishwater, looked foreign, frightening.

"What do you mean?" Yet Sarah, blinking rapidly, scrunching up her nose with the sting of tears, knew exactly what her mother had been contemplating.

"Just that your father loved those cows," her mother answered quickly.

Sarah thinks that history is liquid. When people say that the past is fixed, solid as rock, they are deceiving themselves: they'd rather not believe that things ride on something so unsteady, sliding away and yet surging up unexpectedly

101

beneath them. Sarah, on the other hand, knows that it is all, in the end, a flood; she concentrates on staying afloat, bailing herself out. The other day, she poured a memory out alongside that conversation with her mother and watched the layers, the years, flow through each other: the day the barn burnt, when her father was not to be found, Shamus had appeared – almost magically, as though he had been waiting in the wing – to take care of the animals.

Sarah remembers him leading the cows into the rickety old trailer that rang tin-hollow. The horses, sweating and wild with fright, went two at a time, paired as on Noah's ark, but Shamus managed to fit all three of the old spotted cows at once. Sarah wonders what it was that made Shamus cram all three of those cows into the trailer at once, whether Shamus feels the same way about the cows as her mother does. She wonders if her mother and Shamus might be more alike than her mother and her father.

About Shamus: he is a man, a miner, a farmer, a believer. Sarah's father was not a farmer but an idealist whose day job in insurance bought the land and, to be honest, sustained the farm; Shamus was his first advisor about farming after the column in the local weekly. Shamus was not a farmer, either, really, at least not in the way that folks around here meant, but he did have a quiet authority that passed for authenticity. After his father died – lung cancer – and he had come into some money, he had started from scratch, made his way to the Appalachian Trail and hiked north until he liked the lay of the land in the valley below.

He came down off the trail in Southbridge, found the post office by the American flag outside, and asked at the counter where the best farmer in town lived; then he walked out to Bud Stockard's and offered himself as an apprentice. Sarah's father loved Shamus' earnestness, the thing that made him work for an older, wiser man even though he had the money to start for himself. But more, even, than this, her father stretched thin the story of Shamus walking away from everything in Pennsylvania – Sarah had heard her mother tell her aunt that 'everything' included a pregnant girl – traversing miles and miles of mountains alone in autumn without hiking boots or a sleeping bag, finding a new life as matter-of-factly as most people fill prescriptions.

In Pennsylvania, Shamus had lived in a town with the name of Centralia, as bland as its houses, which the mining company had hastily thrown up against the sky when surveyors found a vein of coal. It was no surprise – people who lived around there already knew about the coal, so pure, so spongy, so black, it sparkled – but the railroad and its riches made the discovery as lucrative, as exciting, as a gold rush. Sarah loves the idea of treasure disclosed in things that have been known for a long time, of train-food.

All the towns in that area looked pretty much alike, Sarah remembered her father saying; the mining companies manufactured them almost as by-products. She looked for Centralia once in the road atlas, combing through the points and lines all the way across the great orange rectangle of

Pennsylvania, even though she remembered Shamus saying that it was in the middle.

"That's how it came by its name."

She hadn't found it. Now she knows why: he showed Sarah pictures when he came back from a visit. It took her a moment to register what was wrong with the town: the streets, regular as tic-tac-toe grids, were empty, and the electric lines strung along them were not connected to any houses.

"Well, the lines are cut," Shamus said, as though it were only logical.

Then he explained: Centralia was a ghost town, but not like those in the West, with their shanties and swinging-door saloons abandoned when the gold – what little there was – had been panned out of the town's bend in the river. Centralia had been abandoned not for lack but for abundance: there was a hundred years of coal still in the mines, there, but it was burning under the earth.

"A-N-T-H-R-A-C-I-T-E," Shamus spelled it out for her. Clean and slow-burning, the diamond of the industry.

Shamus showed her hills barren as tundra, ground smoking ominously, elms blanched to look like birches, grass tall and dry as straw. He showed her houses that had numbers spray-painted on their porches, marking the order of their demolition, and the columns the squatters had built along the sides of houses that used to be supported by their neighbors but now stood alone. He showed her the old gas station, which the government had closed when the fire had begun to heat its tanks. He showed her the way Highway 61 had buckled under the terrible heat below, the vents that had been dug along the breakdown lane.

Sarah shuddered at the long slash – it was too uneven, too violent, to be the work of a human. She squeezed her eyes and tried to picture the earth yawning, but the asphalt was torn so savagely that she could only imagine demons had rent it, trying to escape the molten river below. For the first time, Sarah thought that hell might really exist, that it might be just below, that coffins only delayed cremation, that it got everyone eventually and maybe – just maybe – could get everyone now. The invasion had begun.

But so had the trenches been dug. Shamus had taken a picture that looked down into the vent; its walls glowed faintly orange and seemed to extend forever. She peered into the picture as she would have peered into the chasm: the steam that rose off of it was like a veil across the photo. She could not bring herself to ask why they had bothered digging the vent, since the road was already ruined. She knew: the smoke-spirits must be let out slowly, though the trees fall and the air poisons, so that the earth, Earth itself, would not be lost to the fire.

Last spring, Sarah saw in her mother's *Good Housekeeping* that you could make a playhouse for your child with sunflowers, planting them close together to suggest walls that would grow to her neck, her chin, her eyes. She imagined the sunflowers' stalks gnarling to form fairy-tale jungle walls; she imagined, slightly more faintly, the flowers braiding together in their stretch to the sun; and she stretched to conjure an image, wispier still, of sharing this flower palace with her own daughter who – she could just make out – was wearing a tiny eyelet pinafore with nothing at all underneath.

Sarah knew that her mother would say that she was too old for make-believe houses, so she tried to make a science-fair project out of her sunflower labyrinth: phototropism, it is called, whatever it is that would make the sun-flowers slant together as though the palace were being sucked away from the Earth through the hole that was the roof, the sky, the sun. But her mother was not fooled by the scientific term, and – pre-empting argument in the same way she always does – brought home seeds and bulbs for a vegetable garden. "You can do that project to see which vegetables work as batteries," her mother sug-gested, swallowing, putting her fork down, clearing the table, already, with the calm efficiency that made (that makes) her seem infallible. Sarah acquiesced, although she knew that it was lemons – not even vegetables – but even now, until her mother gets home, she studies in a make-believe make-believe house, curled up in an old quilt against the radiator in the tiny bathroom off her mother's bedroom.

Still, her mother was right about the garden – these days, Sarah loves its yield, its yielding. The garden is simple, practical, like Sarah's mother; they only grow things to eat, only as much as they need, and only things that read-ily grow in the rocky soil of the Berkshires.

Today she is pulling up root vegetables for a roast. It is late for the onions, early for the carrots and potatoes, and Sarah holds her breath, hoping that they will not be runty and withered, as tubers sometimes are when they are pulled up: light-deprived fish from the ocean's bottom. She is already counting days until everything comes up lush and fleshy; in the summer, her favorite part of the day is going light-footed through the damp, fragrant plot, squeezing toma-toes tenderly, giving them another week, day, afternoon, picking them with one person in mind. Sarah and Shamus like them just past ripe, so lush they take on the blue blush of a ruby; Sarah's mother likes them firmer, still pink on the inside, like meat cooked perfectly. Sarah could not bear to cut the last of the late yield; looking, cringing, looking away, she sat at the kitchen table while her mother – always steady, always competent – quartered them neatly.

The fall and winter vegetables have to be cooked to the fleshiness of toma-toes, but they have their own splendor. Sarah spreads her bounty on burlap: potatoes with their gnarled and dimpled complexions, filthy carrots that wash to an unbelievable orange, onions with crisp, translucent skin. She carries them inside to wash and then begins shucking the onions as she does summer corn: if she unpeels onions layer by layer they do not make her cry. You have to let them give up their own secrets, she thinks – they shy from the thin clean truth of the knife.

Shamus watched her carefully while she looked down, down, down through that smoke, into that vent, and then he told her why he left Centralia, although he had stayed out the relocation, although he had the settlement and the house (and the girl, Sarah added in her mind). It was the most she had ever heard him speak; and he touched his crucifix several times while he talked. Although Shamus, who believes in predestination, insists (in his gentle way) that the 'h' at the end of her name signifies the Sarah of the Bible, Sarah-with-God, Sarah does not know very much about religion; nevertheless, she knows a story of transformation when she hears one, and she understands that faith, for some, is snatched from fire.

He had been out for a walk in the hills; it was what those who stayed did, climbed up to survey the town from above, to mark the slow evaporation of their town, to mark that they themselves – watching it disappear – were still there. The sun was ferociously orange, the way that it is, most places, only in the nakedness of winter, and burning so dully that it could only be a hole in the sky, the empty center around which everything else turned. Shamus said that, more than the landscape or the loneliness, this is what makes Centralia different, the way the air has such a hazy heft that you don't see the sun as a presence but an absence, the hole that its heat burns in the smog.

It was a good climb, up to the summit on the far side of the valley, and when Shamus and his cousin – everybody in Centralia was cousins, Shamus said – reached the top, they were breathless. The air was sulphurous and the ground was, of course, smoking. In any other town, the day would have been damp; in any other world, it would have been mist.

Then, as though it was what he was climbing for, the ground opened up below him. Subsidence, they call it – as instantly as a shaft of light, the earth discloses a shaft of dark, a shaft to darkness.

"What was it like," asked Sarah. Like falling out of a tree? Jumping down from a building?

"It's different when it's the ground," Shamus said. "There is no lurch. Sort of like floating, but floating down. Like an anchor settling to the bottom".

"The bottom of what?"

Shamus was quiet for a long time.

"They say that we were high from the gas," he said next. That I didn't feel the fall in my stomach because of the carbon monoxide. But they're wrong. I held on. I knew enough to hold on. I held on.

His cousin ripped off his shirt and extended it down the shaft; Shamus, wilting rapidly, climbed up the vine toward the light. The soles of his shoes had softened, and they stank as rubber does in heat; the surface of his hands had burnt away. This is the part that bothered Sarah the most, when she heard the story: that while his instincts sang in his spine, telling him to snatch his hand away, to get out, Shamus had to clutch the rock, to hold on, and that somewhere, twenty, thirty, forty feet down, Shamus' flesh still clings to the rock of the mountain.

There is an arrangement: Shamus takes care of the animals, Sarah takes care of the garden. Last year, back when Sarah didn't get along with her mother, when she didn't like working in the garden, she asked her mother why *she* didn't have to take care of anything. Sarah was ready for her mother to snap back at her, ready to stomp up the stairs, but her mother just said, "I have to take care of the two of you." Sarah was halted in her hot anger, but not by truth: Sarah didn't think of herself as needing much taking care of, and Shamus was a grown man, an old friend of her father's. Rather, it made Sarah stop – it made Sarah shiver – to hear her mother pair her and Shamus, like they were siblings, like they were lovers.

And this is Sarah's secret, too rich, too decadent, too nourishing to be told: that she is in love with Shamus. He fascinates her: his skin, even in the winter, has the red-brown of desert sand; his voice is always a moment later than she thinks it will be. His hair – always a bit unkempt – is shot through with grey; Sarah thinks that it must have been singed, marked by his encounter with fire. When she was younger, she used to watch him mow the lawn, chop the wood, her eyes slow and wide over the windowsill. She told her mother she was watching for deer. If she was paying attention, her mother would suggest that Sarah would have better luck when Shamus wasn't working outside.

Even before the fire, it was almost as though Shamus lived with them; Sundays, he shared with Sarah's father the sections of the weekly, which they saved from Thursday, and they alternated weeks in the leather armchair. When he was at the house, Sarah would try to be in the same room as he. He would be reading or fiddling with some appliance or absorbed in his tea and she would almost have given up, almost, when he would noiselessly bend at the waist and put one arm up above his head and she would feel his arm trace her leg, up, up, up, and then she would be sitting on Shamus' slender shoulders, her feet folded securely underneath his arms. "Hang on," he would say, laughing, and then make a huge yawning sound, bending forward (carefully, carefully) to rear back, using his arm to mimic the curled trunk of an elephant.

It seems like forever that she has loved Shamus, but she remembers the start of it all. She would almost rather that she didn't – that it seemed like the barn's fire-flower, blooming slow as sunrise – but she knows that when people say that something happened 'over time,' they mean only that they have forgotten the exact moment when. Time, change, motion might seem slow enough to be imperceptible–things might seem to happen gradually – but nothing is 'over time,' there is nothing outside of time. Sometimes – she considers it a mark of her maturity – she can step back far enough to watch the instants slap against each other like pages in a flipbook. Things happen, and the whole world shifts and shifts again; the kaleidoscope twists, or is twisted.

Many things happened the day that the barn burnt and Sarah's father disappeared; the moments crashed up against the two dimensions of what is and stuck there. And here, among them, is the moment Sarah fell in love with Shamus: when Shamus got back from taking the cows to the stables where he worked, he joined Sarah and her mother in the gully across the dirt road. It seems like days that they stood there, until the fire stopped, until the trucks had coiled up their hoses and rattled down the hill, until just the north face of the barn remained, burnt black and crisp and depthless as a shadow. The smoke's viscosity made everything seem underwater: Sarah next to her mother, her arms folded across her tender chest, Shamus, his hands in his pockets, standing off to the side at first but gradually, oh, gradually, moving closer.

Shamus taught Sarah to ride soon after he moved into what had once been the servants' quarters. ("So that he can have his own bathroom," her mother explained to anyone who thought Shamus deserved better, doing a widow – for this is how people thought of her – a favor.) This was two years after the barn burned, when they had not given up but had given up knowing: the forensic experts and the firemen agreed that there were no human remains, but they also agreed that the fire had burned so hotly that there would not have been even if her father had been inside. The report she found (her mother had hidden it) used the word 'vaporized,' and she looked at her arm and tried to imagine bone gone to liquid and then to gas.

Her mother had at first objected to Shamus' offer.

"Isn't she a little young to be on a horse?"

Sarah wonders now if she was just stalling, waiting for her husband to walk through the door: these were the days when her mother made work for herself at the kitchen sink so that she could watch the hills from its window.

Shamus laughed.

"You're a city girl, Gwen. Farm girls start early."

Even at eleven, Sarah heard the unspoken corollary – that Sarah's father had set out to raise her as a farm girl. She was thrilled to be united with Shamus against her mother, and she wanted to learn because of him, not because of riding.

Until she tried it. Shamus swung her up onto the horse that first time, up and over the horse's flank to nestle her in the saddle. Mounted unsteadily atop the horse, she imagined him climbing up behind her, holding her around her waist, directing the horse toward the mountain with subtle movements of his legs. His arms around her unfolded into a thousand different love stories in the short interval before he coaxed the horse to move.

Then she was consumed by the sensations of riding: the stretch between her thighs, the burning of seams of jeans against legs, the jostling of even the slowest walk. She could not think around the intense pressure of the horse on her legs, her legs on the horse, the sound of the hoofs, the rhythm of the ride. Holding herself like a queen on a sedan chair, she could not concentrate on how Shamus' arms might feel, what his mouth might do, what love might be. Later, though, in bed before sleep, she used what she had learned riding – the registers of tension at various depths, in various places – when she wake-dreamed about him.

Sometimes these days, though, when her fingers are crushed down between her legs, Sarah's mother rises up out of the field, an apparition rubbed out of a magic lamp. Sarah doesn't know, really, what goes on between Shamus and her mother, although she is suspicious. Her father was too, or so it seems to her now: he told her, one night at bedtime, that she was very lucky to have the mommy and daddy that she did, because her mommy had almost married Daddy's friend Shamus.

"If that had happened, you wouldn't be here at all!"

This is the way the talk ends: while they sit quietly on the bed, Sarah asks her mother about what her father had said. Her mother contrives to laugh, but not about her and Shamus. "Your father would never have said anything like that to a child. Think how much it would have frightened you, to think you might not have been born at all!"

Sarah's mother is uncharacteristically late with 'the talk.' Sarah's old best friends made more of the talk than the blood itself, and so Sarah – who antici- pated the talk with both excitement and embarrassment – was surprised when she got her period, not because she didn't know what the cramps were, what the blood meant, but because it seemed as though it shouldn't have come unin- troduced. Nonetheless, Sarah knows how to deal with a crisis; she turned busi- ness-like and self-sufficient, following the instructions folded inside her mother's box of Tampax, calling to hear the recording about the dangers of the dangerously-named Toxic Shock Syndrome, steeling herself against them.

Tonight – it is soon enough after her first period that Sarah wonders if she has left a wrapper somewhere conspicuous – Sarah's mother comes to her like a child sent unwillingly to apologize. She opens the door and glides in silently, without knocking, holding a book from one of those racks at the doctor's office. Sarah is disoriented by this outreach, feeling for the first time cheated, even offended by her mother's earlier negligence. She does not know how to respond – whether to announce the point is moot or listen attentively for the secrets grown-ups know – but she does not really have to: they sit side by side on her bed and stare at the book in her mother's lap so they won't have to look at each other. It is open to a page that shows the uterus progressing through the month, its crimson quilting thickening and thickening until – with some impa- tient shrug, some inaudible click – it reverses itself, disintegrating and seeping out.

Her mother turns the page, and all of a sudden it is as though her mother's voice is very close, closing out all other sound. Sarah wants to curl up with the book, curl into the book, into its pencil sketches of hollow bodies enclosing sonograms of a soon-child. Sarah forgets herself and traces with her finger the outlines that shelter the child as it grows and then the tiny fetus, which itself curves protectively about some unspoken treasure.

But most fascinating of all to Sarah, as she stares at the book, is what lies beneath: the gentle curve of her mother's abdomen, where all of this has already transpired. She tries to imagine herself so close to her mother that she is inside her mother, enclosed by her mother, tries to remember the movement out, the progress toward the light. She wants again to nestle down in the cul-de-sac of intimacy with her mother, wants to confess, broadly, indiscriminately. She cannot find words to lay bare to her mother the things that already feel so raw and exposed to her – what are these things that she knows but she cannot say?

She feels this silence as an answer to her mother's, even as she watches her mother's lips curve around words ('uterus,' 'menstruate') like soap bubbles. Now, more than ever, Sarah senses that the boundaries of her world are fixed by things that she does not know, or things she knows only to be secrets. It is as though she and her mother share a pact of secrecy, but somehow her mother has forgotten to share her secrets.

Emboldened by this accusation, Sarah asks one of the thousand questions she has always wanted to ask, after her mother is finally done and they have floated through a long pause. When her mother says, "Think how much it would have frightened you, to think you might not have been born at all," Sarah remains wordless and thinks about how much it did, while the real question, not about her memory but about Shamus, chases her mother down the hall.

Later that night, Sarah is lying in bed, still a bit dizzy from her mother's approach and retreat. This is something else about how things are, she notes carefully: reaching out and pulling away are the same movement. She puts her arms up in just that movement, as she has done many times before, dreaming of Shamus; this time, though, it is an open invitation, and Sarah wishes that her mother, rather than fleeing, had embraced her and sobbed into her shoulder, like one would the shoulder of a confidante.

For this is what Sarah saw chase her mother out of the room: the barn like a great angry bloom against the sky, and Shamus, just a bit too close, just a bit too captivated by the blaze, just a bit too near his nature, maybe – just maybe – just a bit too enthralled by his own work, by the ease with which he had cut one character out of a story and substituted himself, a fairy-tale hero.

Sarah wishes – oh, how she wishes – for more strength, but the arms that she opened for her mother finally, by degrees, curl tight around an imaginary Shamus, who is carrying a fairy-tale version of herself, not her mother, away from danger. He ravishes that frail, glamorous Sarah on a hillside; they both smell strongly of smoke, and the love they make is asphyxiating. When Sarah's qualms intercede, the brave, bold heroine of her fantasy pushes Shamus away, but finally, inevitably, he finds her again.

Sarah is righted in her allegiances when she lies still long enough to hear something like sobbing. She tiptoes barefoot down the long hall, grateful for all the late-night trips to the kitchen that mapped the floorboards' silence. Now she thinks the sound is instead the tiny coo that her mother (and Sarah herself) makes before sinking into sleep. She stands before the door with her hand on the tarnished brass of its knob, and is about to glide in – she has memorized this move of her mother's – when she realizes what the sound is.

Sarah goes downstairs and outside, her steps measured, rhythmic. She does not hear her own feet; she does not close doors. She sits on the ground in her garden, between rows of carrots, and waits for her mother to come out and scold her in the voice that pretends Sarah is crazy. "How could you be doing anything? You can't see a foot in front of your face out here. Come on inside."

"Come on inside. Come in, and you can have your bedtime potion."

It comes back to Sarah like a creature stirring from sleep: the way her father would coax her inside, late on a summer's evening. When she realizes where this cartoonish voice so unlike her mother's comes from, the parental alchemy her mother has attempted on her behalf, Sarah can, just for a moment, feel her way back inside her. But then, the sounds, which Sarah can still hear if she listens – but she does not, she will not.

Over this, the burning barn, the world on fire. Sarah remembers sitting across the dirt road from the burning barn, as she was told, holding her knees to her chest, while her mother talked to the police and the chief of the volunteer fire department. Sarah remembers how poised her mother was, even when they asked her if she knew where her husband was. Then, her mother's composure both calmed and frightened her, and it has the same strange effect on her now. She wonders how long her fantasies about Shamus obscured from her the hijacking, the fairy tale that he and – maybe, just plausibly – her mother had rewritten without her father.

The idea of the plot, strangely, placates Sarah – to know, whatever it is, just to know – but its success bothers her. For now, when she tries to think of her father, mostly, she thinks of his absence. She thinks of the day of his disappearance, the heat of the vast heliotrope against her face, her bewilderment as she watched the barn burn. And when she remembers this, she is bewildered all over again, bewildered that she felt no impulse to disobey her mother, run closer, pluck the flower with her small, tender hand, pull her father back from the burning threshold – to what, where?

Sarah cannot keep herself out of the conspiracy, now. She can feel herself disintegrating – how easy it is, to go to vapor – and it seems that all there is to do is lie between the rows of her garden, straight as the rows themselves. Though she was cold when she came out, now it is surprisingly warm and gusty, more like August, really, than October. The bed of the garden is soft and dank and moist, and she presses herself hard against it, spreads wide her arms and legs. The breeze empties her; the mauve sky swallows her whole, and she hears, dream-distant, her mother's murmurings.

And when she hears Shamus' grunts, a pig resisting slaughter and then, inevitably, succumbing, then – she cannot help herself, she cannot be brave – she scrabbles at the earth beneath her, with the urgency of a woman buried alive, pulling up carrots with an assailant's violence, twisting their hair to wrench them away from safety.

Sarah is making a carrot cake with the carrots she pulled up that night, now almost a week ago; she cannot bear to look at them hanging over the kitchen sink nor to waste them, although they are really much too young to eat. She hears the door creak, and Shamus blunders in. This is the first time all week he has come to dinner, which is just fine with Sarah – everything is easier to ignore when she does not see them together. Sarah does not think of that evening – she does not know how to – but the tint of that night sky seeps into her thoughts and colors them purple. Even the shade of the evening seems deeply criminal.

Sarah overheard Gwen, as she is practicing calling her mother, telling Aunt Maggie that Shamus has been going down to the Florida Lounge between putting the animals back in their pens and feeding them for the night. Before she realized Sarah was listening and shut the door of her room, Gwen also told Maggie that she disapproves of Shamus' new habits. When she comes in from her errands, she watches Shamus lumber around unevenly for a moment before she asks him pointedly how he is.

"I am just fine, Miss Gwen-do-lyn," he replies, exaggerating his accent. Sarah has always understood that part of Shamus' reticence is an embarrassment about the way he talks – not like the plain, clear voices of the people around here, and especially not like her mother's. Tonight, though, he is uncharacteristically silly. "Just fah-yun," he repeats.

Sarah's mother is uncomfortable, but she busies herself pulling the casserole out of the oven and putting serving spoons in the vegetables. She looks sharply over at Sarah and shrieks, grabbing her hand away from the grater. Her knuckles are spectacularly red with blood: Sarah has worked through the runty carrots and kept shredding until what fell to the bowl was flesh. She cannot say whether she felt the pain.

"We don't need carrot cake," her mother mutters, dumping the carrots into the garbage even before she pulls Sarah's hand under the faucet. "I just don't understand how that happened," she repeats again and again, binding Sarah's knuckles with a bleached rag she rips in strips. Sarah tries to shake her off, protesting that she's overreacting, but her mother is working with an efficiency like rage.

Shamus observes them philosophically, lolling back in his straight-backed chair at the table, waiting while the food gets cold. All in one movement, her mother ties the bandage, sits down, and announces with weird triumph, "You'll have to eat with your left hand tonight."

Sarah feels as though she should not argue, tonight, and after a second's pause, things set themselves in motion. Shamus piles green beans onto his plate before passing them to Sarah's mother. He says, a bit too loudly, "Let me ask you again whether you don't want me to order a bull for your cows this next season."

111

Gwen wipes her mouth primly with a cloth napkin. "Shamus, you know I don't know the first thing about farms or cows. You do what you think is right. You're the expert."

"Well, real farmers, businessmen, like, would think it wasn't worth your time. Betting against the odds, they'd say you were." He lifts a finger to correct himself. "They'd say we were." Sarah pretends to be consumed by the task of serving herself chicken casserole with her left hand.

Sarah's mother repeats, "You're the expert. That's why we have you." Sarah, hearing the sullen emphasis of her mother's voice, watches the two of them closely.

"But then you've never run this farm like a business," he continues cruelly, as though he did not hear her. "And I guess somebody's looking out for you, because no one would ever have thought that Ginny could have had a baby this time around, and here we are drinking her milk . . ."

Sarah's mother has set her milk down solidly on the table, presses her napkin against her mouth, then her hand against her forehead. "Shamus, do what you think is right, but for God's sake let's not talk about it." Sarah is shocked by her mother's tone: these last words would have been in small capital letters, if she had spoken them with a typewriter.

There is a long pause. Sarah says, "I don't know what 'ordering a bull' even means." She does, of course, but she also knows how to defuse tension by playing the child. This reminds everyone that she is there, that they are adults, that this is a family. Her mother is a teacher.

Sarah's mother seems to be counting the grains of pepper on the carrot she has speared on her fork. Sarah looks at Shamus. He says softly, "It's how we get the cows pregnant. They've got to be pregnant to make their milk."

Gwen chews and chews and chews. Sarah remembers in a quick, hot flash the way her father would laugh when he asked her a question at dinner and her mother raised a finger to signify that she would answer when she had swallowed that bite. "Well, Sarah-warah," he said, "Looks like Miss Manners is in our midst. You'd better get your elbows off the table." While her mother chewed patiently, Sarah and her father would careen into giggles: her elbows hardly reached that great oak table, the same table around which the three of them are spaced evenly now.

To disguise her reminiscing, she turns her head to Shamus, who is continuing, "How did you think they got pregnant, silly? You know all our cows are girls – they milk."

Sarah catches the glint of his wild eyes and thinks, hopes, that Shamus knows, even in his drunkenness, that she's pretending to be a child, that she is really mature, old, much older than her mother thinks, old enough. "So they aren't monogamous?" she asks. This is a new word for her, from the last chapter in her biology textbook, about modes of animal reproduction.

"No," her mother answers shortly, suddenly remembering her job at the dinner table – curbing inappropriate conversation.

Shamus chimes in with a terrifying bitterness, "Yup, just the once. They just fuck the once." He holds his fork and knife for a moment, one in each hand, then drops his arms and carries them from the table with him.

Sarah's mother – 'Gwen,' Sarah's lips form the word – stares at her plate without eating. She excuses herself to go to PTA without even asking about Sarah's homework.

That night Sarah wakes when the sheets pull down toward a weight on the edge of the bed. She sees the light in his eyes first and knows it is Shamus. Later, when she will think back on this moment, she will not be able to remember whether she moved to the far side of the bed to escape or invite, whether out of fear or desire, whether her mind was blank with threat or cloudy with sleep.

"Sarah." Shamus says like a statement, and waits for a long time. She just lies very still, and finally he asks, "Are you awake?"

Sarah merely nods, though the room is almost black. She hopes that he cannot see her trembling. "Listen," he says, but then he does not say anything else for a long time. So Sarah listens, and hears the friction of a tree branch against the roof in another part of the house, the earliest risers among the birds, a distant truck pull away from a stop sign quickly. She closes her eyes and hopes indiscriminately.

"I don't know what you heard," he begins. She looks at him, and it is his turn to close his eyes. "Well, I do know. Your mother thinks that you hate both of us. You should know that, that morning, when…when we didn't know where you were" – Shamus does not mention his glimpse of Sarah on the way to the shower, the soil she smelled of, the grime under her fingernails, the dirt she trailed – "she was desperate."

Sarah is unconvinced: the only thing her mother had said to her that morning she said through the bathroom door, while Sarah was showering, and by the time Sarah toweled off, she was gone.

"We didn't know where you were."

Shamus senses her skepticism, and continues in a low voice, "When she called the police, all she would say was, *everybody's left me now, everybody's left me.*"

Sarah reads the hurt on Shamus' face, the pain that he – probably holding her mother in the bed they had slept in together – didn't count as somebody who had stayed with her. She is sure, now, that her father was right, that Shamus loves her mother, that he probably always has. Shamus shakes his head subtly, quietly. "You have to forgive her, is what I'm saying. You're all she's got."

Shamus' eyes drop, and Sarah realizes she is fingering the top button of her pajamas – either she realizes that she already was doing it or she begins doing it. They look at each other for a long moment, and then she weaves her fingers together on her lap, as though Shamus were offering a prayer.

113

Shamus rises abruptly. "There's one other thing you need to know. You can hate me about...your mother, and maybe you should. But Sarah, listen to me. You think what you want about the barn, but I knew your Dad as well as anybody. He was a gentle man, and I can't tell you how much he loved you. I don't know why things happened like they did, and I never did. I swear that much to you."

"Everyone – *everyone* – gets a little crazy sometimes, and you and I both know that there are things you can't undo." Sarah hears the momentum in Shamus' voice and knows already that he is going to say something that can't be unsaid.

"But I reckon that if you can't take them back, you can't call them mistakes, and if he wanted to be here with you and your mom right now, he would be." Shamus lays a chapped hand on her cheek, just for a moment, and she closes her eyes – there's too much, too much. She realizes he is gone only when she hears his boots on the stairs.

Sarah's hand is burning now – whatever anesthesia she had while grating the carrots has worn off. She unwinds the bandage. The sight of her knuckles makes her nauseous, even dizzy. She buries her hand under her pillow and lies back down.

Before she knew about Shamus and her mother – before she was excited by a criminal Shamus, a Shamus whose lust demolished buildings – she thought that if her father hadn't died in the fire, he had fled at the sight of the fire in his barn, started by some accident, some undiscoverable convergence of natural causes, some horrible miracle. She has read stories of men leaving their families in the wake of the Great Crash, unwilling to live where their former life used to be.

Some of them, of course, were unwilling to live at all, as there have been people unwilling to live before the Depression and since. And maybe, just maybe, she had gotten things turned around, had the instants out of order. There was the conflagration motivating the death, or the death motivating the conflagration, the fire and then the flight, or the flight and then the fire. There was no knowing what the firefighters called the source. The experts agreed: the evidence that they needed had been consumed; cause had been subsumed by effect, and all that was left was the scorched earth below.

The blackened land behind the house is just barely distinguishable, now, as the sun begins to pull itself over the mountains by its halo. Sarah, fading back into sleep as though she had never really been awake, sees on the face of the opposite mountain the dull glow of yesterday's leaf-burning with a courage that usually only comes to her with pastel dawn. Above it, smoke curls lazily, and above that, there is – Sarah tries half-heartedly to prop a seawall against reverie – a figure against the pasture land, climbing faster than the smoke. She will think she remembers this in the morning, sort and sift the dream-debris again and again as soon as she wakes, before anything else deteriorates. Now, though – now, for the first time, Sarah feels her father float up, up, up toward the sun, through its gap in the horizon, away.

To the Empty Chair
Dave Thorley

[Joe "Tricky Sam" Nanton]

San Francisco, Please Skaggs Hotel:
no vacancies. The orchestra's asleep.

This summer lunchtime's whistling
fast coagulating tunes

and last night's smoke is setting in the lungs
and last night's tinnitus is nibbling in the ears.

At three, Please Skaggs starts up –
bugle-blast post-horn wake-up calls.

At five, one's still not got himself downstairs;
(elevator, swingdoors, hallway, room still latched).

At eight, the ripple-pool radiowaves
are one trombonist short of a jazz band.

This evening we're broadcasting from Vallejo…
and this one's dedicated to the empty chair.

A Selection from the Last Ten Years:
May Anthologies 1992–2001

Foreword

I was flattered to be asked to edit this retrospective of poems and short stories. The job seemed simple enough – to pick ten short stories and ten prose pieces from a short list of twenty – but as soon as I began reading them I wished I'd not accepted the job.

I found the pieces in turn confounding, frustrating, exciting and inspiring but all of them without exception beautifully written – writers telling their stories.

How can one say one is more deserving than another is?

So congratulations to those who have made it and my apologies to those that didn't and my best wishes to you all.

Nick Cave

The Sea and the Land

Seamus Perry

And there was no more sea.

(Revelations, 21.1)

From this the poem springs: that we live in a place
That is not our own, and much more, nor ourselves
And hard it is, in spite of blazoned days.

(Wallace Stevens)

And now in my old age, I wake, and this journey really exists
And I have to take it, inch by inch
Alone and on foot, without a cent in my pocket,
  Through a universe where time is not foreshortened,
No animals talk, and there is neither floating nor playing.

(W H Auden, 'Prospero to Ariel', *The Sea and the Mirror*)

THE SCENE

Having left the island (*The Tempest*, V), Prospero recalls his farewells,
and reads the ship's Bible: the Book of Revelations. He drifts into sleep,
and dreams of providence poetry and endings.

I

Strings over the side. Sea salt drawn to spray
Crispens up the quick crew's expert faces.
Boyish they are with all things being simple.
Easy sunlight. A firm wind from the West.
All eight sails filled and pulling on apace.
Their crowded unmarked ship, Milan bound, fastens.
No one confuses. The old man, by himself,
Not stirring. Nor attending to the noise.
But unheard music, providential isles,
A shipwreck, well meant. Unsought storms, also.
My daughter is in love with someone else,
And I alone, and age, and this is my Art.
Antonio, black below decks, is very quiet;
And Gonzalo hugs himself and can't stop smiling.

II

He had gone to say goodbye to Caliban,
But nothing there was uttered in the end.
Black scared sullen eyes intent as love.
Once I thought he held me as his God,
Despot, arbitrary. This was vain, and wrong:
All things are dark abysmal mysteries
For him. Such terrible days, catastrophes,
Such bloody, wild mundane. An always doomsday!
Empires collapsed upon the fall of trees,
While magic visitations came with swallows.
Once, a dead hawk. The ghetto children perished.
So in the thick of things, "you wouldn't know
The numinous if it hit you on the head," –
Ariel overheard, taunting his frightened brother.

III

Stay still! My life with you was underscored
By how I'd say goodbye: and you won't listen!
But should have seen that coming. How can angels
Know farewells? Unknown to substance, sadness,
Or surprise, his light world pure as reason,
Ariel fidgets: *Why going is better…*
But don't ask me. For wisdom's worldly. Off.
In old eyes, tears. A long time. Then their calling.
A raucous laugh, loud suddenly. *Calling me?*
Fishing. His gaze swam back to sacred pages
Turning, ending. Poetry after truth
By names confused. Nearly finished. Nearly. Oh…
Prospero dreams apocalyptic dreams.
Dark sea slowly shifts its weight to port.

IV
(Prospero's First Dream)

Here was someone. He said: *History*
As poetry. What is too much for soul
Is not its secular confinement. Passing
Agonies may be shared amongst the bones.
Too terrible is the aimless soul, adrift
In unmapped currencies of wandered luck.
The damned at least must know where they are going.
Though ways are strange, immanent. These soul endures.
My Ariel could read the landscape like a love
Lyric, coax the music out of fruit-trees.
I cannot. I long for Ariel hourly,
But Caliban's felt minutely in my bones.
This figure's breath was sweet as Ariel's too.
Cried Prospero thickly, *Ariel!* All at sea.

V
(Prospero's Second Dream)

One waiting for the end. Be-all and End-
All. To be the figures living last!
Sighs as signs. Unmissable. Arcs complete.
Things not themselves, but as their deathly symptom.
He said: *The very soul, like Poetry*
Exudes like scars from that remorseless tissue,
History, its roots in blood. And cut
Without Alas. What else could one expect?
Poetries of endings. Collected voice
Of cries, unwitnessed martyrdoms, lament,
So in the dark. And but the shapeliness
Of tragedy to withold such ancient griefs?
Clouds by winds are moved like model armies.
If I were not asleep I'd know you wrong.

VI
(Prospero's Third Dream)

No end in sight. No tricksy spirits home.
Prospero reeled. This was a different tack.
Things happen. Some more often. Habits form.
You come to rest within the place you are,
As though it were the only you could be.
Not true. But then that hardly matters to
Your one-off point of struck contingencies.
The heart lands where the heart has chanced to be.
Prospero, weakened, sank, was told: *Say truths*
Wryly. No. For what's this final 'You'
Who trails these commentating ironies
On all that's sad, or true, or loved? The world
Alone does not exhaust its empire... But
The swell. He drowned, and half-awoke at sea.

VII

The world is not our own. Is not a home.
Each form the unresisting soul pursues,
Caught, persuades us further of our loss.
Still tuneful isle where all our deeds pertain.
And John, and Ariel, forge poetry out of lives,
Or words, and give some show to satisfy
The anxious, realistic heart. But he
Shall not atone, whose blood avoided Time.
The shadows move. Prospero wakes to find
That sky at dusk, at morning, can be poised,
Pending, indecisive, between two weathers.
(As I that morning, with you, walking, love,
Over the common, never known so happy).
O sea baffles. Is one green, and another.

VIII

He said: Not God, but of a kind with God.
God is not all, or even most, of world,
As poetry is not all, or most, of poems.
Poetry, pure and terrible as angels,
And poems show how little angels know.
And so, with God, Love suffers to amuse
Ariel with the recalcitrance of men.
His impatient talent wth dogged Caliban.
And all these days have hallowed comings-home
My love, this *Revelations* of my own)
Things found, the old world gained, rediscovered.
As Prospero, home from black and random sea.
Pompous kindly speeches. Then judgment, mercy,
Violence. Such slight and real apocalypse:

Dry land once more. And there is no more sea.

Wince

Tim Hancock

"...and she never even said goodbye."
– he'd be slapping on the irony
like a pissed brickie by now. I can see
prints splaying from the corner of each eye:
a permanent feature left by some magpie
who'd flown too high, or had one too many
and jerked about on the still-sticky
sidewalk. His sense of humour was so dry
it seemed like the jokes were cracking him; as
though he could only handle some words
in the pincer-grip of inverted commas –
shiny ones like 'tears' were swooped on from above,
and as for the solemn vowel of 'love'
well... (I thought I had cupped this like a bird).

Ilse's Mother
Jane Rosenzweig

It is 1973 and Ilse's mother is not afraid of dying. At least that is what Ilse's father says in the car on Hallowe'en morning when she presses so suddenly on the brakes. Ilse's mother is driving her to school and her father to the office where he is a lawyer. Sitting in the back seat with her seat-belt on over her Wonder Woman costume, Ilse hopes the plastic tunic did not tear when she was thrown forward into the belt. Her father says, "For God's sake, Ann-Marie, watch out."

"It's not my fault. He wasn't paying attention," Ilse's mother shrugs. "Truckdrivers." She doesn't raise her voice, but her "r's" come out too harsh; Ilse has learned to identify her mother's bad moods by the strength of her accent.

Ilse's father glances over his shoulder, quickly surveying the back seat as if to make sure Ilse is still there. Ilse pretends not to notice; her Wonder Woman mask hides her face. She squeezes her eyes shut and she is speeding away in her invisible plane, the sky stretching out for miles with nothing in her way.

Ilse had wanted the costume more than anything, but she is disappointed that it doesn't look at all like the Wonder Woman on television. The tunic is plastic and shiny and the bathing suit is just painted on and the mask is hot. There aren't even any wristbands to keep the bullets away. But she still can't believe she is actually wearing it. She hadn't really expected her mother to say yes so quickly or to drive her to Randall's Toy Store and buy it for her even when she found out it was $9.95. When her father saw the flimsy mask and the long tunic he had looked at Ilse's mother without smiling. "How much was that?"

"I paid for it," Ilse's mother answered.

"That's not the point," Ilse's father had said. "She's eight years old and she'll never wear it again. What's the matter with just dressing her like a ghost or something?"

"Ghosts do not belong in a celebration," her mother had said, turning away. That was the end of the conversation. Ilse did not understand why her father gave in so easily. She doesn't know that what her mother had not said, he already knew, that she would have liked to be Wonder Woman, that in Holland there was no chance for that kind of imagination, and when she came to America it was too late. That is why she can't say no.

Now with the truck long out of the way, Ilse's mother speeds up again, and her father sounds angry. "Ann-Marie, for God's sake slow down. If you won't think of yourself, at least think of Ilse."

From the back seat Ilse can see her mother's mouth moving, but the noise from the open windows drowns out her words. She sits perfectly still so that she won't mess up her costume. She can feel the drops of sweat forming under the Wonder Woman mask. The holes for the nose and mouth are in the wrong place and Ilse feels like she is going to suffocate. She concentrates on the frosted strands of her mother's hair, whipped by the wind. Her father grips the doorhandle as he says, "I'm not kidding, Ann-Marie. Slow down." And Ilse from the back seat does not say anything; she can't say that her face is sweating in the mask or that she likes it better when her father drives.

At the school her mother stops the car and Ilse climbs out carefully. She pretends that the car is her invisible plane taking off to refuel. When her parents are out of sight she pulls off the Wonder Woman mask and wipes her sweating face with her plastic sleeve.

1979. By the year of her thirteenth birthday, this is what Ilse knows about her mother's past: That her parents named her Ilse for her mother's sister who died in World War II when the Jews in Europe were murdered. To Ilse, this is simply a fact, like the knowledge that her mother was in hiding in Holland for two and a half years, or that her father was born in Pittsburgh; Ilse doesn't remember when she started to know these things or who told her. Every year in Sunday School they show pictures of the concentration camps but she is pretty sure her mother was never in a place like that.

What Ilse knows is that her mother came from Holland after the war and lived with relatives in New York, that during the war she hid from the Germans with a cousin named Harry and his girlfriend Eva, that Harry died when Ilse was a baby, that her mother never mentions him. Once a year a beautiful hand-painted Christmas card comes from Eva, blank except for her signature.

Ilse pictures her mother in a house like Anne Frank's and since she has never really heard about her mother's family, she imagines them as Anne's cold mother and perfect father, only they lived somewhere far away from her mother and could only write her letters. She imagines her mother all alone in the Secret Annexe with no family and no potatoes.

By the time she reaches her thirteenth birthday. Ilse is growing out of her clothes; her arms seem to get longer and longer and her legs are too skinny.

It is 1939 and the girl who will later become Ilse's mother is eleven years old, riding a train alone across the German border to Holland. There she is at the last station in Germany, standing on the platform with her terrified dark eyes, begging the German conductor to give her back her passport. Without it she will have to turn back and she has not even enough money for that. The girl who will become Ilse's mother pleads in German with the conductor, I have to meet my cousin, he is waiting for me, and the train is about to leave, please give me my passport, sir. The conductor laughs. Later she will remember this as though it happened to someone else, a scene from a movie.

I don't remember laughing at all during the war. Years later, this is what she will think when she hears that conversation in her mind. She will remember the war as though it had happened in English, all the German gone with that part of her life.

In 1939, this girl who will be Ilse's mother looks at the man next to the conductor for help. He won't give me my papers and I must go, she says to this soldier with the large stomach. And something, she will never know whether it is an act of kindness or of indifference, snaps in his face. He nods at the conductor and she is again clutching her passport. She hurries to board the train, but in front of her the tracks grow longer from beneath the moving train and she is left alone on the platform, waiting.

After dinner in 1978 Ilse's father with his American Reform Jewish upbringing has been convincing her to have a Bat Mitzvah. "It's up to Ilse," her mother shrugs, lighting one cigarette from another. "What do you want to do?"

Ilse starts to say that obviously she doesn't want to do it since it was she who started this argument, that Hebrew school takes time, that she wishes she could run on the track team instead. She can only mumble, "It takes so much time."

"You'll be glad later," her father insists. "I felt the same way when I was twelve. And when it's over you can run track for the rest of your life. You're not even in high school yet."

"Is it really so important." Ilse doesn't say this as a question, she just lets out the words. She looks at her mother but her mother is staring out the window.

Ilse finally agrees because what she is afraid to say is that she doesn't like learning Hebrew, that she hates the way it sounds and doesn't see the point in being able to read words of a language without knowing their meaning.

1974. It is Yom Kippur, the one holiday when Ilse's family goes to synagogue together. Her father's brother, Maurice, and his family join them and they all go back to Maurice's house in the suburbs to break the fast at the end of the day.

Ilse has not fasted – her mother says it is not healthy for children to starve themselves – but she is hungry anyway by the time they get to Maurice's. His wife Candace has hired a caterer. Food stretches from one end of the dining room table to the other, and Ilse walks along slowly, deciding carefully which items among the bagels, salads, breads and cakes before actually filling her plate. Ilse's mother points to the cherry cheesecake. Ilse's favourite, and warns, "Watch yourself with the cherry juice on Candace's white carpet."

Ilse scowls and turns away, waiting until most of the adults have served themselves and moved into other rooms before finally serving herself. As she is reaching for the last slice of a chocolate cake her cousin Roddy grabs it. "You didn't even fast." He and his brother Jeff snicker at her. Ilse blushes with shame and takes her plate with no dessert to the couch where her father is sitting. She picks the tomatoes from her salad while her father listens to Uncle Maurice talking about Israel.

This is the conversation that Ilse hears and remembers later but does not really understand:

Uncle Maurice is saying "It makes you wonder, to think about last year this time, and how it could just keep happening unless they are always prepared now we see why we need the army service if the Jews don't stand up for themselves then no one will for godsake we've all learned that," and helping himself to more pie.

Jeff and Roddy are sitting at snack tables next to their father. Roddy's face lights up when he hears his father mention last year's war in Israel. "We were talking about the Yom Kippur War in Sunday School this week and Eddie Kaufman thought the US fought in it. Boy is he dumb." Roddy is eleven. "I mean..."

His brother Jeff who is almost fifteen interrupts: "Joel Weisberg went to school on Rosh Hashana last year and he heard a bunch of guys telling Jewish jokes in the library."

Roddy: "Oh yeah, I remember that story, they didn't see him because he was sitting in a carrel reading and they thought no Jews would be at school."

Uncle Maurice says, "His parents never should have let him go to school."

"That's not the point," Ilse's mother says. She has joined the group quietly and is standing behind Maurice's chair. Now everyone looks at her; Ilse's mother never speaks when they talk about Jewish things. Even she seems surprised to hear the words coming out of her mouth.

"I would've beat them up," Jeff says.

"Me too, I'd get myself an army and blow them away. I would've just beat them up." Roddy sounds excited to be agreeing with Jeff.

"What were you going to say?" Maurice turns to Ilse's mother.

"Nothing."

"Well," says Ilse's father. "Well."

Maurice turns to his boys and starts talking about something else, but Ilse stops listening. What Ilse will remember long after she has forgotten the exact words is how suddenly the whole atmosphere changed and the room seemed too big.

"That's why I never say anything. I hate the way they all looked at me," Ilse hears her mother say to her father that night as they drive home.

"What way?" Her father keeps his eyes on the road.

Ilse's mother lights a cigarette, rolling down the window slightly to dump the ashes. "And that woman. I'll never understand what Maurice sees in her. What on earth does she want with all that white carpeting?"

It is 1982 and Ilse's mother has been invited to a dinner in honour of being named one of the top ten Pittsburghers of the year.

Sitting in the audience, Ilse sulks because she is missing the eleventh grade dance to be at the dinner. She listens to a man in a tuxedo say all these things about her mother, how after she stopped working in the office of the Pittsburgh Ballet, she continued to dedicate her time to fundraising for the Ballet, how she worked to bring important exhibits to the museum, how she has served this board and that committee, how she has been a "key force" in rejuvenating the cultural life of Pittsburgh. And how at the same time she has planned benefit performances for the Cancer Society, for the American Heart Association, for the Women's Shelter.

Personally, Ilse wishes her mother had a regular job; she doesn't see what is so great about doing all this volunteer work just because her father makes money and doesn't think his wife should have to work. She has been reading about the women's liberation movement and she wonders if her mother is happy doing all this.

Strangers stop at their table to congratulate her mother. Ilse had no idea that her parents knew so many people.

When they are alone in the ladies' room her mother applies her lipstick, combs her hair and then looks at Ilse. "If you would just stand up straight you would look so much better."

Ilse stares at herself in the mirror. Next to her mother she is a giant. She hates her height and the straightness of her hair.

Looking at her mother in the mirror, Ilse says, "I'm not sure I want to go to college." She hates herself because whatever she does is not enough. They leave the room without speaking.

In 1979 Ilse can't say no and she knows if she does, all the Hebrew school will go to waste and so there she is in a blue dress, standing on stage speaking in a cool voice which doesn't seem to belong to her. Speaking in Hebrew and then in English what she has memorised. She quotes the book of Genesis, the words of God to Abraham, words which seem beautiful when she skims them: "I will indeed bless you, and I will multiply your descendants as the stars of heaven and as the sand which is on the seashore. And your descendants shall possess the gate of their enemies, and by your descendants shall all the nations of the earth bless themselves, because you have obeyed my voice…" Ilse stops in the middle of the passage when she suddenly knows something, that this has nothing to do with her.

Ilse, standing on the pulpit, can see her mother in a green silk dress, her face unreadable. She stares out at the congregation. The rabbi nods encouragingly, as if she has lost her place. As she stumbles through the rest of the passage, she realises that she has spoken the Hebrew over and over without thinking about the words or even that it was words, and now she tastes the words and remembers her mother's indifference about the Bat Mitzvah, she finishes the words but she does not hear them anymore. She is wondering if her mother thinks the same thing about this ceremony, that it has nothing to do with her.

131

Right in the middle of her own Bat Mitzvah, she finds herself wondering if her mother even thinks in English; Ilse has never heard her speak German but she has never thought before about whether you can learn to think in a new language.

After the service, at the reception, her mother remains cool, perfect as usual, thanking the guests for coming, small talk rolling off her tongue. The guests are mostly friends of her parents. The only relatives are Maurice and Candace. The cousins who kept Ilse's mother when she first arrived from Holland live in California now, and with the exception of occasional letters, Ilse knows nothing about them. Ilse blushes as the guests congratulate her. She runs a hand nervously through her hair, messing up the already flat bangs she fought about with her mother this morning. Here she is on the day she is supposed to be a woman, hating her mother for the curl in her hair and for not allowing Ilse to read her thoughts.

If someone asked Ilse's mother why she doesn't talk about the Holocaust, doesn't speak of it to Ilse especially, she would probably say, I don't want to burden her with my story, I don't want her to spend her entire life trying to make it up to me. That is only part of the truth. The rest is that none of it seems real anymore, she can barely believe that these are parts of the same life. The rest is that what happened was so long ago that the words are not enough. If Ilse's mother were to tell her the story, she feels she would be telling a story of someone else. She can never make Ilse feel what she felt when so often she can no longer feel it herself. She can never tell what it was like because a story is always different when you don't know the ending.

It is 1942 and the girl who will become Ilse's mother convinces herself that she is someone else. She spends hours staring at the set of fake papers that Eva, her cousin's girlfriend, has given her. In the papers she is still German because she would never be able to speak Dutch without an accent. In the papers she was visiting friends before the invasion and then they thought it better to keep her in the healthier climate of the Dutch countryside. She sits in the attic of Eva's country house all day, memorising another person's life, answering imagined questions over and over until she can barely remember who she was.

By 1942 there are no more letters from Germany, she stops reading the last one because it is much safer to forget. Sometimes she wakes from dreaming of her mother's parting words to her when she left Germany: "…only he who abandons himself is abandoned." In the attic she has no family and never thinks of the past except when waking from these dreams when she wonders if it is precisely this kind of living which her mother has warned her against. Later she will shut out thoughts that in her new life in America she has abandoned herself. She will tell herself that for survival she had to start over, that there was no self left to preserve.

They hide in a country house outside Amsterdam which belonged to a Jewish couple before the war. Eva has purchased the house for next to nothing;

there is a huge well-tended garden which Eva attempts to cultivate, and four empty bedrooms. More than once late at night there is a knock on the door and they think it's the police but it is the man and the woman, holding a battered suitcase and explaining that they have been expelled from yet another hiding place with nowhere to go but here, their former home. Other nights, the Dutch police come with a warning of a Gestapo raid and then there are long nights alone in a foxhole behind the house; even with false papers it is a risk to be found. The risk is that the girl who will later become Ilse's mother might forget who she is supposed to be.

One night, Harry plays the piano and the music pulls the girl to the foot of the stairs, but just as quickly she runs back to the attic; it is too dangerous to allow herself to slip back into her own mind. She cries only once, when she hears that her bicycle, the one she used during her first year in Amsterdam, has been taken into custody by the Dutch Nazis.

In 1984 Ilse's mother has begun to talk publicly about her Holocaust experience. She has been giving speeches for almost four months; she started soon after she went back to work full time, directing special events for the Carnegie Museum. Home from her first semester of college for winter break, Ilse accidentally discovers what her mother is doing.

While looking for a stamp on her mother's desk, Ilse sees a letter from the principal of Reizenstein Middle School thanking her mother for coming to speak about "her experiences during the Second World War." Ilse sits at her mother's desk and tries to picture her mother at the front of the auditorium of her old middle school, telling her secrets to a room full of strangers. Middle school strangers who will forever associate their knowledge of the Holocaust with the sweet baking smells from the nightshirt of the Nabisco factory next door to their school.

When her mother leaves after dinner one night in January, explaining vaguely that she has a meeting "over at temple," Ilse does not need to ask questions. When she hears the car pulling out of the driveway, she wanders into the living room. "How long has she been doing this?" she asks her father.

He is sitting in his usual chair, looking at the newspaper. He doesn't seem surprised that she knows about the speeches. "About four months," he says. Ilse wants to ask him a question, something like, "does it help her?" but since she doesn't know what it is her mother needs to be helped from, she doesn't know what to ask. Instead she tries to sound normal.

"I think I'll go over to the mall." She knows he will not expect any details. Probably because he is used to the secrets of her, Ilse's mother, he never does.

At the temple, the lecture hall is crowded. Ilse stays in the back of the room; part of her does not want to stay. Her mother stands poised on the podium. Ilse wonders what the audience thinks of this beautiful German woman with barely a trace of an accent. The room is overheated and Ilse standing, has nowhere to put her coat. Her mother quotes a German poet, Heinrich Heine, something about books burning and people burning. Ilse is surprised to hear her mother talk of poetry. She slips quietly out the back door, knowing that her mother has not seen her, feeling guilty for having stolen information that her mother has not given to her.

Outside, yesterday's snow looks gray and dingy. Ilse walks past her car and onto Fifth Avenue. She wonders if her mother will offer to answer questions. She identifies the feeling she had standing in the lecture hall. She had felt suddenly American, having a nationality, something she imagines you don't usually feel in America where everyone is American. She thinks of her father reading the paper and wishes she could ask him if he feels American, if her mother believes anyone can understand, if he does not ask questions because he does not want to hear the answers. She wonders if she herself really wants answers.

It is 1986 and in college Ilse has discovered writing. She drinks words, sees putting them together in the right way as an answer to everything. Her professor says write what you know and over and over Ilse writes instead what her mother knows. Ilse struggles to analyse; her professor says I am not so interested in meaning. He is a young man who borrows words that he has heard elsewhere to explain to the class what he means:

"If you are writing about a hat, of course you can explain how the colour of the hat symbolises innocence, how the shape or size of the hat is a symbol of the secret which the protagonist carries. All of that is no good if I don't see the hat, its shape, its size, its colour. Show me the head, if there is one. Show me the hat. *Most of all, I am interested in the hat.*"

Ilse sees that everything is connected, that there is no such thing as words without meaning, that you cannot contain your life and your family through the shaping of a sentence. She does not discuss this with the professor because she thinks he probably would disagree. She studies the Bible in an English literature class and reads poetry but there is nothing beautiful about the tightness in her chest when the story of Abraham comes back to her as the feeling of emptiness she had at her Bat Mitzvah. She stops writing when she realises that even words will never help because the hat is not hers to describe.

It is 1991 and Ilse's mother has died thousands of times so now she is not afraid. Ilse sits in her hospital room making small talk and writing dictated thank you notes for cards and flowers. Ilse's mother has no words to explain that dying is easy.

It is the summer of 1983, the night before Ilse will leave for college, and she is having a nightmare. She rides alone on the merry-go-round on the Washington Mall in her Wonder Woman Hallowe'en costume, only she is seventeen and not eight, and the horses suddenly come alive and run away in the rain. For a split second she feels completely free, galloping across the mall.

Then her legs grow more and more tired and the voices swirling around her speak another language and the grass has stopped growing.

One voice, as if over a loudspeaker, repeats words from a book review Ilse once read about a book on the Holocaust. *Jews, check your passports* and in the dream Ilse screams, not me, and the ground ahead bursts into flames, but just for a second and then there are her cousins Roddy and Jeff, and their friend Joel Weisberg, the one who went to school on Rosh Hashana, and although she has never met him, he has a face, and even in her dream she wonders how she can see him when she doesn't know what he looks like, and she cries for him hiding in the library carrel, and the horse runs faster but her mother is in Wonder Woman's invisible plane and Ilse cannot catch up.

When she wakes up she is sweating and as she stands by her open window, she can see that the driveway cement is wet from rain. As she thinks, this is the last time I will sleep here and really live here, her dream is already fading so that she will not remember it by morning.

It is 1975 and the last helicopters are lifting out of Saigon on the evening news. Ilse's mother fixes dinner. She does not speak throughout the meal. People run after the helicopters, hanging on as they rise, left behind for lack of room. When Ilse sees their faces she looks at her mother, but her eyes are unreadable and this scares Ilse.

It is 1973 and Ilse's mother stands on the porch, watching Ilse ride down the driveway on her bicycle. She has been practising all day on the steep driveway and she finally has it.

"Did you see me?" Ilse turns the bicycle on its side at the curb and runs up the front steps, waiting for her mother's answer.

When her mother nods, Ilse cannot see that behind her mother's eyes another bicycle exists, another pair of legs pedalling as fast as they can, pedalling faster than the speed of light through the countryside of Holland. Somewhere behind her mother's eyes, the railroad platform is always an island, the attic is always dark and lonely, there are always a thousand deaths, and the girl on the bicycle rides as fast as she can. And Ilse, releasing the brake slightly to feel the thrill of coasting down the driveway, will try, but she will never understand how it feels always to live with the fires, how inside each fire there is always more fire, memories packed so tightly they can barely breathe.

Free Will in Humans and Fish

Nicholas Sparks

Before I was fished out
in the billowing cold I
saw a running salmon force
its way past – its sideways snap
of tail breathless jaw
and eye-sided face

The Origins of Exile
Stephen Henighan

We didn't hear the door open. An autumn chill brushed the backs of our necks, stilling our supper time conversation. Deirdre cocked her head to one side. My mother cast a quick, nervous glance at my stepfather. I heard a languid clicking sound stutter from the mudroom, like a faint, lazy clattering of dice. My stepfather pushed back his chair from the head of the table. The clicking grew ponderous; the kitchen was getting colder. My stepfather, his expression tense behind his shaggy beard and long hair, gripped the flared handrests of his wooden armchair. A soft thump stifled the clicking. I saw a large skunk tumble down the step separating the mudroom from the kitchen. The animal landed with its legs splayed, righted itself and dawdled across the burgundy tiles, its tail curled up over its striped hindquarters.

"Eddy Munster!" Deirdre shouted, leaping up from her chair. The mudroom floorboards creaked with the weight of a second, heavier tread. The front door closed and David Larsen, the sheath containing his hunting knife strapped across his buckskinned thighs, followed his skunk into our house.

· · · · ·

The severed paw rose through the water like a shaggy trophy imprisoned in a gelatinous coating. The fur looked grey and oily in its sodden thickness; the bright pink flesh glared against the dull day.

"Muskrat," David said, prizing open the jaws of the trap. The paw dropped onto the matted brown grass. "Muskrats are the first ones to chew off their paws. A beaver will try to yank the trap loose. They can be big galoots, too. You've got to anchor your traps right in case you get a beaver." He reset the trap and lowered it into the gurgling black water of the swollen drainage ditch.

"Do you use snares?" I asked, as we set off again. Drab fields stretched out on either side of us. The spring thaw had left the ground too waterlogged for the farmers to plough it up and plant their corn. The fields before us, used for hay, lay flattened and colourless beneath the tangle of last fall's post-harvest growth. Beyond them, the swamp began in a crooked thicket of knobbly black tree trunks knee-deep in stagnant water. I thought of the coils of golden snare wire I had bought with my pocket money. I hardly ever spent the fifty cents I received each Saturday, hoarding my money as a bulwark against sudden change. But as soon as David invited me to accompany him on his trapline, I had begged my mother to drive me to the hardware store in the village. I kept my coil of wire in my bedroom, looping it into snares and yanking them taut, cutting off the circulation in my index finger or wrist at will. I weighed the coil in my palm and dreamed about the day when I too would earn my living selling pelts.

"Snares work best in winter," David said. "You can get rabbits by setting snares on their trails in the snow. In summer there's too much undergrowth."

I bowed my head, dismayed at the thought that I would have to wait until next winter to begin trapping. My mother having thwarted my efforts to obtain traps by mail order, snares had seemed to offer my only hope of starting this spring, before the season ended. The brown April landscape still harboured patches of glazed, gritty snow in its more wooded recesses. Next winter! I would be ten before winter returned.

The next trap held a mink. It floated dead on its back beneath the water-line, the dimpled jut of its snout drawing ripples in the current. The water had combed the mink's lithe body to a flossy brown softness. The trap had closed on the animal's left hind leg, flipping it over, dragging it under and drowning it. David dropped to his knees and went to work. Mink was the best pelt the swamp had to offer; in Ottawa they paid five to eight dollars for a tanned, unmarred mink pelt. I watched David's big, chapped hands open the trap. The mink's body slithered, eel-like, onto the dun-coloured grass. The trap had seized the animal high on its leg, yet as David probed the fur, I saw that the pelt had not been gouged or torn. The mink's value was intact. David would need the money it brought him: there would be no trapping over the summer, as the fur-bearers lost their thick winter coats. David would go to work part time gutting fish at La Pointe's in the Byward Market, or plant trees for the provincial government. He would sleep in our old shed or set up his tent in the swamp or paddle his canoe west across the country. I envied him his freedom. I had to stay cooped up in school until the end of June. I was the only boy at school with long hair, the only kid whose family had not lived in the Ottawa Valley for six generations, the only one whose parents were divorced. My teachers told me I had an English accent. Provoked by my long hair and my strangeness, groups of boys beat me up at recess. I responded by exerting myself until I became the class brain, recasting my undeniable weirdness as a source of defiant superiority. I was happier now that I could hold my own. My private world, fixed on the farm and fantasies and books and my mother and my sister, was the existence that counted.

One morning as the school bus was clattering along a dirt road cutting through the swamp, David stepped out of the bush carrying the twenty-two calibre rifle he used to hunt groundhogs. His chin was dark with stubble; his brown moustache drooped over his cheeks. His tightly braided pigtails, extending from beneath his wide-brimmed hat, trailed over the collar of his fringed buckskin jacket. He wore his knife in his belt; a necklace of beads, interspersed with shards of bone, hung draped over his chest. "Dirty hippie!" the two guys with whom I was playing cards yelled out the window. Every kid on the bus jumped to his feet, howling and jeering.

"My old man says that guy should go to jail," a burly Grade Eight boy said, as the bus rattled between the skinny, birches studding the outskirts of the swamp. "Goddam hippie."

"He lives at our place," I said. "He's a friend of my parents."

Everyone fell silent. Loose gravel smacked against the floor of the bus. The big Grade Eight, a full six inches taller than me, wasn't to be deterred. "He lives with your parents, eh Oliver? And where's your dad live?"

"In Ottawa."

"Ottawa? Holy Jeeze, he's getting closer all the time. I heard tell he was in England."

"That guy doesn't live with my dad," I said. "He lives where I live, with my mother and…at our place."

"Tell me about it," the Grade Eight said with a twisted smile that raised snickers. "Your mum ain't even married, Oliver. You're illegitimate. You're all gonna go to jail for the stuff that goes on up at your place."

• • • • •

The farm was my mother's last legacy from England. Descended from the ruddy, fiercely Christian, football-and-cricket-worshipping branch of a family renowned for men with white handlebar moustaches who ran Lloyd's of London and slender perky women who expected to receive sports cars as twenty-first birthday presents, she had inherited a slice of the family's diminished fortunes on her own coming of age. Enough of the money remained, at the end of her marriage to my father, to cover a downpayment on a 125 acre farm in the Ottawa Valley. The farm was cheap. It was too far from Ottawa to attract the middle class, and the area's supply of young men willing to contemplate a lifetime of farming was beginning to falter. For the last 25 years, the two storey redbrick house had been lived in only during the summer; for most of that time, the second floor, blocked off by a sagging wood panel, had remain uninhabited. Bare lathe ribbed the walls, the floorboards were a conglomeration of buckled knots and ridges, field mice shuttled in and out of the kitchen through thumb-sized passages confiding glimpses of the high grass of the yard. The first night we stayed there, Deirdre and I slept on wire-framed canvas cots in the kitchen. The pattering of rodent feet awoke me half a dozen times to the unbroken blackness of the rural night.

How did we live? My father, far away in England, fell months behind on his support payments and eventually defaulted altogether. My mother, shattered by the divorce and busy with Deirdre and me and the house, lacked both the self-confidence and the time to find a job. In order to do her shopping she bought a gigantic silver station wagon for a pittance from a professor who was dying of cancer. The monster drank gas at a rate of nine miles to the gallon, refused to go more than forty-five miles an hour and predeceased its former owner. Unable to cook in the bare kitchen, my mother hired a man with the inauspicious name of Gamble to build her cabinets. He wandered off, leaving his tools strewn over the rough floor. Appropriating his scraper and goggles, my mother scoured the house with the asphyxiating odour of paint remover as she sliced through layer after layer of leafy wallpaper and fading, garish paint. When her labour exposed smooth wood panelling, she varnished it to a crystalline shine; the pocked walls above the panelling she daubed with plaster and coated with three or four layers of white paint. Deirdre and I delighted in each advance. We turned somersaults the day we came home from school to find a carpet in the living room, even though we knew the house would never be as plush as the ones we saw on TV.

Our mother was strict about TV: we were forbidden to watch more than an hour on weekdays, three hours on Saturdays. We both had to be in bed, in twin beds in the only upstairs room sufficiently finished to sleep in, by nine o'clock. We ate vegetables from the garden. Our mother dressed us in clothes that she ingeniously sutured each time they ripped or wore out. We made the transition to long, lank hair more as a result of parsimony and neglect than as a declaration of hippie allegiances. The farm was a fastness where our future selves put down roots in a sediment of gnarled, ingrown tension and therapeutic silence. Once Deirdre and I had stepped off the school bus and wandered up the half-mile laneway to our house, we were home for the evening. No playmates lived nearby, no other children resided within walking distance. The front fields swelled like a wave in the ocean, blocking off the view of the highway. The evergreen plantation fringing the left-hand verge of the final stretch of the laneway led into my mother's vegetable garden and the semicircle of slouching grey outbuildings below the house. A ten acre patch of mixed bush, separated from the house by a trench-like field where our neighbour's Holsteins grazed, covered a broad, rock studded rise; behind the house, a sunken landscape trickled away towards the swamp. All of these places contained mysteries. Fossilized fish embedded in sandstone nestled in a cove of loose dirt on the edge of the conifer plantation; the ten acre sprawl of bush opened at its high front crest onto the clearing holding the foundations of the first house and barn on the property, destroyed by fire in the 1860s; an abandoned car listed in soft soil near the swamp, where hawks planed overhead in summer and tuft-headed snowy owls gazed around incuriously in broad daylight during winter. I would ramble from one spot to the next, walking off the tension that built up among my mother, Deidre and me. Some nights, re-enacting the turmoil of my parents' divorce, we would argue compulsively until all three of us burst into heated headache-causing tears. I shouldered much of the guilt in these anguished recapitulations. I was the male: the incarnation of my father, who had fled the family hearth, and even of my grandfather, who had abandoned my mother by disappearing into death during her adolescence. These two vanishings – one spurring my mother's flight from England in her teens, the other consolidating my own rootlessness – consigned us not to fashionable expatriation, but to the internal exile of brokenness, fragmentation, emotional incoherence.

Loneliness and guilt only strengthened my devotion to the farm. I felt knocked out of shape when strangers intruded. One day an exuberant, prematurely white-haired man with an English accent and flesh of boiled lobster appeared, trying to ingratiate himself to me with effusive, ill-informed assertions of interest in baseball. The cynicism and condescension bristling behind his remarks about the game he kept calling 'rounders' made me stiffen with silent,

140

hostile suspicion. What did he want? I had my answer when, creeping upstairs well after my nine o'clock bedtime – I was now sleeping alone in a sliver of a downstairs room occupied until a year earlier by goats – I realized that he had not gone home. I gazed for a long time at the closed door and tarnished doorhandle of my mother's bedroom before returning to my bed. The next day the man was still there, sipping tea with my mother in the kitchen. I went upstairs in search of a book. As I started back down the staircase, my gaze snagged on the sight of my mother's doorhandle. I stumbled forwards, feeling faint and sickly. A velvety blackness swathed my brain. I jarred back into consciousness as I hit the floor at the bottom of the staircase. I broke into surprised, shaken tears. In an instant my mother's lover was leaning over me, lifting me up as he enclosed me in the flaccid cage of his pink fleshy arms. He carried me into the kitchen. I kept sobbing, feeling no tenderness in his embrace, only containment and an unwillingness to let me go to my mother or stand on my feet again once my tears subsided. His disappearance, two weeks later, restored the farm to its full, unblemished identity as refuge: as bastion of my privacy and independence.

I was playing baseball the evening my stepfather arrived. I had bullied my mother and Deirdre into pitching to me so that I could practise switch-hitting. The ambiguity of the switch-hitter intrigued me; writing with my left hand but throwing with my right, I considered myself a natural for the role. But I had no one with whom to practise. My fascination with baseball marked me out as an anomaly. The other boys at school followed NHL hockey and CFL football; at noon-hour we played soccer. Even the awarding of a professional baseball franchise to Montreal, less than two hours' drive away, had failed to stimulate interest in the sport. But I had become obsessed with baseball statistics – far more intricate and elegant than the figures generated by hockey or football. I chased their supple formulations down the backs of baseball cards and through the pages of baseball annuals. By developing my switch-hitting, I hoped to induct myself into the game's occult statistical universe. I envisaged my own baseball card, years hence, bearing the legend: *Throws: right – Bats: both*. I never imagined myself as one of the game's stars, but rather as a canny journeyman wise in the lore of the bullpen and the bench: a dexterous utility infielder, a specialist relief pitcher brought on in the thirteenth inning to confound the opposition with an unfathomable fork ball. In pursuit of these dreams, I harassed my mother and Deirdre into pitching to me. But most of their underhand tosses reached me as head-high lobs or bowling shots, irrevocably out of my strike zone. When they protested at my failure to swing my bat, I replied that a disciplined hitter did not swing at pitches that were not between his knees and his shoulders. "Don't be a bloody prig, Oliver!" my mother said. Deirdre, looking confused and offended, drifted away. My switch-hitting practice was about to end, when my stepfather came walking up the long laneway.

I knew him as Mr Fraser. He, his wife and daughters had stayed with us in our previous house – the house where my parents' marriage had ended – when they had arrived in Canada from Scotland. The Frasers had lived with us until

141

they found a house of their own, and my mother and Mr Fraser – both practical British people who had ended up in Canada in the company of temperamental New York spouses – had become friends. My mother, the entire expanse of the Ottawa Valley at her disposal, had bought her farm a mere mile and a half from the house Mr and Mrs Fraser had moved into. After the demise of my mother's silver station wagon, Mr Fraser would occasionally drive us on shopping expeditions. He had once snapped at me not to call him Mr Fraser when he was driving because it made him nervous. He suggested that I call him Callum. Mr Fraser told people to call him Callum even though his driver's licence, which he had shown me, identified him as Calvin. His parents had been in England at the time of his birth; the local authorities had refused to register him under a name that was not English. All his parents' efforts to register him as Callum had failed. It was only after the Second World War started, and he was shipped off to the safety of his aunt's croft in the Scottish Highlands, that he took up the name his parents had intended for him. Since that time, he had felt that he belonged nowhere. He was, he said, essentially a displaced person.

Despite being Scottish, Mr Fraser had lived in New York and California: he understood the subtleties of baseball. He took the baseball from my mother. Twisting his mouth and the curled goatee below it, he concentrated on an imaginary strike zone to the side of my body. His pitches flew in straight and low through the leafy dusk as crickets shrilled and the arid redbrick face of the house, safely uphill from my longest fly balls, softened with evening dew. I slapped at Mr Fraser's pitches right-handed and left-handed until the ball began to get lost in the deepening dusk. After that, he always seemed to be there. One morning I came upstairs to find him standing with his shirt off, hefting Gamble's discarded crowbar. "Now watch my dust fly!" he said, as he flung himself into demolishing a wall whose presence had become an obstacle to my mother's renovation plans. Lathe cracked, powdered plaster spewed up, then filtered down through the air. The next day Deirdre and I stared at each other as our mother and Mr Fraser – I called him Callum now but still could not think of him in that way – embraced in the middle of the kitchen, whimpering into each other's ears. In the morning Deirdre knocked on my door and beckoned to me to follow her upstairs. Backing into the doorway of her own bedroom, she pointed towards the enlarged upstairs room Mr Fraser had built for my mother by knocking out the old wall and installing a longer wall, running at a more generous angle, made of whitewashed gyproc panels. The door of the room hung ajar. Deirdre and I crept in on bare feet. Our mother and Mr Fraser lay entangled and asleep beneath the covers. Deirdre laid her hand on my mother's shoulder. "Mummy," she said. "Put some clothes on."

My mother yawned. "Does the human body really disgust you, dear? What have I done to get such uptight kids?"

The longer Mr Fraser stayed, the shaggier he became. His goatee spread into a broad, full-fledged beard. His hair grew long and thick. My mother's hair, on the other hand, turned stringier as it grew down to her shoulder blades. She called it wartime hair: a consequence of having been born during the Blitz and brought up on the poor nourishment of rationing. At Mr Fraser's urging, she cut it short. I was aghast. I sobbed all the way home in Mr Fraser's Cortina the day we picked up my mother from the hairdresser. When I was unable to stanch my tears over supper, my mother sent me to my room. "He's changed you, he's changed you!" I shouted, slamming my bedroom door.

My mother decided that I needed organized activities outside the farm. I was enrolled in the village Wolf Cubs. The Wolf Cubs met in the gymnasium of my school on Tuesday evenings. Knowing other boys who belonged, I warned my mother that their meetings did not end until nine o'clock. "I'm sure they end earlier than that, Oliver," she said. They didn't, but I was still driven down to the village to join. My mother decreed that I could go to bed at nine-twenty on Tuesday evening; the rest of the week I would continue to go to bed at nine. The Wolf Cubs barked out ritualistic chants and played rowdy games. At Christmas we took to handicrafts, fashioning wooden letter holders shaped like rabbits as presents for our grandparents. Unlike the other boys, I did not have grandparents in the village; I did not even – a fact the Cub leader refused for two weeks to believe – have grandparents in Canada. And I had no grandfather; my foreign grandmothers both lived alone. The Cub leader finally assigned me surrogate grandparents, an elderly couple who lived above the village gift shop. One night before Christmas I rang their doorbell, dashed up the stairs, thrust my letter holder at an astonished old man and fled.

In January the Wolf Cubs hosted a father-and-son night. There were to be competitions for teams of two; each boy was expected to bring a father. If your dad had to work on Tuesday night, the Cub leader said, you could invite a friend of the family. I explained this provision to my mother and Mr Fraser as they were watching television. "Will you come with me, Callum?"

"Of course, Oliver." He glanced at my mother. Their faces trembled with smiles of triumph as their eyes met in sharp, delighted union. I revelled in their pleasure, reassured by my continued ability to make my mother happy. Feigning an acceptance I did not feel, I had regained her approval, reinforcing my man-of-the-house autonomy within our new living arrangements. Mr Fraser might have settled in, but his advent would not dent or diminish my claims to the farm, my mother or my own impulsive freedom.

· · · · ·

"You should know the way," Jack Ship said. "It's your country we're going to."

"I know the way."

"How come you're leaving Delaware? You quitting college?"

"No, I like college. I just need to get out for a year." He gave me a look of jaundiced appraisal. Jack Ship was three years my senior, but he seemed a decade older. He had dropped out of a good East Coast college at seventeen to become a union organizer. He worked for an outfit whose acronymic name,

ACORN, he expanded as American Communists for Revolution Now. Jack Ship had little time for the dreams of social transformation nurtured by the eggheads in his office: he helped working men get a better deal. He had brought unions into companies in New Orleans, Chicago and half a dozen other places. In every city he had confronted an exhausting struggle; in most, he seemed to have met a woman who had become his lover. Now Jack Ship had a problem. His latest woman was in Montreal, and soon to head for Vancouver; his current union battle was in Wilmington, Delaware. The ballots in the vote on whether to establish a union would be counted by midnight. Jack, his car and belongings had to be in Montreal by the next afternoon, when his girlfriend was planning to set out for Vancouver. Since he couldn't do all the driving himself, we arranged to make the trip together. He picked me up at six in the morning, having left the union victory party at five. The speed he had swallowed kept his small body perked up with bantam alertness behind the steering wheel until just north of Poughkeepsie. Then he pulled over and fell asleep. I drove the barren stretch of Interstate 86 up to the Canadian border. I felt grim and confused and elated with Jack's Bruce Springsteen cassette grumbling from the tapedeck, the thickly wooded ramps of the Adirondacks rearing towards a sullen sky and Jack snoring away in a black T-shirt emblazoned with the logo *DARE: Detroit Alliance for a Rational Economy. DARE to fight! DARE to win!* I was glad to put the United States behind me. It was not merely that I was bitterly, traumatically unhappy in Delaware. After two years on a college campus, I was starved for movement and change: two years represented the outer limit of my tolerance for sticking with any place, person or project. The prospect of tearing up my life and ranging off in search of a new existence enabled me to breathe. It bothered me that most other people weren't like this. Even Jack claimed that some day soon he was going to ditch organizing and settle down with the right woman. But I couldn't imagine a time when I wouldn't relish flinging everything away and striking out into exile.

Twenty minutes before the border Jack woke up and told me to pull over. He tossed his remaining speed pills out the window. "You clean to cross the border? You're not carrying anything?"

"I'm clean."

Canadian Customs let us past with a cursory interrogation. When the official asked me what I had been doing in the United States, I replied that I had been attending university. "Listen to the guy!" Jack said, as we pulled away. "When I pick him up this morning, he's Mr Preppie talking about his college. We hit the border and he goes all Canadian on me. 'I was going to uni-ver-si-ty.' How can you change that quick?"

"I've had lots of practice."

•　•　•　•　•

"What did you do in the States, David?" I squatted on my haunches in the snow. I had discovered a technique of crouching flatfooted and slinging back my weight that avoided tiring my legs. I could sit this way for hours. Had I adopted the posture in the schoolyard, I would have been ridiculed – the stance suggested someone hunkering down to defecate in the woods – but while elsewhere this might have concerned me, on the farm and with David, it did not matter.

"I screwed around. My life here is better." He turned over the pale bread cooking on the low, lapping fire banked against a semicircle of flat stones. The bread, pinched between the two wings of a hinged mesh grill, puffed up around the metal struts holding it fast. Crisp, musty-smelling brown spots scarred its pale crust. David set the grill on a stone, opened it and cut us each a big slice of bread. I pulled off my mitts; my frozen fingers fumbled my portion. The bread fell, landing on a stone. David caught my elbow. "Your hands freeze up like that and you can get into trouble. If that ever happens, you shove them down in here," he said, pointing to his crotch. "That warms them up."

I nodded and bit into my bread, concealing my disappointment. I ached to ask David about the details of his departure from the States. I knew, of course, why he had left. Like the others who passed through our farm, David had escaped from the States because of The War. Sometimes the only way people in the States could avoid The War was to come to Canada. And once here, they had to remain. If they went home, they were sent to jail. David could never go back. He was a deserter; that was worse than being a draft dodger. Deserters had lost their homes forever.

I longed to be admitted to the thoughts and impulses that had prompted David's flight. If I could understand why David had fled to Canada, then perhaps I would be able to make sense of my parents' precipitate moves from Germany to England to Michigan to Ontario and all the confusing events that had taken place since our arrival. I chewed the dry, heavy bread, tasting of stone and woodsmoke. The bare grey trunks of the trees leached the deep snow of its gleam. I had woken up early that morning – going to bed at nine, as I would continue to do until the evening of my sixteenth birthday, when my mother finally relented, I was dressed and alert by quarter past five. I usually read British mystery novels at the kitchen table until the rest of the family woke up. Today, in a fit of restlessness, I had headed for the woods. At the bottom of the garden I surprised a rabbit, its white winter coat standing out against the grey shed where Callum parked his snowblower. The rabbit thumped its big rear leg against the hard crust in a tomtom beat of warning to other rabbits. It bolted. I raised my slingshot to fire one of the harmless paste bullets my mother baked for me. I underestimated the rabbit's speed: the bullet dropped into the snow as the creature scooted away. I crossed the low field next to the house and roamed through the ten acre bush until I found David. I had hoped he might be around. There were moments when my need for the example of David's introverted self-reliance keened through me like a sonar wave. During periods of less biting stress, watching Callum apply the honed method of his carpentry skills to renovating the house sufficed to satisfy my yearnings for a male example. Some days, though, I awoke feeling that I could not stand to know anything about being male. I would cling to my mother until she ordered me to stop following her around the house; I would go to play with my sister, who received me with a fractious uncertainty. When the disorienting volatility of my moods threatened to pitch me into crushing gloom, I complained about them – about life – to my mother. "You'd better get used to dealing with being depressed," she said. "It'll only get worse when you're older."

Today, though, was a David day. I leaned forward, rapt and attentive, as he showed me how to extinguish a fire with snow. I waited to see what would happen next. I couldn't bear the thought of returning to the house alone. Yet I didn't dare formulate my wishes into a request. The strength of David's self-absorbed silences, the wild energy of his rare outbursts of emotion, frightened me at the same time that they reeled me towards him. The precise, caressing gentleness with which he hefted his rifle riveted my attention. He glanced down at me as he slid his grill and the leftover hunks of bread into his pack. I remained squatting next to the extinguished fire, staring into the snow.

"I'm gonna go hunt a groundhog for your folks," David said. "You want to come along?"

· · · · ·

David had entered our lives as a result of Callum's work with draft dodgers. A member of the final generation to be kidnapped for two years by Britain's National Service scheme, before the policy was abolished, Callum had turned to helping the bewildered young men who fled The War. Many of the draft dodgers entered Canada illegally. In order to make their residence claims they had to be smuggled back into the US posing as Canadian tourists, then cross the border again and declare their draft dodger status at the Canadian Immigration post. From our farm, Callum could do these runs in about three hours. The house would fall silent while he was away, my mother preparing endless cups of coffee to soothe the draft dodger's girlfriend as she paced out the minutes until his return. Everyone knew or had heard of somebody who had been tripped up, identified and grabbed by the US government on one of these forays. But Callum always brought his passengers back safely. A floating community of exiles, with David as its mainstay, sifted through the farm. They would sleep for a night or two in one of our sheds or in an unfinished upstairs room, or don broad-brimmed hats dripping with mosquito netting and accompany David back into the swamp. Some of them worked on the endless, ongoing renovation of the house. One day the local plumber, whose two sons were my schoolmates, came to install a new faucet on the mudroom sink. He stopped short at the sight of Callum and two long-haired guys hammering and nailing while one of the youths' girlfriends helped my mother tin beets. Buffalo Springfield was blaring from the record player; Deirdre and I ran errands, zigzagging through the confusion. The plumber tilted back his construction helmet. "Is this one of them communes?"

Callum assured him that it was not; yet the stories rushing through my school pounded roughshod over his denials. Weird stuff was happening up at Johnny Hall's old place. Hippies. Drugs. Sexual depravity. It was only a matter of time

146

before everybody up there was carted off to jail. Daydreaming in a math class where I already knew the answers, I would armour myself against the verbal assaults sure to batter me at recess by imagining a ragged commando of draft dodgers, led by David and his thin-faced friend Doug, and Gord, who had found a cache of marijuana in a ditch and used the money to buy a farm in Quebec, advancing across the schoolyard, hunting rifles at the ready, to liberate me from my bored ostracism. The Ottawa Valley farm kids, their community so tight that they were all each other's distant cousins, shared odd beliefs, local prejudices, timeworn lore and a distinctive accent. Wanting what they had but knowing I could never gain admittance to their clan, I imaginatively wove my parents' circle of ragtag drifters into a cohesive social fabric. When we drove into Ottawa, I would tell my mother that I had spotted Doug or Gord or one of the others on a street corner. She would tell me to stop making things up. Yet two or three nights later she would come into my bedroom and wake me, telling me that this or that person was going out to British Columbia for a few months and insisted on saying goodbye to me. None of the others, though, made the same impact on us as David. The night he and his pet skunk, Eddy Munster, whom he usually lodged at another farm, interrupted our supper, we all leapt up to greet him. David had good news. The National Film Board wanted to make a short film about his life. He had accepted their offer, anticipating with glee the day when he would be able to induce a cameraman to wade after him through fetid, waist-deep swamp water. His jovial, brutal mood endured for the entire three days he stayed with us. He cooked us squirrel stew and broke into an evil grin as I struggled to choke it down without betraying my revulsion at the meat's stringy texture and liver-like mustiness. He left us to spend two weeks planting trees in a provincial park. I asked him if he was still intending to make the movie. "Sure am," he said. I clapped my hands. I could hardly wait until my classmates, confronted with the film on their television screens, were forced to concede that my world was as authentic and legitimate as theirs.

· · · · ·

We were both foreigners. Despite our shared passion for losing ourselves in the country's language, literature and politics, we kept sliding towards each other. At one point I lost track of her for a month. I learned that she had moved into a room in an apartment in the poor south end of the city. A phone number was offered; I dialled it. When Erica herself answered, I identified myself in Spanish by first and last name. She laughed. I asked if we could get together. "Sure," she said. "How about tonight?"

She told me which bus to take. I stood in the crowded aisle for an hour as the bus rattled along potholed streets. The profile of the mountains changed, thrusting unfamiliar green indentations and rocky peaks to the crest of the skyline. My body lumbered me with a stubborn erection that refused to be muted by the sight of the ghastly slums rolling past. I found Erica's apartment without difficulty. Her landlords had finished with the kitchen for the evening and retreated to their

147

room. We stood hip to hip cooking arepas on the gas stove. We ate them on plates on our laps, leaning close to one another as we talked about our families. The low-cut V of Erica's blouse, tilting the tender white tops of her breasts before my eyes each time she bent forward, cranked up my arousal until I was on the brink of gasping. Erica intercepted my scrutiny, smiled and, the next time she reached forward, dipped her body a fraction lower. We stashed our dishes in the sink and went to her room. I turned to her, waiting for the tremor of assent that would permit me to wrap her body in my arms. We had been distractedly discussing the possibilities offered by the working world for jobs involving social activism. "This group I worked for in Delaware," she said. "Everybody calls them American Communists for Revo"

"ACORN! I got a ride to Montreal with a guy from ACORN." I outlined the story of Jack Ship and his girlfriend.

"So that's what happened to Jack! None of us ever knew. He got the union into that plant, then he disappeared in the middle of the victory party. We never saw him again."

We stood staring at each other. Outside the window a donkey brayed and a woman began berating it in peasant Spanish. My penis was no longer erect. Erica's body grew still, the busy, welcoming animation of her gestures subsiding into enervation. The sex – perhaps even a shimmer of love – that we had both been anticipating withered, blasted by serendipity, reminders of the claims of other lives, and by the disconcerting discovery that we were already socially linked. It was as if the crossing lines of our pasts, cancelling out the exhilarating tension created by our strangeness to one another, had made a sexual relationship superfluous. I spent the night sleeping on Erica's floor; she, a hand's width above me, slept on a foam pad. Waking in the morning, I told her I was leaving the city. There was a six thousand mile journey through the rest of the continent that I had been yearning to embark upon for months.

Erica listened to my announcement in silence. "This is obviously something you have to get out of your system," she said. "Come and see me when you get back. You and I still have a lot to talk about."

• • • • •

"This is a film of somebody else's ideas about David," my mother warned Deirdre and I, as we walked down the hall to the theatre of the National Library of Canada. "It's not what David thinks about himself."

The film opened with a close-up of David's face in profile. The grainy texture emphasized the snouty Nordic set of his features. As the camera drew back, a frozen landscape spread behind and around him; The crunch of David's snowshoes on the icy crust became audible. The camera cut to typewriter keys pecking a white page: *Larsen, David Frederick. Born Chippewa Falls, Wisconsin, September 3, 1946. Drafted into the United States Army for service in Vietnam. Assigned to Fort Bragg. Failed to return from weekend leave March, 1968. Status: Absent Without Leave.* The camera cut to a shot of David scaling a wind-carved drift in his snowshoes.

The shot stilled into a photograph of soldiers going over the top. David thrashed into the bush, glimpsed a rabbit, lifted his rifle and fired. A still photograph of a Vietnamese girl staggering from a gunshot wound filled the screen. David checked his trapline: each mink, skunk or raccoon he had caught dissolved into a slaughtered Vietnamese. I heard Callum grumble and rock in his seat. The film switched to interviews with David in his camp. As the camera panned the denuded shrubbery of the frozen swamp, David's voice said: *"Sometimes I contemplate suicide. I'm twenty-four. I can't accept that I'm going to have to live to twice or three times my present age before I die naturally."* The camera homed in on the camp. I was startled to see a woman I knew, a spooky younger cousin of Callum's ex-wife, huddled in David's tent. Her hair fell over her face. The interviewer said that she had met David when she had come up from New York to get away from a father who beat her. They were two Americans sharing their exile in the Ontario bush. The interviewer asked David why he hadn't found a Canadian girlfriend; David didn't reply. The film cut back to the snowy wastes of the winter fields: more hunting and trapping, more dead animals metamorphosing into Vietnamese bodies.

The lights went on. "Why isn't David here?" I asked my mother.

"David's already seen the film."

"Are they going to show that movie on TV?"

"No," my mother said.

"Good." I couldn't articulate the reasons for my relief, but I could sense that this film would do nothing to improve my classmates' image of the world I inhabited.

A few weeks after the screening, David took the train out west to buy a tract of bush in northern Saskatchewan. When he returned he had shed his buckskins in favour of blue jeans and a functional workshirt. A group of Indian men on the train had hooted and jeered at his old garb; one of them had poured beer over his fringed jacket.

David gave away Eddy Munster to the family with whom he usually lodged the skunk. He brought his family up from Wisconsin to join him on his new homestead. He had a square, sturdy mother, a burly younger brother who looked much like him but for his short hair and beardless face, and a distant blonde sister who rarely spoke. No one mentioned his father. His family stayed on the farm for a few days before piling into a rusted camper van and driving away. Later, David sent us photographs of the house they built in a clearing in the bush. His younger brother grinned in the doorway, holding up a canoe paddle like a javelin. David's letter described the northern Saskatchewan bush in musical prose that Callum read out admiringly from the head of the kitchen table. The next day he wrote a reply to David's letter. When, after a few weeks, he had not received an answer, he wrote again. There was no reply. He asked Doug and Gord and the others who remained in the area if they had heard any news. They shook their heads. Nothing.

The next news I received of David came twenty years later. I was looking after the farm for my mother and Callum while they were on vacation in Europe. Lounging on the plush furniture and meandering through the house's large modern interior felt like an immersion in stunning luxury after the suffocating dinginess of my Montreal apartment or my rented rooms on other continents. I could work on the computers, toy with the VCR and listen to music on the compact disc player. Late one night the telephone rang.

"Goodday," one of the local farmers said, speaking, as Ottawa Valley telephone etiquette dictated, without introducing himself. "You know David's on TV?"

"David?"

"David that used to live up at your place."

I clapped down the receiver with the scantiest of thanks and dived for the television. I rifled through the channels until I found him – on the local newscast. David was in Ottawa! The screen showed a chisel-faced man in his forties, his hat tipped back to reveal a receding hairline, his braids turned grey and flimsy. He had squatted on a vacant lot in Vanier, setting up a teepee amid the rubble. He wore a threadbare US Army jacket with somebody else's name on the identity flash. His explanations of what he was doing there verged on incoherence. The camera switched back to the anchorman. "Mr Larsen says that he lives a traditional hunting and trapping lifestyle because that's what he likes. And what's more, he wasn't even brought up in Canada. Mr Larsen came to the Ottawa area in 1968 as a deserter from the United States Army…"

I turned off the television and stared at the screen. Two days later, when my mother and Callum flew in from Athens, I told them about the broadcast. They were intrigued to learn that David was living a mere twenty-five miles away. All through supper that evening we reminisced about David. None of us ever went to look for him.

• • • • •

I returned to the city months later, bearded and sunburned. Solitude and distance had given me a wary, circumspect approach to conversation. I had lost twenty pounds from a frame that could ill afford to lose weight. My Spanish had grown idiomatic and accentless. With my fair colouring, people told me that I was a Spaniard, a German-descended Latin American – anything but a gringo from Canada.

It took me a couple of days to locate Erica. We finally got together in an empanada joint downtown. It was late at night. She touched my elbow as we met. We spoke in a desultory way for a few minutes, then she said: "Oh yeah, I did something while you were away. I fell in love."

"That's not a bad thing to do," I said.

She told me about her lover. He was a painter, an artist. "A real artist, not a fraud." I nodded. Erica's mouth twisted. "You seem so much older now. If you had been this together when I met you…"

"Don't say it," I said.

She smiled. "Okay, I'll just think it… You know what, Ollie? You should fall in love with a *latina*. Then you could stay in South America."

I thought of a woman in Cali who had gone back to her apartment to send her mother out to visit relatives so that I could come over for the evening. I had stood the woman up and caught a bus to the next city. I said: "Me and a *latina* wouldn't have worked. I've been here long enough. It's time to move on."

• • • • •

David led me through the ten acre bush and out onto the silent, snowbound fields. The early morning cold was debilitating, but with the warm bread inside me and David breaking the trail ahead of me, I felt fortified. At a fenceline two-thirds of the way back to the swamp, he motioned to me to crouch down. "There's a groundhog hole over there. They've come out of full hibernation. If this sun holds, they should pop up in an hour or so."

The sun held, glazing the snow to a wavering white brilliance. We sat in silence. I forced myself not to fidget or mind the cold. Callum, who had been a weapons instructor during his National Service, said that David was more patient lining up a shot than any man he knew. David possessed the patience of the wilderness, Callum was steady and methodical, my father was impulsive and intuitive. I felt I must reconcile these differences and did not know how to do it. I stared across the field listening to the day's first remote hints of human activity: the far-off hacking of a chainsaw or snowmobile, the lowing of a Holstein during morning milking in our neighbour's barn. My gaze remained fixed on the groundhog hole.

I saw David's rifle swing up before I realized that the groundhog had emerged. He squinted down the barrel from above his frost-beaded moustache and red-stung cheeks, tracking the animal's foraging swipes at the snow. His rifle twitched to one side then the other as he readjusted his aim in response to each twist of the animal's sleek head. I was shivering with the cold by the time he pulled the trigger. A hundred yards away, the groundhog spun around and went down. It got up, lurching on all fours towards its hole. David shot it through the head and killed it.

The blood was still bright on the snow when we reached the groundhog's body. David picked it up by a hind leg. "We'll take it back to camp and skin it."

I was delighted. If I was going to make my living as a hunter and trapper, I would need instruction in skinning animals. We walked across the last of the fields and tramped over an expanse of snow-bent sedge enclosed by high, scrub-by bushes. I followed David down into the sunken maze of drainage ditches and along narrow arms of water frozen solid and dusted with snow. Gaunt trees and clump-like brown bushes poked up all around us. The day was silent except for the distant buzzing of snowmobile engines. David led me into a circular clearing on the edge of which he had ensconced his winter-camping tent under the cover of a snow-drift. He ducked inside to drop off his rifle and pack. Returning to the clearing, he pulled his knife out of its sheath. The grinding roar of snowmobiles grew louder. "They're getting closer." He hefted the knife. "It's like this a lot of Saturdays." He sank the point of his knife into the groundhog's thorax, slit its hide from forehead to anus and peeled off the pelt as though he were undressing a tod-dler. "Groundhog fur's useless. But the meat's good." He eviscerated the animal, spilling the warm coil of its guts onto the snow. As he did so, the red, forty-horse-power Arctic Cat belonging to Mr McFee from the Fourth Line blasted over the sculpted lip of the far snowbank and landed in the middle of the clearing with a metallic crunch accompanied by a wild war-whoop. No sooner had Mr McFee skidded past than the yellow hull of a Ski Do bearing the older brother of a boy I knew at school came careening in his wake. The snarling of half a dozen other snowmobiles mangled the air. Portly figures in thermal suits wearing helmets with dark plastic visors clung to their machines as if they were wild steeds. The stench of burnt fuel stung through the penetrating cold. An errant beer bottle bounced off the side of the tent and rolled across the snow. The racket degenerated into a disorderly growling as the snowmobiles, having made one pass of the camp, regrouped and turned around. They gunned towards us again.

"Get into the tent!" David shovelled me out of the snowmobiles' path. I landed flat on my back on the tarpaulin floor. David reached over me to retrieve his rifle. Sitting up, I saw him rearing back like a cornered Kodiak bear as the first snowmobile, taking flight from a hard-packed snowdrift, hurtled past him in midair. He staggered backwards. Regaining his balance, he seemed to become charged with a mad gusto at the prospect of defending his camp. "Wahoo!" he shouted, jabbing his rifle in the air.

"Get your hippie ass out of here!" the village insurance broker shrieked, driving over the groundhog's spilled guts.

"WAHOO!" David yelled, as another snowmobile's runner nearly severed one of the tent's support strings. Spreading his arms wide, the barrel of his rifle flaring skyward, he sprang forward to challenge each snowmobile in turn as it roared out of the frayed shrubbery. Arctic Cats and Yamahas swerved and skidded. One teenage driver nearly flipped his machine. The last snowmobile crossed the clearing; the sound of their engines began to recede. This time they weren't coming back.

David picked up the skinned groundhog, its carcass miraculously unmarked by the tumult. He stumbled into the tent, laid his rifle on the floor and sat down. He shook his head, gasping as though winded. "Assholes…"

"I know," I said. "I go to school with their kids."

"They get tanked up and they go crazy. Just like my old man before he took off… My mom used to have to slug it out with him. We kids would sit upstairs and watch to see which of them was winning."

"Is that how come you left the States, David?"

"Look, Ollie, take this to your folks, will you?" He lifted the skinned ground-hog, prodding the right hind leg into my palm. I stood up, pulled on my mitts and took a grip. "Can you carry it?" David asked.

I tested the groundhog's weight. I nodded.

"Good. Now get moving."

I stood up. I could feel icy wind roughening my cheeks. The flap over the entrance swung back like an opening door. I stepped out of the tent into the glittering, frozen world beyond.

Unventing Myths and Monsters
Helen Cleary

A fictional essay inspired by Marina Warner's *Indigo*

A woman knitter once wanted to learn how to spin her own wool
and found the directions in the handbook on spinning hard to follow.
When she actually picked up her spindle and began to wind the
threads through it and to twirl it in rhythm, she found that her fingers
already seemed to know how to perform motions arcane to her
conscious mind. She coined the term unventing for this rediscovery
of a lost skill through intuition, a bringing of latent knowledge out of
oneself in contrast to 'invention' from scratch.

> *Annis Pratt*
> *Archetypal Patterns in Women's Fiction*

When we think of the octopus, we think of that mythical monster who lives
deep, deep down at the bottom of the ocean along with pink, anaemic fish (the
ones that you can see straight through to count every bone in their body) and
prehistoric relics that look as if they have been roaming the sea for millions of
years. In the octopus we see a great, threatening hunter who will lunge out of
the dark, swirling great tentacles at its victim, which, once caught, will be
squeezed and sucked till there is not a breath of air left in its carcass. But that
is because civilisation is afraid of the unknown, of the sea, whose power and
immensity can crush and swallow human life in a matter of seconds. We no
longer have a symbiotic relationship with the god of the ocean; he is not a
provider of sustenance, his waves rarely lap tenderly against the curve of our
bodies without a fear of depth and death touching us.

Once, however, when we were as relaxed in the water as we are on land,
the octopus (who did not go by that name at all) was our great friend. She was
called Sisijubo, which is translated as 'many legged lover'. Then she symbol-
ized an all embracing love, a love which offered a security and an innocence
beyond the imagination. She lived in warm waters around an island called
Sethea, which today we would locate in the Caribbean on a contemporary
map. She hated cold and damp, she knew that she would not find play or love
in such conditions and although she had heard of the great whales' journey
across miles and miles of ocean, she herself had no desire to seek adventure.

At any time of the day one could hear the screams of laughter and joy in the lagoons where Sisijubo dwelled and where the children chose to play. Sisijubo could take three or four children at any one time and throw them into the air, letting them dive back to the silky bottom of the lagoon. They would also ride on her back as she whooshed gracefully through the water; Sisijubo never moved quickly or abruptly. For many, many years Sisijubo lived this peaceful life. None of the villagers living in Sethea knew how old she was or even dared to bet on her age – any such gambling or bets were against the islanders' moral code. Everyone could claim to have been held in her many arms and for this reason every single person had been blessed with love and innocence and Sethea was a very happy place. The islanders knew that to guess at the age of Sisijubo and to question her beginnings would bring a curse upon the island and upon the great many-legged creature herself. To talk of Sisijubo was to celebrate fecundity and fertility, to shout her praises from the top of banana trees and mountains. Any other mention of her name was hushed up.

Yet, there was one young boy, called Bacalin, who knew nothing of this. His mother, who had died giving birth, had not been able to teach him the lore of love. As an orphan he had been fed on the milk of shoats, and as everyone knows, this is no substitute for the milk of one's mother. As a result, he had been a sickly child; unlike his contemporaries he had not been able to experience the vital warmth of the lagoon. He had not swum to its silvery bottom on a quest for a twist of shell that was home to various tiny sea creatures. He had not played amongst the reef, chasing fishes, nor had he been exhilarated by seemingly heroic dives from rocks like the other children. Instead he had spent many days in the shade sweating with fever. He was small and thin and twisted and pale. His skin did not possess that sheen of health that is particular to young children and lovers. It was somehow dull, unusually antiquated. Sometimes his eyes had the look of an old man. For this reason, and also because of the sudden death of his mother, the rest of the community feared him. Some whispered that he was the cause of the young woman's death and thus he must be a curse. Because he had not felt the brush of Sisijubo's love it seemed that the villagers could not find it in their hearts to love him. They found it easy to support their rumours that he was the devil in disguise, by citing his pallor and ghostly appearance as evidence, "He is not like the rest of us," they said: "He is white, his whiteness is obviously an attempt to hide his darkness inside."

Suddenly everyone was discussing the matter of Bacalin's skin. They hid in corners, in the shade of the palm and, huddled in groups, they whispered ferociously. Some old men jabbed their sticks into the earth in indignation, and others' faces twisted in contempt and hatred – Sethea was no longer a happy place, it was full of the whisperings and hissings of deceit and discontent. The island's great Papa, to whom everyone went for advice, began to fear for the future of his people's happiness. He felt an overwhelming desire to rid Sethea of its hatred. Late in the evening, he would lie in his hammock and look over to the place where the frail child was sleeping restlessly. Bacalin, caught in yet another fever, muttered and groaned some unknown pain and the setting sun picked out drops of perspiration above his top lip and on his brow. Yet Papa could find no compassion for this child, he could not explain why he felt such contempt and frustration welling up in his heart when he considered the child's situation. Although Papa did not know it, the people's feelings had been forced by their own failure to tend to the child and offer him the opportunity to play, like all the others, in the ocean. Bacalin had not felt the benefit of Sisijubo's healing contact. Papa succumbed to a blindness like all his community and it was with this disability that he made a fatal decision. For many hours, when the sky was black as indigo, he wrestled with Sethea's problem. As much as he hated to choose a culprit, he decided that the child was to blame for the island's unhappiness, and therefore, the only way to deal with the matter was to make the child disappear. If Bacalin could not be seen, the islanders would soon forget his existence and peace could be recovered. So Papa decided that Bacalin should be taken to the hills where he would live alone and tend to the indigo plant which was used to dye the cloth used by the islanders for clothing and decoration. Having settled the matter once and for all, Papa fell into a sound, contented sleep shared by all those who have swum in the arms of Sisijubo. Early the next day Papa strapped Bacalin to his back and swiftly made his way up the mountainside in order to return to his community before the sun rose to awaken the village.

To some extent Papa was right – it was not long before the people forgot about the little boy. Oh yes, there was some gossip as to the cause of his absence; some explained that he had been taken by a wild dog, the devil's companion. Others said that Bacalin had given up any attempt to destroy Sethea's peace because the place was obviously so happy. Papa frowned on hearing this, had they already forgotten the whispering and hissing? He felt apprehensive that they were so self-righteous, so indiscriminate. He wondered if this lack of perception was not an omen itself. He feared that his decision to move the child away was unjust and Papa himself began to look a little pale. The very next week, he once again made his way up the mountain to seek out Bacalin. He found the child working hard at the indigo plants which were difficult to tend. Bacalin greeted him without any hint of bitterness, but Papa saw a shadow in the child's eyes that caused his heart to shrink, and the boy still looked so ill. if not worse than before. His breath was snatched in rasps, and sometimes Bacalin coughed, little barks that sounded like the scrape of a brush in the bottom of the women's pots. Papa left plenty of food, as he had done last week, but he noticed that much of last week's supplies were still untouched at the foot of the tree under which Bacalin slept. As Papa made his way home he feared the worst.

It was not long after Papa's second visit that the great storm happened. The island and its inhabitants had seen nothing quite like it and there was no example to be found in the old people's stories (that are handed down from generation to generation) that could compare to the rage that fell upon Sethea. The angry storm sneaked upon the village in the deepest, darkest of nights. The day had given no hint of what was to come. As usual, the children had swung in the trees and leaped into Sisijubo's many arms. Sisijubo, herself, appeared to be especially loving. Perhaps, somewhere deep inside, Sisijubo had sensed the great change in her life that was about to happen (through no fault of her own). At her most energetic, she appeared slightly sad and her tentacles were wrapped tighter than ever around the children's waists. Her grip became almost claustrophobic. Some of the less patient children ran off to play with seaweed at the shoreline, out of her reach. Later that night, the villagers awoke to the roaring sea shouting its indignation at them. It was some time before they were able to calm themselves and gather their few belongings in order to flee the shoreline where their huts huddled together. The men helped their elders, whilst the women strapped their young to their backs. Their hands were dexterous, despite their desperation. It was just as well; no sooner had the villagers began to wind their way up into the jungle than the sea surged onto the beach, ripping away the village as if it were made of paper. All the animals were pulled, screaming, into the waves. All the crops, including the village's own plantations of indigo, were swept away in a matter of minutes.

The storm continued to rage and scream until dawn broke. The sky flashed its disapproval and crackled its hatred vehemently. As the islanders turned to each other for comfort, under an unfamiliar jungle canopy, they began to question the meaning of the sea's and sky's rage. As the children stared, wide-eyed into the unusual and frightening sounds of the jungle night, Papa made his confession to his people. The occasional burst of lightning illuminated the face of a tired and guilty old man. The villagers later commented that they had never seen such pain on Papa's face. As they heard Papa's confession and how he had dealt with Bacalin, they knew that they had mistreated the child and were being punished. They also guessed that the child had died that day and their fear was confirmed shortly after dawn, when a scout returned with the news of the damage and Bacalin's fate.

The scout described how he had found the child lying curled amongst his seedlings. His face was peaceful although more drawn and pale than ever. All the little plants were withered except for one and that one was held in Bacalin's right hand. This plant was healthy and had dyed the boy's forefinger and thumb purple. The scout paused and said, "But the most unusual thing to relate is that I found something else in the child's other hand. At first sight I thought it was the seaweed that is regularly washed up onto our shore. But when I got closer, I realised that it was the arm of Sisijubo. I wept at the sight of it, and the child, and ran to our village (or what remains of it). I shouted for Sisijubo and plunged into the lagoon. But I could not find her." The villagers stared in astonishment at the scout and his report. After a long silence the scout added, "I cannot understand how Sisijubo's remains got so far up the valley. How did her arm come to rest with the child among the indigo plants?"

Sisijubo, who is now called the 'octopus' (because now, most definitely, she has only eight legs) is never to be found in shallow lagoons. Instead she is a very shy creature, who hides in crevices and caves deep, deep down in the ocean. You will find that if you do try and approach her she becomes very defensive; she will squirt a jet of purple ink at you in order to blind you. Actually, the colour of the fluid might best be described as indigo. This defence mechanism is most unique, quite unlike any other marine creature's manoeuvres. Poor Sisijubo – of what is she so afraid? And if you ever go to the island that was once called Sethea, you may hear the story about seaweed and a mythical sea creature that possessed the power to love and also to inspire a love that was so sweet and innocent; it was as pure as the pearl made by the oyster. In this place, seaweed is treated with superstition and it is said that it is an aphrodisiac, but that it can make you go blind with love. When the little children of the island hear this story, they take fright, and run to their mother, who bathes them in the sea to calm their fear.

Tiresias

Stephen Burt

squinting, comes to us in a pair of half-rusted
faces on a coin, or as both sides

of one coin. When he wakes, without breasts
and horrified, the gods

can pummel him with questions: where
is fancy bred, the heart

or your old head? Since you're a man
again, which sex

is better? He won't
answer, but their ex-
cruciating thunder can divine

what he can't hide: exposed, his outward parts
curl up, a rosy snail
that wants to be a rose.

His flat pale nipples, like shut eyes,
contract in disbelief:

now that he's voted the wrong side
his own thighs are the last of what he sees.

• • • • •

Blinded, he learned the delicate arts

of teaching heroes to expect disasters,
but saved one truth for preadolescents, old men,

spinsters, and unmarriageable bastards –
a truth which might be engraved in this odd coin's

insides, between the obverse, a scowling patron,
and the flip side, where a sky-blue patch obscures

either a beardless pikeman with an eyesore
or a distraught girl lifting a carnation.

Anonymous Bosh
Ben Teasdale

This is the last chapter. Don't pick up the phone. COME ON COME ON COME ON COME ON. Is this your second-best second guess? I think you've crunched the numbers like a clockwork crocodile; I think you've tracked down the other tapes and are sitting there surrounded by printouts and it's no news to you that I'm sitting here with Henry's letter and the keys to Heaven and Hell, trying to figure out which one is the Word so I can eat it before the lexicographers – the police – whatever – get here. Are you one of them? Are you my friend or my enemy? Are you sheep or goat?

A word for our hosts. I'm sorry for the intrusion; I didn't always used to do this; this is a long story and you've only got a short one. But you must have figured that that the beginning is always a wrong number. Life progresses by wrong numbers. The DNA's straight and then it kinks. Three years ago I called my boyfriend, 221395, and a voice answered, 221395. A woman. Hi is Phil Phil who he's my there's no but that's his Phil sorry. Here. Sorry. Click. Wait. I rang again. Long. Then Hi. Hi. Hi. Eventually I figured it. I must have dialled a digit wrong. She'd done the same thing, only inside out; dialled the wrong number out loud, the number I thought I'd rung. Just one of those stupid coincidences; but for about seventeen seconds it had dropped us both into another world. When Phil and I broke up I found myself wanting to talk to this virtual girl, thinking that as we'd shared a little derailment she could sort out the big one, make it make sense. So I started phoning around his number, trying to recreate the mistake, figure out the permutations. If I'd just got one number in the wrong place that was 36 combinations. If I'd actually misdialled any of them, that was 60. Two and we were into the thousands. She sort of got lost in the numbers. Eventually I got into the habit of dialling totally randomly, just to see if there'd be a connection; just to have a conversation. I checked the time by the speaking clock; I shopped with imaginary credit card numbers; I got off to prerecorded voices, ate to 0898. We evolve. The tape revolves.

Everything blasted to ash. Prise up the stone of the sky an inch and peer at the leeched life beneath. Light a remembered umbra only. Lost in the numbers. The year nothing. Every dead object turned survival freak, bristling with unnatural spars, great thorns of ice. Dead weight of white. Paralysed pugilists. Barbed wire on the barbed wire.

And a butterfly on fire.

No, no, said Henry Ling. No. ParLOURment. Not the other. You sure? I always yeah I'm sure.

He received, it says here, a dull sceptical stare tempered by genuine animal perturbation; not that the owner of said stare would have put it in so many words. Lose sceptical, for a start. Far too expensive. And tempered? Perturbation? You crazy? You wanna break the bank? More plausibly the look might be captured with some degree of verisimilitude, if you were prepared for an entire fucking Wall Street of a sentence, by one of those slightly undergound suburban painters, semi-eliciting in their semi-illicit studios; where men moved by muted ghosts of feelings would come in with dislocated tread and stare silently at the pictures and wonder without words where the words were. Bells without tongues.

Not ParLIA no, believe me. You wanna watch yourself. Henry strode swiftly away from the mark. Never hang around after passing off a counterfeit. Dumb alarums.

Henry Ling is a semiotic terrorist. A serial surrealist. He is the man who flamed the prime minister's favourite hedge so it read DYSTOPIARY in six-foot high smouldering vegetative letters. He is the man who made the House of Lords advertise itself as the Louse of Hoards for a week and a half. He fucked McPriest's word processors so the executive committee spent an unwitting fortune exhorting their Massburger-chomping clients to think deeply about their Christianinanity and submit to the Lard of the Ward. He wants to freak the Phoneticians and fuck the Philologists. Most of all Henry Ling wants to fuck English PLC.

The counterfeiting is the simplest racket. If the fuckers have privatised your language, undermine the currency. Defile the dialect of the tribe. Dump non-Lexicon pronunciations and constructions over the country like chaff dumped by bombers – everyone's paranoid about committing neologism, so do it with conviction and watch their words twist like strips of silver. Scare the radar shit-less. Or more properly the guys in the monitoring room. feeding glucose to the machines that maintain every account from Economy to Executive, keeping a cathode screwed eye on the security analysis as the numbers come up from the banks of conversations being randomly scrutinised. Henry, of course, wears a doctored monitor that bypasses the mouthpiece and continually broadcasts the numbers of banal, uncontroversial, cheap communication. But someday they will rumble him. His number will be up. Do you think they see, the privileged few, hunched in this chamber where the semantic atom has been split, its energy harnessed, signifier and signified sundered, each word given an atomic number and a price tag and banished from view, seen but not heard, do they perceive, crouched in this universal lughole, surveying the speech-acts of a species, a pattern to it all, a common voice, a collective expression, a logos, a harmony, a symphony? Best not to ask. Questions cost more.

I have this recurring dream.

I'm in a payphone, hanging on to the connection like an umbilicus because this time, finally the information I have to convey isn't just empty sounds, this time it's life-or-death, vital signs, vital statistics; and when I open my mouth to speak all I hear is bleep-bleep-bleep-bleep bleep-bleep-bleep. Out of units. Another coin and another breath for mouth-to-mouth, and all I get is more monotonous binary fucking morse from the fission fucking muse. Another coin. More bleeps. More bleeps. I pull out my wallet, rip it open, grab at the clatter on the shelf and I'm shoving in fives, tens, twenties, pate de fois grasing the fucker with fifties, pound coins, bleeps, fivers, tenners, bleeps, twenty pound notes. Try to speak. Bleeps. Skitter out plastic and ram in a phone card. Units snap down and out. Bend it out blind and slam in my bank card. Numbers tumble, race to OD. Credit card. My house and my car hanging upside down in my retina. Charge limit exceeded. End of the line. The wire unwinding. Roar like an ape and smash its fucking face in until the buttons are bruised and the card is snapped off in its slot, tongue bleeding, and there's blood dark bright and slimy like snail trails on the metal. And a long continuous bleeeeeeeeeeeeeeeeeeeeeeeeeeeeeeeeeeeeep.

And silence.

How did you get this number?

And suddenly I'm on fire with fear.

Laser-sighted bats are the worse. One of them could have your eye out, soon as look at you. You have to sneak into their caverns wearing mirrored glasses and radio jammers, then flame-thrower as many as you can until they're dropping like swiss army rats and you can finish them off on the floor before they get their aim together. Can't do that with the petrols, of course. At least not inland. When they're swooping down to siphon off moored boats and parked cars about the only thing you can do is armour-plate; hope they'll break their beaks, the little buggers. Electric cages around gas stations. Not like the old days, when all you needed was a good slick to bring 'em all down. Sometimes a whole squadron of the bastards will mob an oil rig or a tanker; fuel themselves off the spill for months. Most people don't realise that there's a war going on under their noses. Anti-Evolution is the second biggest branch of PLC. Second only to Devolution – handing people the choice about their vocabulary back to them and all that. Of course, all of this is strictly strictly. All that stuff about Domesday even more so. Schtum. Life and death. We may be about to turn the war around.

Not a typical conversation.

A typical conversation:

Fuck?

No shit.

SHIT??

No, fuck!

No fuck? No shit!

SHIT!! SHITTING SHIT!!

Twenty-four minutes earlier Henry Ling had been standing in the devil's mouth, trying to find a way to crawl down its oesophagus. The Anti-Evolutionary department is, like any PLC building, an anonymous office block that would never admit to its function; but, thought Henry, rounding the corner past the girls and heading for the Bibliotech, once you've located one of these unmarked markers, once you've drilled into one of these concrete teeth and found the gum you should begin to be able to map the cavities, trace the labyrinth to the Lexicon, find a route to the offices of English PLC itself, the place so deeply buried even its inhabitants don't know its location, incarcerated in its hollowed-out jaw bone. The devil's mouth is a city: it is one flat palate randomly crammed and crowded with broken molars and incisors, irregularly worn down, every tooth a mouth, a mouth full of mouths. Orthodontists shiver in their sleep.

He had passed each word and swiped his swiped card. Then in a cage of hanging plastic strips Henry had found a cat clamped bolt upright to a metal pole, limbs splayed out like a man gesturing sitting down. In a strange flare of compassion he had released it, and as he had done so it had raked his uplifted forearm with both front claws and then coiled into the corner not like a cat coils but like something reptilian, staring at him with snake-mouth wide open. On his arm was a perfect barcode of blood. Quickly he had pressed it onto a sheet of paper, watched it shine to dullness.

Then got the fuck out.

And in the Bibliotech, closed, surrounded by barcoded versions of the trashed classics and the classicised trash, each thoughtfully devolved of any provocative and therefore over-expensive content, he plugged a reader into his monitor and read what his blood said.

I don't know. I don't know. I'm only reading what he's written. I'm not sure what I'm doing here. I only have half the story. I don't even know if its you I'm talking to. Maybe I've been deceiving myself. Maybe this whole thing is just going to go banal and some poor granny in flatland is going to complain to the council about the voices coming out of the new wiring. To tell you the truth I'm shit scared. I don't know if it's the local devils they've sent after me or just the guy trying to get my rent. What's worse, I'm not sure I'd know the difference any more. Or if it mattered.

Did you hear that? I thought I heard something.

I was there, you see, and there was a scrum of figures and in the middle of it this guy with all these bits of wire and metal sticking out of his head and they were trying to get him into one of the cubicles and he was fighting like a mad thing and one of the nurses turned to the desk and said Christ, give us a hand and there was a rip, you could hear it, and one of the wires came out and there was blood coming out of his head and a piece of wire sticking up like an antennae.

Henry's no hero. He's just another fuck-up.

He plays all the parts.

With his scuffed toe he idly pokes the shards of a broken angel around the floor.

Henry sits at his desk, writing a letter. With curves, not parallel lines. When the letter is finished he puts down the fountain pen next to the pots of ink and begins to pull on his asbestos suit; boots, body, gloves, hood. He moves slowly to the door and, bracing himself, opens it. Blasted back by the heat. Head down, he steps, ponderously, stoically, poisoned, out into the flames.

The world is on fire. Still. Henry treads slowly and heavily down what was once a street, wading through the slow liquid of the tarmac, an intermittent flare bursting from the top of his head as he labours his breaths out. He stops briefly to peer through his small square of smoked, melting glass at the great lung of flame that was a tree, stumped charcoal spear just visible or imaginable at the darkness of its heart of heat. New kind of respiration.

He kicks his way through the incinerating remains of some crashed cars, this millenia's or this morning's, swaying clumsily as they crumble. He finds his way not so much by sight but by the shifting landscape of sound, the varying timbres of different materials forced to burn until they can only keep on burning, the different currents in what used to be the air, the patches where the fire itself has become self-feeding, self-sustaining.

Henry Ling stops in the town square. He approaches the marshmellowing postbox, reaches deep inside an asbestos pocket and pulls out his letter. It flames immediately. He pushes its emptiness into the postbox as best he can, wiping the still-burning ash from the gaping, giving lip and dutifully knocking it in.

He is tired. He is poisoned. He stumbles out into the middle of the empty square. A man is making his way across the other side, trailing the flaming mass of what was once a dog.

He reaches for his glove.

Another long dark night of the bowel. I'm sitting on the shitter like a spirit level, not knowing which way it's going to go, this mass, this pressure, this presence stuck inside of me. My body is crying out to be a wind instrument and it can't, it's blocked, the breath cannot pass through me. I'm gulping at the air trying to burp it out and it's like I'm trying to articulate a word, a word stuck inside of me I have to get out and I can't say it, I can't get it out, it's turned to poison inside me, bad biological alchemy.

Henry is shoved back into a chair. One of the Lexicographers draws up another chair and sits eyeing him with a tight, feral smile, pen poised over precarious pad of paper. The other strikes a foppish pose in front of him, long fingers unconsciously creasing the folds of the air. Now Henry, before we begin I think it only fair to warn you that we already suspect you of gross and unprecedented crimes against the glorious construction and institution that is our language. God, vast and impossibly grotesque monster, frail shaven-headed old man in Belsen, is shoved back into a chair, strapped in crackling bands of antimatter. And whilst we're enjoying our little badinage, our little game of verbal badminton, my colleague, Mr Cognomen, will be algebraically analysing your speech for the slightest signs of deviancy, do you follow? What vocabulary did you say you were paying for again? And they lever open that horrendous multiplied shark's maw, that multi-dimensional saliva-coated cogwheel and tap until they find a tooth with a worm in it. No, I'm sorry, I don't understand. The Lexicographer's pen mosquitoes across the page, scrawling a complex array of longhand sums. There's a rattling at the window. The Word is here somewhere. It has to be. Very good! Very good. Absolutely Standard. Now Mr Ling, here's the rub. I want you to justify the pursuit and study of English language and literature. And whilst you do, I'm going to be applying some of these devices you can see here. You begin, I'll just fire this baby up. They take it to the military. Extraction of root from any given power. Swarms of locuses. And with a phonendoscope they take down the numbers of the Satan muttering to itself inside. Domesday book. Lexicon. The ultimate weapon. No more need for fusion bombs or antimatter missiles – crack one of these open over your enemy and you can literally turn a place to hell. Or just synthesise the key and release the chemicals into the water supply, increasing the dose day by day until they're all gradually damned. You can even do it to a specific individual. An animal. Watch them spiralling tighter. Winding down. Pages of sums on the floor. Henry reaches for his glove. You see we think you have something we want. Stuck inside of me. Too long. I can't find it. They're breaking in. I can't find it. The Lexicographer turns the head of a tiny acetylene torch tighter until its fat blue nib is an elongated quivering scalpel, plays it back and forth on his gleaming teeth, face looming, twisting to face Henry's. Too long. Henry tears off the glove. Is this with flaming hand he tears off the other glove. Logogram Logograph Logogriph. He pulls off his boots. Crib. So he pulls off the body. God creche-lands on earth. He rips off the hood. The Lexicographer stares down at him in disbelief, torch still flustering in the air. Got it. Naked in the blaze in the square. Same word on both sides of the page. Context. I can feel it boiling over. The door splinters open. Sum done wrong. I open my mouth, swallow, and dislodge a vast, cavernous, genesis-and-apocalypse reverberating animal of a

GHOTI.

He not laughed, laughed, then not laughed again. Bosch process. Hydrogen. Hits the invisibility of the torch. SCHTUM. Homophone. Cri de queer. Tongues of flame. Salvador Dali's face in the Garden of Earthly Delights. Sound of shattering angels crashing down from countless shoulders. Spirit glue. Potable phone. Gargle to get the dialling tone. Hell is an LP. Volution. B-side. Blaze whites him out to the white. Los Angeles and San Francisco pass each other like ships on a raging sea of rock. Berrocal returns to colour. And he's naked and sane and standing in the middle of the square, arms coming down from outstretched, suddenly hit by a gentle reflex of embarrassment. And cold. And a slight drizzle. VIRTUALLY NO TRAINS. FATTY ACIDS. Madam, are you Alexia Martins? A SUPPOSITORY OF WORDS! DECLARE A PEACEFIRE! And a girl looking at him peculiarly. Are you alright, mate? HAND ME MY METAMOMETER, SPOCK, AND SET PHRASERS TO STUN. Yes. thanks. I'm okay now. I'm fine. HELLS BELLS! I'm fine. I'm fine. I'm FU-

New Year's Day, 1996

Arnie Guha

For Ben and Jessica

"I would be a good boy, mamma,
but someone is following me..."
– Blind Lemon Jefferson, 1927

"Play me some blues then," she says.
And the rough groove renders half its soul
to the outdated stylus. Round and round,
the uncut sound from 'twenty-seven
swirling vintage, slow.

Along the seafront, at Leigh, I hear
the masts of boats at the yacht club, covered,
sleeping, clack-clacking to the wind
like children in their dreams turning
and in this room, about five minutes
from the tidal beach, the gulls,
the blues on this old machine employing
the dead in sleepless twang-twang calling
twelve-string tales of woe.

From what I know of fishing, I think
the trawlers are now hauling in their nets,
their people and soon the *Bembridge* will be
an insect-dot by the station and the gulls
will disappear for those whose morning
comes in dreams of salty, swarming
monster eyes aglow.

The Newspaper Man
Zadie Smith

1

Fathers are creatures of the night. They do not arrive home until the sun disappears over Kilburn, and then only for a few hours, gleaning their strength through the blood of mothers, and leaving once more in the morning rejuvenated from a night of vein-sucking. That is why they look so bedraggled in the evenings, and eat no food at breakfast. They have been sated already. When they come, they come with newspapers which have comics hidden in their middle pages, to distract the children Mickey says. He is a real boy, and is interested in the insides of pigeons. Mickey says this to me when we are nine, and when all adults live in a world of ghouls, bloody bed sheets, fangs and strange aromas. We are never afraid though, because fathers never eat their young, this is well known. Instead, claims Mickey, they never really die, but haunt us forever, caped in black and as insubstantial as the air yet with wiry moustaches. The world, we decide, is a graveyard of fathers, covered in red earth, with their coffins ajar.

2

At some point one must leave England. Must stop dotting the i's in correspondence with malicious intent, searching for good oranges, glaring at children and despairing of the British press. One must simply pack the bags. notify those who matter, and escape to foreign shores, the final opportunity to be a little out of context. For most, this point comes around retirement, the autumn years, when many realise England does not love its older citizens, but instead shuffles them into corners with no heating, where they remain out of sight and silent, too feeble to reach the polling station.

For me the decision to leave comes a little earlier – I am a dumpy, sprightly, woman; what the lonely hearts columns call "young 50", which means I do not yet wear skirts shin length and pleated or let brown stockings collect around my shoes like the ankles of elephants. I sometimes cross the road if I think I am about to encounter one of these women. The shuffling of their feet, their creakiness, bothers me. It is a dislike as irrational as the ones we have against the obese or the blind. Pure fear. I am not like them. Am rarely seen coaxing young boys out of their seats on public transport and have no great insights to offer on the subject of the British weather – since childhood I have had an uncanny feeling of what middle age should mean.

A great flight lifted by the wings of experience. Just that. For me the decision to leave my place of birth was far easier than I had imagined; it starts as an itch on the Finchley High Road during rush hour, within a week it is a tangible idea, in a month it has evolved into an appointment with Gatwick, gate six, and a meeting with destiny. My personal assistant Katie, had pushed the idea over the line into decision. With the flippancy that comes of being twenty-three and exorbitantly paid, she argues the question can be easily answered by a simple table – Reasons to Stay (1 st column), Reasons to (as she puts it) Get The Fuck Out (2nd). Twists her gum around her middle finger – monumental events. she mutters, have been decided on lesser grounds. So I spend a nostalgic evening with a bottle of Bailey's and a large piece of paper, mulling England over, holding it up to the light and measuring where the shade falls. Think about corners of it, break it into pieces, moments, trying to get a little closer to an essence of England, one to take up and hold to the heart, or reject and turn my back on. The sweet complacency of the place keeps returning to me in waves; how long it takes to stir the English and then how it is only the silliest things that stirs them in the end. I have always been a quiet fan of English complacency, nothing scares me more than the radical, the fundamental, all big gestures that make a difference send me running for cover.

And then I have a pang of affection for London, which I think of as an enormous inner city mural, effortlessly multicultural but with cracks in the paint. It is a metaphor I heard at a party.

These and other things... but they are not enough. After four hours of concentrated musing what ties me inland amounts to scones, the cliffs of Cornwall, St. Martins in the Fields, and British comedy.

On the other side of the coin, a million things called sweetly from European shores like sirens for a sailors heart; their song, irresistible, soon begins to chip away at my flimsy attempts at national identity. Living in England is just a bad habit which has become, over the centuries, hard to shake. It is simply comic to feel serious, angry, dedicated to England, but it is easy to feel comfortable, centred and cosy about her: she is a giant pair of slippers and a mug of cocoa in front of a television, where faces flicker through a light tube as things go on in far away places. Apart from the obvious benefits of the continent; sun, sea, sun food, sun (I note these down in quick succession), the things England excels in are to be found across the oceans, too often done better and with more class. And yet, England is, it stands, there is something - the unnameable quality which one ums and urs about in bus queues cannot be worded and so does not go down in either column. England takes another right hook to the chin. I feel guilty, beating up England in this fashion. But I am English only by virtue of an English father, and he is English only due to an accident of birth, his Irish parents moving to England because money was owed somewhere to someone. These are too many accidents to amount to an identity. Homes are accidents, or at least all mine have been. I stub a cigarette into an overcrowded ashtray and trace the scarcity of the left hand column with a finger. Responsibility - is added as an afterthought. A little later, Dad.

I am not married. I have no children. No men pace the floor of artistic flats in West Hampstead wondering if I will call, mad with jealousy, desperate at the prospect of desertion. Neither are there older, Christian gentlemen who enjoy country walks and opera, queuing up to open a claret for me. Suddenly I feel elated that I have managed to amount such a lot of nothing in my life. I must be a true artist, I am rootless. Usually at this age, a great deal of baggage has been amassed. As a child I walk down supermarket aisles searching for the old men and women who lug around tons of bags and shopping. They usually dribble and have peculiar stuff in their trolleys. Powdered milk, olives, prunes. Powdered milk and prunes. This is my brother, Mickey's, favourite gruesome dish. You know what you're getting for your birthday...? (every year this ritual) Powdered milk and prunes. These old people and their food are endless entertainment. They fascinate me. My brother and I imagine what's in the bags, and who they are going home to. Who are their children and their children's children? Because though they are only comic old people to us, they are somebody's mother. We find this hilarious, and look up at our own mother, who is still ebony coloured and beautiful. I am not a supermarket granny with bags of life shoved in a trolley, or cutting ridges into the palms of my hand. But there is some luggage, a divorce, which was acrimonious. The difference between a good divorce and an acrimonious one, being that of the mirror which breaks simply in two and the one that shatters, compounding bad luck upon bad luck, its multiple shards never entirely removing themselves from the carpet. You cut your feet when you are least expecting it. His toothbrush in the crevice of the sofa. His name still on the phone bill. Splinters.

And we had been told it would not work, that as a "mixed" couple (as if we were a salad – vegetables not suited for each other) the chances were lower, harder. The Seventies said it's a miracle that man and woman meet, ying and yang, it is a miracle if the outer poles of their experience meet at their extremes – add colour and you're heaping madness onto misery. But I was half Jamaican, half English (had been told once by a rabbi that my soul was Jewish and in 1974 such things, along with wearing yellow and brown, were possible), Jake was Russian, Jewish, Polish, Irish and English by degrees: love had laughed these things free – when there is so much difference the lines become shady, and difference stops being that poisonous thing that stands proud, its feet on somebody's back. And we were both artists, and art transcends -at least the history books always say it does, and as we were not there, we always believe them. Ruth and Jake. Jake and Ruth. Marry with flowers in their hair and are divorced by Palmer, Keely and Michaels in a dingy office on the Old Kent Road. England is littered with similar failures. I place my pen on the second column and underline two words in green felt-tip. English men.

• • • • •

"What is needed, Mrs Boyd –"

"Ms Boyd"

"Ms Boyd. Is for you to take your son in hand. He needs a little discipline, however unfashionable that word may be in modern education…"

Liz Boyd is my oldest friend. We have been through punk, funk, eighties Romantic, late eighties mod-art-school, clean-cut academic men and deconstruction, together. It seems natural that Liz, in the absence of the father, should take me to her son's parent evening. I want to see Liz as much as possible now as we come to terms with me leaving. We are being adult about things.

"Let me get this straight. He's not failing anything, in fact as he has again confirmed this year, he's about the most bloody gifted kid in this shithole. Did I dutifully send my son to the worst comprehensive school in the borough, to hear this crap?"

There are a few sighs from nearby parents, themselves answering twenty questions across the little desks that are dotted around the hall like drowning men without life rafts.

"I think, Mrs Boyd, we could try to be a little more constructive –"

"Bollocks".

I, who am better at constructive than Liz, step in.

"I think what Liz means, is that she's unclear what the problem is. given that his marks are so above average"

"The problem Miss…

"Mackintyre"

"Lies in his behaviour. He is disruptive in class, it's as simple as that. Very disruptive."

"If this is about those leaflets, I'm in complete support of my son. What are you running? A police state? What happened to bloody freedom of speech? I can't help it if my son has opinions"

Caspian, who is 12, has handed out leaflets during Physics proclaiming the joys of an anarchic state. He led a large proportion of 7b on a mission to seize control of the staffroom and reclaim the dinner tickets for the students.

"He created a fire hazard."

I briefly recall how many things were banned in our own school in aid of fire prevention. It seemed a child couldn't visit the toilet unaccompanied lest they spontaneously combust.

"This is not about fire hazards, this is about my alternative lifestyle, which this school seems to take issue with. How I bring up my son is my own business."

Quite. And yet when one brings up a son in a commune of ex-prescription drug addicts, keeping him home two days a week to model for a sculpture class, you feel a school, no matter how comprehensive, how liberal, how often splashed over the local tabloid, could conceivably take issue. I love Liz, but she has that unconditional love for her child non-parents find inconceivable. The teacher looks at me in despair, I find it easiest to sigh non-commitantly. As usual I am on everybody's side.

The argument escalates I turn my attention to the many grooves gauged into the table, like a map of Africa carved up, each party staking their claim. Ben was 'ere in ninety three. Many are like this, unable even to assonate their own graffiti. You love it. Or Don't drink and drive when you can puff and fly! and Exams are mind control. Free yourselves from the mental dictatorship. Ignore what you have just read. Smartass. Thankfully someone has retorted underneath, Fuck off you sad wanker. Voices bounce off walls up and down the hall. Parents defending sons, Teachers attacking parents, children attacking the furniture. Gum under the seats. Biros forced underneath the table varnish, so cracks materialise and zip along them like a domino rally. Schools exist in time warps. This hall is a dead ringer for the one in The Blessed Saint Mary Girl's school, my own long lost seat of learning. I come to parents' evenings with my father, who is inevitably dressed as a Monty Python extra – bowler hat, long umbrella – looking as if he has a penchant for spam, or would pay five bob for an argument and be shortchanged. This is his manner. We walk into the room, and even at this young age, I can see his defence mechanisms spring into action. He is afraid of schools, knowledge, education, he feels at war with them and so stiffens his umbrella arm. People, even the teachers, do not understand who he is. Over the years I will get used to this. To the passer-by I am his secretary, his shamefully young girlfriend, in later years, his nurse. But never his daughter, our skins deny it. It is such a simple equation for me, for Mickey, yet so inconceivable for England, that likes consistency in all things. We go first to the English teacher, because surprisingly it is my best subject. I hate art in school because I cannot do portraits – no, because I do not see the point in them. Once we are asked to paint from a photograph of an old Mexican basket-weaver. I ask what the point is. Thrown out of class for this, it will be years before I understand the importance of the question.

· · · · ·

The English teacher is my first female hero. Her hair is red, which I think is pretty cool to start with. But she is also opinionated, bossy, domineering, and choosy. This is what I like best. She chooses me as one of her "special people", and no matter how cruel she is to others she is nice to me. She has no time for idiots whatsoever, a trait I wish for. I will suffer fools gladly for hours rather than have the audacity to turn and walk away. This is a Caribbean education, politeness at all costs. My father sits down and immediately things go badly. He begins to talk about my favourite book *Pride and Prejudice*, and it is painfully clear that, at most, he has seen the film, possibly the television serial. Miss Lorca nods dutifully and I know deep down, deep down, her stomach is being ripped to shreds as mine is, we are both being murdered. Now he is on to *Wuthering Heights* and it is impossible to stop him. I want to cry, "Miss Lorca! Forgive me, I am not of him, we are separate, I am of you, we are together", and what I mean is something even more sinister than this. He is working-class I mean, and I am educated. But as of yet I do not know the words. There is a feeling in the school, in the belly of the school in the recess beyond language, that I am smart because I am half-white. There are a group of black girls, fully black, really black, not milky coffee like me. who have exotic names: Latetia, Odessa. Jasmine. They are what my mother calls the bad influences, and my father would not deign to mention. I walk past them snootily in the play-ground, can see them now, heads bowed to the floor as they go from desk to desk preparing for a lecture. But I am secretly fascinated, and a little in love with them. They play rope games which involve multiple, impossibly compli-cated jumps, and tease even the most popular white boys with incredible ease. They talk loudly at the back of the class, and sing in Biology about things I do not yet understand. Most alluring is their hair, cain rowed, or tied in elaborate red bows – they are beautiful. Most nights I wish my hair thick, black, plaited and bowed. Others I wish it straight, silky and falling over my shoulders and into my eyes. These are the most secret wishes in the world, only my pillow is privilege to such information. But during the day none of this is known, I hardly know it myself. I am just the smart girl, and I collect gold stars like other kids catch colds. Your daughter is a very unusual child, Mr Mackintyre. And I know what this means. It means I don't plait my hair, I can't suck my teeth in the playground. Can't sing:

Two, six, nine
The monkey drank wine,
He fell from the trunk of an Elephant-ine
The boat sunk,
The monkey got drunk
And they all went to Heaven on a little row-boat,
Clap your hands!

I can't sing that. Yet I am black. Yet I am smart. "You have a very unusual daughter Mr Mackintyre, she's very bright. You should be proud." My father smiles broadly, and pats me on the head, smoothing hair that stubbornly refus-es to be smoothed. "She gets her brains from me," he says, "and her looks from her mother".

• • • • •

I do not want to be here, helping a friend through the private/public school decision. I don't want to see my peers asking "pertinent" questions about chil-dren/staff ratios. In 1972 Liz puts a safety pin through my nose in the back room of her mum's house. During the delicate operation we make the first of several pacts never to sell out or stop, as they put it then, noticing the bollocks. About '82 we decide men can in fact be lived with (which was fortunate as we have both already married some), but there is no point having boys because they only grow up to hate their mothers and get interested in ammunition. When Caspian is six we go to a series of conferences on the crisis of meaning in post-Hiroshima Western Culture. Liz gleans from this that everything means nothing, and nothing has visuals known as MTV. She buys a computer and leaves Caspian with his grandmother for two years. During these two years we are like schoolgirls again, dying our hair and sleeping over at each others houses now the divorces have come through. Late at night we phone up radio talk shows, the problem hours are our favourites. Liz is a transvestite who carries her dog with her in a caboose. I am a seventy-eight year old virgin, who believes its never too late. Desperately we try not to giggle in the background.

Camille Paglia convinces us we should be lovers and we try it one night after a bottle of vodka and orange, but we giggle too much. "I'm not licking that," laughs Liz, "if it smells like mine". Things, in short, used to happen. Now Liz is a successful journalist and I am, I suppose, a successful artist and we both no longer speak to our parents. Every expectation, every predictability has materialised. We have similar crises at similar times, see similar therapists, have similar results. I remark once, over a post-divorce depression lunch, we could swap couches and it would make no difference. I could have a solved Liz-Life, and Liz could have a balanced Ruth-life. Because it doesn't matter who is cured, or "comes to terms", as long as somebody does, as long as we get the kick, the catharsis. This is what Oprah is for. Liz accuses the Maths teacher of being a fascist. The Maths teacher looks tearful. She is not paid enough, she says fighting a wobbly bottom lip, to listen to this kind of abuse. A cacophony of educator's and parent's neuroses rise from the crowd and settle like a smog just above our heads. The evening is winding down now, as parents and teachers unite in mutual contempt of the government, I was an art teacher for two years, and remember this enjoyable middle ground. Nothing changes. It is the same government still cutting the same funding. Even the staff are eerily familiar: the well-worn northern Technology teacher, the English teacher in Indian caftan, the History man with leather elbows. The meeting is momentarily beautiful, but the moment passes, and personal acrimonies resurface like enemy submarines.

"Why should she learn Italian if she wants to learn Latin?", comes the jungle cry of a parent head to head in desperate dispute

And as simply as that, Italy looms large in front of me like an inevitable phantom. Italian vowels wash over me, it is Petrach, and it whispers of hate and love, and heat and warmth. Seasons are in it, and it ends with Autumn, melancholy but mature, the month that stretches summer proclaiming that it ain't over till its over. Words sound correct, musical, sensuous in this Italian tongue, and as I whisper the poem to myself I discover for the first time since school, how poetry can occasionally spark an action as surely as if it pushed your hand. Italy it is. In a second it becomes my heart's home, and England just a place my body has not removed itself from yet. Immediately, essentially, irrevocably Italy enters me like an injection, clinical in its precision. Monumental events, have been decided on lesser grounds.

3

Italy is the place. Deciding to leave is relatively easy, moving to Italy, natural, practically unconscious. Like most artists I have little imagination beyond the obvious – I am a painter, Italy the canvas, I am a sculptor, Italy the clay. I will set up home in the Tuscan hills overlooking Florence and re-present the obvious through my own eyes, simply overbrimming with that stuff the Evening Standard has called "…the sparkling, down-to-earth originality and simplicity of Ruth Mackintyre". My art is attractive, minimal, consistently good, though never brilliant – the kind of thing that can be hung on a Hampstead suburbs wall or shoved in a Hampstead suburbs hall appearing to be simply what it is; stylish and unpretentious, art one can discuss at a dinner party without reducing a room to either awe or derisive laughter. I will not go down in the history books, but might have a coffee table book in my memory, a retrospective at Goldsmiths or in the Sainsbury Wing – this is enough. It feels wonderful to finally realise one's limits, shed unattainables like old skin. And Italy enables me to continue with these quiet aims. There is a Tuscan home and fresh bread delivered every morning, an extra studio in the centre of Florence, and a friendly rapport with the few Italians I come in everyday contact with; the fish man, the security men at Sante Croce, my maid, and my agent, Phillipo Correll, a short, sweaty, but amiable man with an undisguisable love of money. Your Art…(he says it with a capital A) it is great, taking time…this OK, artistic integrity, this is fine…but Ruth-a…, somebody gotta pay the bills around here, capiche?

It is Phillipo who accompanies me as we wonder through Sante Croce, a church that, even to this damaged artistic retina, can only be seen as wholly beautiful. Not beautiful-ironic, or beautiful-classical, or beautiful-tedious, but simply beauty in a manner we hardly believe in anymore until it accidentally makes us gasp. Sante Croce echoes like a shrine and sparkles like a palace, frescoes swim across it like overlapping waves littered with pink babes and fleshy Gods; it is entirely gaudy, mercilessly tasteless and restraint is alien to it. In concept it is not unlike the larger British supermarkets. Yet Phillipo remains unimpressed.

"This place, it is unnecessarily cold…all of Florence it is sweltering, and this thing is as cold as a dead man toes. It is a masterpiece of bad planning"

I draw a finger slowly across the marble.

"It's a church, Phillipo."

"Sinners should be cold? Or Catholics? Too much air conditioning is what they get for their devotion? I prefer my gallery…it's warm, the floors they are heated…"

"And it has my work in it"

"Esattamente. And you may laugh, but it is outselling and may I add, out-reviewing your Mr Ex-Mackintyre in London by a hill-slide"

"Landslide," I correct gently.

"Both."

To avoid an approaching mob of Italian schoolchildren armed with ruck-sacks and questionnaires we sidetrack into an alcove and sit down on a ledge of protruding stone. The spot provides a beautiful viewpoint of the church; halls within halls, within halls, like crevices in an ear, or the curves in a conch shell. All echoes seem to revert back to this point, and all sightlines appear to issue from it. Phillipo's eyes soften in what I now recognise as a peculiarly Italian way used to signal that now we are going to talk frankly, kindly, hold-ing as little as possible back. Such talks I am not overly enamoured with.

"Ruth-a"

"Phillipo"

"Your skin...brown, this looks nice against the white stone"

"And?"

"And I think you should paint it".

"Right. I will. Can we have lunch now? I'm ravenous."

The children pass by the alcove, rising in a crescendo as each new part of the procession scramble by, unable to keep a straight line or a decent tone of voice. A few find humour in the sight of Ruth and Phillipo, like two puddings, one boy thinks, squeezed together on a plate.

"Ravenous...mmm..." Phillipo looks vacantly at the fresco on the opposite wall till the shapes dissolve and the colours separate and dot like a Manet, or a child's first attempt. I have taught him how to do this, how to see a picture in terms of colour and not words.

"Is there something wrong, Phillipo?"

"No..., well Yes..., I mean knowing how you feel, it no importante –"

I feel a sort of impending doom, as if the walls of Sante Croce are about to open outwards, revealing me to the world.

"– is just that your sister call."

"My sister?" It always takes a moment to register this; it is my half sister who I have seen a dozen times in my life, and heard her named thus even less.

"She says your father, he is very ill. And she is coming to Italy to see you."

Phillipo puts his hand over mine and holds it tightly. I feel the pull of expected misery, I must react for Phillipo so we can escape this awkward moment, where death rears its unwanted head in our uncomplicated lives. But I cannot accommodate people as much as I used to, this is what age really means. So instead I say; "At last, thank God", and know that possibly only my sister will understand what that means. I slump into Phillipo's arms like a puppet with its strings cut.

Some noise, some kind of scene is erupting on the other side of the church, Phillipo catches sight of the protagonists over my shoulder. A stony-faced security guard seems to be trying to eject two young women from the church, the fight they are putting up is attracting quite a crowd. I am a merciless lover of scenes. Accidental explosions, lost tempers, I am old enough and tame enough now to be a professional voyeur. People expect the old to be nosy, so now I have a kind of license. One of the women is Italian, and gesticulating wildly, while the other tries to make some kind of peace. As the guard attempts to march them towards the exit from the pulpit, they come more clearly into view. The Italian, brashly attractive with a dusky, honey, brown complexion, all the time pushing the guard away from her, the English girl (she is pale and insipid looking, Phillipo and I assume this was her nationality) attempting to keep the two apart.

"Perche? Perche?!" screams the Italian girl, changing tactics now and grabbing on to the English girl for dear life so the two of them can not be moved. The security guard's face (Phillipo knows him, it is Marco, a nondescript, inoffensive local boy) grows redder, for the first time he raises his voice.

"Dis is a church, chiesa, understand? You cannot do that in here. Cannot! You should be ashamed, aver vergognoso!"

There is widespread support for this, a few men come and align themselves to Marco, shouting at the women. One man spits

"Please, please...leave now," pleads Marco, at which the women scream more abuses, the Italian reaching out to hit him. A larger man prevents her, grabbing her wrist as it nears his face.

"Aren't you cattolico? How can you do this in your Father's house?"

"Si! Si! But my father," shouts the Italian girl, "is not in this house!"

There is a pause, after which the Italian woman spat on the larger man's shoes, and all hell erupts in Sante Croce.

"Ho chiamato il polizia". Marco tries to call above the noise, – "POLIZIA!"

The English woman grabs her friend and kisses her passionately for what we now gather is the second time, at which point the security guard has to separate the increasingly blood-thirsty crowd from the women. In a moment, a policeman was on the scene, surmising the situation from the variously fictional accounts of it shouted by the two parties. For a moment the group appears in a kind of slow motion to me. Mouths open and close with slow violence, veins bulge, arms beat the air like the wings of great birds. These are the women, the harpies, my father sometimes mutters about on long drives. Snide comments about my mother and her friends, and the world weary comment; "you're too young Ruthie, to understand that". These were also the women my Jamaican grandmother mentions when we are in the park one day, and two women, one with short hair, help me on to the swing. "Godless!" my Grandmother cries. "Sister!" the women call back. These are the women I meet in the seventies, comrades in a women's movement, sometimes lithe and elf-like. One, Dolores, is six feet tall with a fabulous afro. She tells me to let my hair free, and I admit to killing it, with bottles of "relaxers" in brown paper wrappers, smuggled in by my mother and reeking their little violence on our scalps as we locked the door behind us. We pleased Daddy that way, looking like Lena Horne. with carefully covered scalp burns behind the ears. These are all those funny women who do without men – I cannot imagine doing without any portion of the human race. I am a mix of so many of them.

After a time the crowd begins to disperse, the women are taken away. Some of the bigger men loiter around, patting the slightly bewildered Marco on the back, "Movimento Femminista" one mutters, and shakes his head.

Altogether, the scene is a messy one – not something, I sense, Phillipo feels I should be witnessing at such a time. Phillipo's paternal instincts have been awakened, and he feels he wants to protect Ruth (but not only Ruth, all women – the feeling was of an enormous responsibility, a trait unheard of in Phillipo's experience of himself) from scenes such as that, from all the messiness and gore of life, that even in Florence occasionally rears its ugly head. Though we are almost the same age he feels at once mentor and father figure, and visibly congratulates himself that this is so. For him, it is quite proper and perfectly timed.

"Phillipo...I want to get out of here, I've got work to do at the gallery. I have to meet a buyer. I'll fax my sister from there."

I stand up and begin to walk towards the exit, a clear urgency in my step. Phillipo, even less aerodynamic than me, struggles to keep up.

"A buyer? I was not informed. For which painting?"

"It's a personal sale, to an old friend. I didn't think you needed to be informed."

"Personal sale means the buyer gets it at an inferior price because they once sleep with the artist. This is not good business"

The mouth of Sante Croce throws us out onto the piazza, where a fountain is weeping loudly to itself, and the opera that is street life, that epic of bad, bourgeois taste, is performing its matinee. Phillipo adds to the libretto;

"Rutha – which painting?"

"The Newspaper Man" I answer.

4

"The Newspaper Man", the largest canvas in the present exhibition, is one that has smouldered in the artist since she was seventeen. In its many conceptual metamorphoses it has been a story, an installation, a film, a poem, and a sentence, but as my talent resides in none of these forms, it has finally been born on canvas and as such is as successful as anything I have done. After all the girls I have conceived; African sculptures of inscrutable female faces, nudes in the Lucian Freud mould, photographs of world weary waitresses and the working class female, this is the first boy – a portrait of my father that stretches the length of one wall. It has taken pride of place in the centre of the exhibition acting as something of a locus, a central point around which the rest of the work circulates like moths round a light bulb, for the rest are all, I now realise, variations on a theme. Standing in front of it is, in striking contrast to the other pieces, an imposing experience. There looms the enormous face of an old Englishman, done in oils, wax, wire wool and newspaper, against a Daliesque backdrop of apocalypse, ironic next to the "little England" that the various newspaper clippings evoke. Its message then (I stand in front of it: people pass, giving it a message, I must offer a meaning too), is one of little sophistication. Here is the Englishman torn between the petty nuances of his life and the adventures of his subconscious – Freud said once of Dali, you murder dreams, and here too is the conscious rendering of the subconscious, yet the picture is not as facile as this diagnosis suggests, though in the backdrop volcano take on the contours of women and the sky proclaims itself menstrual. What rescues the painting from banality is the face. It is one of the few things I am proud of. It manages in its materials, its lights and shades, its many wrinkles and bags, to capture an essence of age, an essence of bitterness and failure, and an essence of a father and daughter; one of the most difficult and inscrutable of relationships. It is a piece of considerable emotional force, something new in the work of Ruth Mackintrye. Many critics say all this about The Newspaper Man. I am a respected artist because of it. On the strength of it I have fed myself in the cold months. I am lost in thought and it is a moment before I register there is a woman standing beside me. She is a white woman with pointed, comic red glasses, and a dress that appears to have no arms and legs, only folds. My gut instinct is to escape. I am wearing jeans with elastic in the waist, and a jumper that has "Espana!" emblazoned across it. I cannot talk about art just now.

"Miss Mackintyre," the woman says, "we talked on the phone. I'm here to buy the painting on behalf of..."

She pauses, wondering how to put him. I kept the name because I wanted as many pieces of him as possible.

"...Mr Mackintyre"

So he didn't come himself. He is not here to see what I have sunk to in my elasticated jeans and badly applied rouge.

"Right, yes, right, of course"

Wonderful. She is probably sleeping with him and I manage to sound like a traffic warden.

"It really is a stunning piece. To be honest, my client was a little surprised you agreed to sell it at such a reasonable price. He asked me to make clear he's prepared to offer more"

Ominous legal language. Once he was the man I loved, Jake, with beautiful eyes and a chest made for me to rest my head on, now he is the client, he has been "the second party" also. At times we were in court and we'd both want to jump up and say Jake! Ruth! Let's just split it all down the middle, we loved and lost! But I am the party of the first part, Jake is the party of the second. I don't want his bloody money. Then why am I selling the painting? Because it is not everyday you get to sell your father to your ex-husband. Mickey would call it killing two ghosts with one ectoplasm.

"No, we've already decided on a price. I want him to have it. It's not something I want around anymore."

He'll put it in the living room. The new wife will look at it. And I will look out onto the new wife. Standing in front of it now, I expect it to be changed a little because its subject is dying, but Wilde was wrong, there is no connection between the subject and the object created in its honour. The two travel in different hemispheres, have no effect on each other as they sit in their parallel galaxies. Father on the wall is still malicious and very much alive, a raging suburban Lear caught in a picture frame looking truly infuriated to be put there. But then he always hated galleries. The university educated "types", the free wine, the glib conversation, the middle class-ness was something he dreaded really feared because, of course, he desired so much to be part of it. Even before I move to Italy he never comes to any of my exhibitions, not even the final year presentation at St Martins. The newspaper man (so called because he arrives bearing them every night at eight-o-clock – my earliest memories of him are as a doorbell ring accompanied by an Evening Standard) had been born without opportunity (he did not go to the local public school because his mother could not afford the uniform – or so the story went), without money, class or education, but he aspires…I remember how much he aspires. England is littered with similar failures.

Once, after a particularly trying night when he comes to see Jake and I (a rare visit, but we are newly wed), it comes to Jake in bed what my father is, or rather, what he is made up of. He laughs uncontrollably before he is able to get it out.

"It's like he's Basil Fawlty. No. not just him…Tony Hancock as well, and Albert Steptoe, and Rigsby, and Tommy Cooper – your father Ruth, is an amalgamation of the British Comic tradition. Is your husband a genius or is he a genius!"

Not a genius, but perceptive. My father is the paradigm of the frustrated lower-middle class snob, of the man who watches the Old Boys network and seethes – I owe Jake for the insight. And Eliot for the words; No! I am not Prince Hamlet, nor was meant to be…it provided a frame in which to see the man, a context in which to understand him. But. But we can dissect a man entirely, measure his self hate, gauge his pretensions, paint them on a canvas and never come any closer to him. And so the Newspaper Man stands, a paternal enigma, a white man with a black daughter, dying in a foreign land. I wish Mickey was here. But Mickey is in America, working on the new campaign for Disney. He has to sell Mickey Mouse to a new generation. I get silly faxes: Mickey's behind Mickey a hundred percent and Mickey's selling Mickey to the kids out here. Underneath them is a little drawing of Mickey Mouse with an afro and a joint in his mouth. Mickey's great at his job, but he takes it a little less seriously than he should. I should call him and tell him about dad – he'll fly home immediately. But I don't want to see family, and sense what they're thinking. That I didn't love him. That I'm not sorry. They will put all the issues in black and white – I am neither of these and cannot think this way. I want to touch someone who knows what it was to be my father's daughter, albeit my father's white daughter.

I want to speak to Laura.

I put my hands on the painting, feeling the surface with my eyes closed, finding it is cratered like the acne of a first boyfriend, or, more aptly, the hardened wrinkles of a dead man. I read the picture like Braille as far as I can reach, then step back and sit on the self-conscious bench that makes its home in all galleries. The woman in red pointy glasses smiles indulgently. She was surprised at my dirty sneakers but now she knows I am an artist. I am eccentric.

Lucky Sylvia, getting rid of your Daddy in one short poem and so well… this canvas is enormous, has taken seven years, and copious amounts of tears and sweat, and yet the black telephone, the crossed-wires that so entangles fathers and their daughters, is still fully connected.

• • • • •

"She," says Mickey with an air of authority, "is the Wicked Witch of the West".

He is wearing ill fitting osh-kosh dungarees, and white Nikes with a big red stripe, and we are in the closet looking at old photos. We have never seen this one before. It shows a woman with her hair tied back into a tight bun, and a large crooked nose. The picture is black and white, but you can tell she is red-headed. On the other side of the picture is my father, long before we ever knew him, and a little girl we have never seen. It's not a normal family portrait but this is not a normal family. It is my father's first family, who for me and Mickey, exist in another time zone, shrouded in myth, mystery and covered in closet dust. There is no point arguing with Mickey about this woman. To him she is a witch, replete with broomstick and cat, who had my father under a spell, until my mother, the beautiful princess came and broke it. Today the girl in the picture is coming to see us for the first time. Mother explains that she is not little anymore but twenty-five, a ponderous age, we think, for a daughter to be. We are to be dressed especially for the occasion, which means being tumbled out of our osh-kosh into floral dresses and grey trousers, and having our hair slicked down by pink gel, which gets rid of the fluff and accentuates the curls. We also have to wear pinchy shoes so Mickey puts bubblegum down the heels to stop them rubbing. I am a girl and used to suffering for beauty. I grin and bear them, practising my walk in the mirror to ensure I stride with sophistication. I am fourteen years old. When the doorbell rings, everyone panics a little. Laura is here and I am not the only daughter anymore. Stupidly. I am surprised that she is white. And though Mickey pretends not to be, I know he is too. The first thing I see is her nose, which is thin and pointed like my fathers, they look alike. They have the same little blue eyes like Mickey's hamster, they are the same height. They look at each other a little while in silence, my father is nervous.

"Come in. So nice to see you again, Laura," says my mother, averting disaster.

My mother has seen her before, then. They have sat around tables, laughed, talked together. I don't know why this bugs me, but it does, like itching powder placed between the skull and the skin.

180

We are introduced and hug nervously. Everyone is saying, take your sister upstairs, show your sister where to hang her coat, ask your sister if she would like a cup of tea – as if this were the most normal thing in the world. As if it is normal that she has a long blond plait down the centre of her back and pink fingers. I catch sight of Mickey from the corner of my eye. He is desperately trying to signal that she has light downy hair on her cheek, sideburns, which signifies she is a witch, though she could be a good one. This depends on the colour of her slip, which we will investigate later as it is not peeping out from under her skirt.

Dinner is confusing. No one is sure how to address anyone else, so we end up calling everybody by their first names very self-consciously. Evelyn, can you pass the salt? I say to my mother. Harold, cut the turkey, Mickey says to Dad. Laura is talking to me about school in those questions that always start with "so…", but Mickey is kicking me under the table at the same time. He signs to me (we have recently learnt the sign alphabet in school and use it to beat witches at their own game) that he is going to drop a fork under the table so he can see the slip. I sign. shaping my fingers furtively below the table cloth, OK Pudding comes, and amidst the noise of people complementing my father on the pastry Mickey mouths the result. White. It is a white slip, and she is a good, white witch. Which is rare, Mickey explains later, given that her mother was evil. It must have been dad's goodness that tipped the scales, just like I have lighter skin than Mickey. But I am not satisfied with this conclusion. I am fourteen, and I feel things now that cannot be explained by good and evil, sideburns and slips. I feel the world impinging on me. and events aren't just trivial, but affecting. I am affected by Laura. Liz comes round in the evening and I tell her about the white sister. She agrees that it is weird, kind of gross, but we have a sleepover to get to and the matter is forgotten as we back comb each others' hair. and draw oversized beauty-spots near our upper lips. We pout in the mirror, wiggling the spot and singing our favourite song in a husky Monroe drawl:

If I invite, a boy some night,
To drink on my fine Scottish haddy.
I do abhor, him asking for more,
'cos my heart belongs to Daddy

We do not know what Scottish haddy is, but we know the song is sexual because Liz's mum won't allow it in the house. We know we have a kind of precocious sexuality with our flat chests, and our improbably gangly legs. When we sing this we become caricatures of sex, shadow plays of the future. We pull up our stockings to our thighs and clip them with suspender belts we have stolen from our mothers.

"Was she beautiful? asks Liz, buckling her winkle-pickers.

"Yes" I say.

"More beautiful than you?"
The cruel frankness of children.
"Yes" I say.

5

Billboards are the most wonderful, nerve-numbing anaesthetic. I am walking through the centre of Fifteenth-Century Florence which has recently exploded with Billboards, much to the consternation of the residents, displaying every type of blandness and mediocrity. "I never thought I'd get EXCITED about Contact lens care!" yells one. "Putting on the GLITZ!" another. You hardly have time to think your own thoughts amongst this ever present jungle of advertising, though you never believe you're actually taken in by the hard sell. My brother is in advertising as my father was. Mickey says you think you can't be sold to, but why do you pick that soap powder off the shelf rather than the other? Why those digestion tablets? We are incredibly brand faithful, apparently. Especially in England. America, Mickey says, is a more fluid-sell market. It's one of those little ironies that Mickey follows our father into advertising. It is this profession, selling to people who sell, that I feel empties my father. It is like the stock-market or high fashion, the business of business, the non-existent product. My father sells for years; newspapers. junk-mail, billboard space, television – if there was a space of air, wall, or doormat his job is to find something to fill it, a bit of nothing for the people. When I am driven to college for my first term, his boss kindly gives me a lift. My father and I sit in the back. My father calls him Mike, but the tone is Sir. Yes, Mike, I'll get onto it right away, Mike. I am just eighteen and all establishment figures are slime to me. My hair is dreaded and half way down my back, my jacket emblazoned with Socialist Worker paraphernalia. my jeans very. very tight and worn at all the pressure points. I am being taken to a prestigious University looking like a dealer from Moss Side. I am a student. Mike Bravo is a sweaty, lower-middle-class-boy-done-well-for-himself-fascist-pig, as far as I am concerned. With his fake Georgian country pad. and his public school children and his wanderings into amateur dramatics at the local village church, he is everything I stand against. And I stand for everything and anything; revolution, small community organisation, sexual and racial equality, Islam, the IRA, miners, the unemployed, abortion, Ken Livingstone, anarchy and free sanitary pads. The drive down is unsurprisingly awkward.

"'So... Ruth. Pretty good all this University bit, eh? Best place for it too, eh? Never went to College myself, more a self-made man like your dad here, right Harry?"

"Right".

"Your dad's worked for me...gawd, how long? Twenty-one years?"

"Twenty-five years, Mike".

"That's right. Not showy, your dad. Just a good, honest worker. Trusted for it. You can always trust old Harry to come up with the goods when you want them, where you want them. Isn't that right Harry?"

"Right, Mike."

"Now me, I'm a bit more showy, y'know. I mean, when you say Mike Bravo, people sit up and listen. That's the only reason I'm here and your dad's in the back seat. I mean no offence taken, eh Harry? But I've got a Merc for a reason...know what I mean?"

"You bet, Mike"

You bet. My father is twenty years older than the shmuck in the front seat. I hate selling from this point on; connecting it forever with my father, the little man with the plain name being stepped on by men with better names. This is what advertising comes down to: the best slogan.

My revolutionary feelings pass, after a few years in the soft lane. I cut my hair into a manageable length and wear long flowy skirts that make me look like a cello player. Now I love advertising, the quick image, the bang to the senses, the hard sell. Long before it becomes popular I start to see imagination in the dunking donut wrappers, a surreal brilliance in the McDonald logos. But I never bring this to my paintings, while others make millions by photographing Campbell's soup cans. I feel somehow that to love these things is a bit of a dirty secret, I fear in art school I will be considered merely a black artist who doesn't know the ropes. I am instead rigorously classically trained, in the hope that it will impress my father, and in somewhere, convince me. Convince me that what I am doing is worthwhile. Laura is a psychoanalyst (he tells everyone this). I make sculptures from razors and diaphragms funded by taxpayers money.

· · · · ·

I am on my way to meet Laura and the air is so thick in Florence that you can taste the smog. Sour lemon, powdered milk and prunes. I am all prepared to go to lunch and sit next to death. Look him straight in the eye. Offer him the menu.

I haven't seen Laura in fifteen years. We seem to only meet at weddings, funerals, and graduations and as a result I don't think I've ever seen her without a hat. I dreamt I met her once at Ascot, and could not work out what portentous meaning this had. The answer was so banal – hats. Dreams are so magical yet fundamentally bland. I keep on playing out this lunch scenario.

First: Laura is pale, drawn, and skeletal, her hair pulled tight in a bun, she has been highlighting her hair. She has been to his bedside, but he would not see her, raging and cursing women, swearing he would go the grave without their contamination. He spat in her grapes, and tore the heads from her flowers. She is hysterical, I am calm, collected. I tell her I have been preparing for this death for forty years so it can no longer touch me, I can no longer be hurt by it. He has died every day since I was eleven. and all my crying, mourning and screaming (she is doing all this at the table, and the waiters are concerned) has been done. I've finished. I leave the bill.

Second: The restaurant has no floor, just a fathomless bog, with a small stone path leading from table to table, which the waiters carefully negotiate, carrying their trays of lizards eye, centaurs entrails and pigs trotters to the dribbling, heaving crowd. Ghouls, wizards, spectres, ogres and pixies sit around the largest table in the centre of their room, eating with their hands and tipping large. There are a couple of Gorgons at a bad table in front of the toilets. The White Witch sits alone at the back, her fingernails so long and curled it is impossible for her to pick up the silverware. She is being fed pasta by a midget in an emerald suit, who sings in a high pitched voice and picks scabs off the back of his ears. He scatters them over her pasta like Parmesan. I am the black witch, and do not ask if the seat is taken. We are here to argue about the King, all niceties are dropped. We both open little compacts in silence and note our lipstick has faded. In unison we bite our lips and smear the blood around. We pucker up. We begin.

Lunch with my father. I am fifteen and the night before have accidentally come across a porno mag in his jacket pocket. My parents are sleeping in separate bedrooms by this point, and I have gone into my father's bedroom to find something, or something, and instead find something. This filthy thing. This disease on paper. He explains it is for his work, I storm out, the next day he takes me to lunch. But I cannot speak to him and I cannot look him in the eye. To me all the waitresses are naked. A couple walk by, with another woman on a lead. The short order cook is chained to the counter and is having lunch inserted into him. The manager wears a black mask as a customer grates his penis. My father does not mention the magazine, in fact. we never mention it again. The only person I ever tell is Liz, and her nose crinkles, condensing her freckles, at the grossness of it all.

"Your dad? Oooh, that's creepy. Mind you, you don't have that women's health book under your bed for nothing"

And that was it. No scream, no outrage, no phoning of the police to protect me from this degenerate man. But it dwells on my mind – this is untrue – it rots and putrefies there. My adolescence never escapes the stench. Later I have other cover-up lunches. Cover-up the relationship is falling apart lunch, cover-up you're failing the degree lunch, and uncountable cover-up we want your money lunches. But this vegetarian curry in Kings Cross is the first. The one that makes me realise people are not infallible, fathers are faulted, children, unforgiving. I wonder if Laura had this lunch too, I need to know she did. That she was not always the right daughter and me always the wrong one. I'd rather we were both wrong.

That lunch my father looks at me sadly, and his eyes say, sex is a part of me. And my eyes say back, me too. In a silent moment, an era ends.

"Ruth…Ruth"

Laura has her hand on my shoulder, I am at the restaurant, though I hadn't noticed. She is speaking to me but I am processing nothing except how beauti-

ful she is. How young she looks (she must be sixty, she looks forty), and how different she looks, yet entirely familiar. She is blond, pale, almost transparent like baking paper. But her lips are thick and red like mine, everything below our noses are the same. Phillipo comes out of the restaurant and meets us on the steps, an Italian girl following behind him. There are four of us then. standing in silence, smiling warmly and thickly as an understanding begins to rise like good soufflé. The Italian girl, hugs me and kisses my cheek. She has heard, she says, so much about me. "And I have seen you," I say. Mouths open and close with slow violence, veins bulge, arms beat the air like the wings of great birds. "From the church," I say. And then with a simplicity that comes before cognition;
"You must be my sister's lover."
Great laughter. A rain cloud gurgles ominously, we go in.
On Sundays in Italy, fathers walk their daughters to church, and in small villages, just up and down the road, proudly displaying their offspring. It is quite a breathtaking sight, the feathers, the gold buttons, the parasols, and we are privileged enough to see it, as we sit in our booth, enjoying particularly good tagliatelli. Lisa, Laura's partner, explains to us that it is symbolic of the father's mourning for his daughter's imminent puberty, when he will lose her, and she chooses another man, and then ultimately God, as her father. Laura laughs. "Such patriarchal rubbish," she says. "Italy is almost as bad as England." Lisa looks a little slighted.
"You may be able still to walk a road with your papa now, no?" she says quietly.
I may well. The crisis is passing, the old bugger, despite twenty cigarettes a day for twice as many years, has pulled through again. I puff on a Marlboro in tribute to him. Laura continues to berate partite to a tired and confused Phillippo. Lisa orders some more wine on Laura's credit card, which is embarrassingly more stretchable than mine. We must compete, after all, over something now. Outside, a particularly resplendent father and daughter team stroll by. They are in matching suits on a sailor theme, with matching gold trim, and white lilies in their respective lapels. The innocence, trust, love is palpable. The security and the faith in similarity, in the concrete fact of beget-ing. It is amazing to me. It is an Eden we love but cannot live in for long the great tightrope of need vs. independence. I asked Liz once in Religious Education what "beget" meant. We were watching a video, nine-part drama adaptation of the Bible and the narrator repeated the word several times to accompanying class giggles. Liz signals for me to put my head under the table where we can talk in relative privacy. We put our mouths together to swap chewing gums. "Mothers give birth, right?" she whispers. "Yes?" I say.
Liz draws a lipstick heart on my thigh.
"Well, fathers beget.

Homecoming
Nick Laird

From the word go the Ulster way was to leave.
And again a son's gone off. Gone across, gone south.
And got lost on the long cast. Gone posh. Gone soft.
But at vacations the reeling-in, the rolling home,
expecting banners, drums, feast-days in his name,
only to find the town unforgiving, furtive,
straddled by an Orange Arch – "Welcome here Brethren",
but not the place's native faithless children.

Learning gone to their heads, back-agains lob questions
like grenades at the dead, assess their own core and character,
talk of the light of Ulster in the evenings. Before retreating.
Emma and I used to throw sticks over the bridge into the river,
to see whose came out from the dark arch first. Easier
to go with that sinewy flow than bed down and raise a stir;
stay. An accent is at least a token vocal gesture,
a hook caught in river-roots while the line spools off elsewhere.

Think of an Irishman, whose boat's come in, sitting
at the airport. Well that's me. I'm the man in the joke.
The lynch-pin of the bobsleigh team, the one that won't begin
'til the track's been gritted. The simple harmless bloke.
But Irish were deceivers ever. Sharing water and air
with those who murder, and doctors, birthdays, names,
taints you. I once became Jesus because of Brummie innkeepers.
Travelling through England after the bombs in Birmingham;
my expansive Dad, Mum large with me, my sister just a toddler,
nowhere would take us in. No inn. The luck of the Irish
where an accent, beard and bulk spelt suspect, terrorist.
Fair enough. But tough enough too. They slept in the car.
Ripples spread outward and outward. And blood being thicker
than an acre of seawater, distrust has more to offer.
I'm scared about that. About what that might mean –
these thoughts of an endless homecoming,

to this over-anthologised province, this skundered hole,
where the gullible and the culpable are forever interchangeable,
along with the good, the bad and the holy, where stray
seagulls swoop low over Lough Erne and Lough Neagh,
watching fishermen, by passed-on legerdemain, conjure
something from nothing, lures from wool and feather,
fish from water, their eyes fat and dead from swallowed lies.
I've always been fingers and thumbs when it comes to tying flies,

blind at reading rivers, at floats and knots an amateur,
but I knew a man who was a master. He knew the sharp tap,
grew used to the strike. He is only ever pictured at the river.
Trees splitting light, the quiet pool lit like a Big Top,
grass ringside seats, and him, ringmaster with a flyrod whip,
in the swim of it, standing in the river's skin, the lash
and crack of line and slack eluding us. I almost gave it up
after learning, at Dee's in Kesh, how to wash and gut the fish.

But riverbeds are not easy left. Old baits sit and wait to hook
your boots. One last cast. That splash. Lost by looking back.
The evening Dad saw an otter or something similar up at Millars'
I caught an eel further along the bank. Hooked him coming home.
A returning one who'd managed to outswim the traps at Toome,
and who wriggled like he was being tickled when I cut him.
For hours after his tail was an epileptic tiller,
his torso a wavelength. Ultraviolet. Even the cats wouldn't try it.

And so I imagine the path of the lure as mine. The bale-arm click
as it snags on rock or weed, the line taut as tendon,
the reel-in delayed, the spoon snug 'til tug or flick
releases it. And then the spinner teasing and ascending.
But I remember how it's common for returning salmon
to leap onto the ground instead of up-stream. And to drown
stunned in that thick shared air. The other way of getting home,

of stepping in the same river, of lastly coming among your own.

Mrs Begum's Son and the Private Tutor

Zadie Smith

So Mrs Begum said to me, "Young man, young man...I can see you are getting some

> ideas. Don't get ideas. No
> ideas round here, yaar?
> My son does not need a companion,
>
> or a friend-type-thing, or
> any of your English moral
> guidance – Magid needs this
> one
>
> thing: A private tutor.
> Question a) – are you
> willing or not, will it do
> or won't it?
>
> Question b) – have you the
> ability? Can you or can't
> you?"

Before I had a chance to answer in the affirmative, she pushed another sticky oil-soaked box of Indian sweets under my nose, while her youngest child, a little girl all in pink, removed one from the box and force fed me. The sweets were pink like the child and tasted pink, far too much so; between this sickly pink, the outrageous red of the carpet and wall (the wall was carpeted), the strident green of the sofa suite, the gaudy orange of the 24 set children's encyclopaedia that dominated the bookshelf, and the blinding yellow of Alsana Begum's selwar khamise – a peculiar synisthesia happened – the room gave you indigestion.

"Mmmm," I said, once I've flicked the marzipan to the back of my throat, "I came for the job of Majid's tutor, Mrs Begum – nothing else".

"Ha!" cried Alsana, continuing her incredulity in Bengali, and, smashing her hand down on the coffee table, flung Geeni's Barbie across the room into a half-packed suitcase. I found later that every room in the house was like this – half-packed suitcases – though they had lived there for fourteen years.

"Young man, you are an Oxford man, is that right – there is no need for stupidness between a man like yourself and I. Clearly, when we say "a tutor for Magid" this will not be a normal-type-thing."

"No?"

I must have looked entirely at sea, because for the first time since the beginning of our consultation, she took pity on me, put her slightly podgy yet elegant fingers on my knee, and tapped one of her many rings sympathetically on my corduroys. "You see that?" she said, as if explaining to a child, and pointing to the television.

"Yes," I said.

It was some kind of Sunday morning Hindi musical, over which the Ceefax weather report was imposed, almost entirely obscuring the two lovers who were darting in and out from behind a tree.

"You see those?" she said, pointing to an eclectic huddle of very old toys in the corner of the room. Amongst them a cuddly octopus, a Fisher-Price car station, a My Little Pony demonised by a red felt-tip.

"Magid never watches that," (she had a formidable index finger), "he never plays with those. It seems to me that here we have the central issues of importance – that there are certain things any tutor of my son should realise. These are as follows..."

I settled down in my chair and waited for another lexical inventory. In the twenty minutes I had known Alsana and in the years that were to follow she never lost her liking for a) listing propositions under letters and b) making whatever was, in fact, very simple, highly contentious and confrontational.

"A) My son is ten years old but he is not a child. He is a man-child, as was the prophet Mohammed." (Alsana was prone to inventing the Koran) "B) My son is pretty clever-clever. No one in this house understands him half the time. His teachers don't, the local education authority do not" (at these words a newly fresh venom came into Alsana's gaze, as if she mentioned the LEA only under extreme duress).

"Probably, you will not. But we must try, that is *someone* must try."

She was determined not to reveal the decision, even though I knew I had the job, that is, that Alsana and I, from the moment I walked up the pebble-dash driveway, had made an immediate, though reluctant connection.

"So, to finish 'B', it has been said in some quarters that Magid is a genius".

I nodded vigorously. At that time, I had been out of University for four years, wanting to write but fumbling into teaching, and every child I had so far tutored had a mother convinced of his latent, disguised, or entirely obvious genius.

189

As Geeni tugged pointlessly at the hem of her mother's skirts, Alsana delivered with thundering emphasis point C, which, as was her habit, entirely explained and consumed all other points, indeed, everything in the room.

"And C) – Magid is a Bengali. I don't expect you to know what this means. You can never be us and we, thankfully, will never be you. Luckily, in this borough, however, we have mutual understandings. We are all *liberals* here! And my brother on the council tells me things are changing, changing, mutual understandings, though –"

She looked at me sharply.

" – there can be too much of that…at some point families should close their doors, don't you think? I think so. And yet there must be *communication*, so important. *Communication…*"

She mulled over the word like a word-taster and then spat out her conclusion:

"…and so 'C': *He must have an English education for one reason only.*"

Neetu Singh crooned in sweet capitulation as Ravi finally caught her from behind the tree and clasped her in his arms, and Geeni, with a childlike desire for correspondence brought Barbie and My Little Pony together in a bestial kiss.

"He must, one day, save his people".

A week on Tuesday then, lessons would begin.

• • • • •

It was a pretty nice road, Alsana's road, although maybe my views at that time were a bit touristy, I don't know, but it still seems to me, now that I'm a fully signed up Londoner, that those long North London roads tucked behind dingy high-streets and lined with bent trees are worth the fuss the estate agents make of them.

The best ones are the ones that end at the mouths of parks like Brighton roads fall into the sea, and you can tell the class of an area depending on whether its suburban road leads up to a park (Hampstead) or down to a park (Willesden). I remember when I first arrived, and spent most of my time walking (even now, I've made few friends in London), I got really preoccupied with the social physiognomy of London parks and roads; realising that an area can redeem itself even if it leads down to a park, by the park itself rising up again in a hill.

This was the case in Alsana's instance, and she was fond of reminding me, when we dragged Geeni, who hated the outside, up to feed the ducks, that the view from the top of Gladstone Park Hill rivalled anything in the more aerial North London boroughs, if one faced East so as to exclude the Bingo Hall that towers over Kilburn to the West – but it was almost unavoidable unless you squinted.

Really, it was pretty.

I'd made a point of making sure all the kids I tutored were within walking distance of Gladstone Park and each other, and so the logic of the roads went something like:

Park, Magid, second corner, ice cream van, Katie, two doors down James, long road, tree roots bursting out of pavement like blood vessels, Anita, Joshua-and-Isaac, lost cat, lamp post, through church yard, Parjev.

Between appointments I was kicking leaves up and down these streets. Autumn lasts forever when there's so many trees.

Magid was the last pupil I got on my books. Before him it was pretty run of the mill.

Joshua and Isaac, two Jewish boys whose parents were friends of the family were my first private appointment; big brown eyes and open plan faces, work always completed with decorated margins; then Katie, fifteen, sulky, petulant, full breasted and prone to inviting her friends over to look at me; James, brilliant lateral thinker but emotionally closed shut and tight-springed like an old music box, beady eyes, baking paper skin; Anita of Romanian descent, a peculiarly pious seventeen year old, wrote all her History essays with clinical adherence to my opinion, but fingered the cross around her neck at the end of each session and swore her allegiance else-where; and finally, Parjev Shastri, the little emperor, only seven in knee high white socks, and while he solemnly nods at the algebra , there is somewhere in the house the sounds of – well, she is a servant, flown in from Pakistan, she is rustling sheets – she changes them.

Alsana actually knew Parjev's family, but there was no conversation to be made out of this, as she despised them and begrudged them their rusty iron, peeling gold plated lions that stood on either side of the gate to their actually pretty modest two-up-two-down.

"Only a Hindu," Alsana would mutter mysteriously, "would have lions."

But soon she would warm to her theme, and up to fifteen minutes of fitful invective would issue on everything from the physically diminutive Parjev: "Runt! I give thanks to Allah my sons are large and my girls pretty!" to the rel-ative shades of the housemaid and the family: "If I was black as that woman (Mrs Shastri) I'd have no cocoa coloured girl in *my* house!"

But I often wondered what would issue from a friendship between Parjev and Magid. During the leaf-kicking I played out scenarios for all my tutees – if, if, if this were not London and people's lives intersected as easily as their roads. Parjev meets Magid, and the two precise little boys create a 'clever-bomb', Anita, solemn-mouthed Anita, teaches Katie to uncurl her snarling lip, or maybe Katie teaches Anita how to French kiss a pillow, how to take a bra off without removing your T-shirt, and Joshua-and-Isaac open the door to James with warm smiles, each take a hand, and lead him upstairs and backwards, back into the playroom. They'd teach him to play.

Though my tutees all lived physically close by, I was twenty minutes away in Cricklewood, which is really a bus-ride though occasionally I'd walk it. Someone once told me that T S Eliot said Cricklewood was one of the most God-forsaken places on earth. That surprised me. It's so forsaken you can't imagine why anyone would bother to mention it, particularly not a founder of

Modernism. What was he doing there? A wrong turn maybe. Wrong concrete jungle. No place for even an urban poet.

I went there because it was pretty damn cheap, and I managed to get a road off the highroad with a few trees. But it's not like Willesden, there aren't really any roads off the highroad. The Highroad is insidious, and the McDonald's cartons and the vomit seep into the turn-offs and the cul-de-sacs like a tarred lung. There are no mouths in Cricklewood.

Covered in shit and marinated in alcohol, Cricklewood air is about thirty per cent proof. My wife used to stay in the back room writing her novel and wouldn't open the windows. She's wasn't my wife, this is 1990 and she's still Alison, my girlfriend, and we've been going out for six months but it's basically serious enough for me to work for a year while she writes and then for us to swap round come next spring.

For some reason, when she works she works in her pants. She'll sit down in trousers, but within the first paragraph she finds them restrictive and they're thrown across the room. Our landlady, who thought I was adorable, thought Alison very peculiar.

On the allocated Tuesday morning I got up and found she'd ironed my one white shirt in preparation for my new pupil .

"Alex, you know, if you're teaching India's Saviour you'd better look the part."

"Bangladesh. Not India. Different places. Anyway, she said 'his people'. Most of them are here in Cricklewood."

"Exodus, Diaspora," said my future-wife. It's a pointless, irritating habit of hers to act like a thesaurus.

• • • • •

The Communist candidate for Brent East lived in Cricklewood. I'd see him every Tuesday around the time of Magid's morning appointment. We both got the bus that packed twice the regulation passenger allowance on it and hurtled down the hill, narrowly missing the lamp posts on its way to Willesden Green Station.

- Without fail there were always two geriatric Jamaican men, one impossibly fat, the other dangerously thin, spitting their back-seat advice into the poor drivers ear:
- – Bwoy, ya never drive a big-man bus before, uh? You gwan kill us all?
- – Rhas-clut…If some one come run for bus let dem run for bus, see? – whya stop?

And there was always the Communist candidate for Brent East sat at the back, crushed between the Mafia of London bus travel: Old Age Pensioners and Pregnant Women With Shopping.

This first appointment with Magid was the first time I'd ever seen this local legend, the Communist candidate for Brent East, in the flesh. It was something like seeing Gorbachev on the bus, so familiar was his face from Eighties newsreel, postcards and badges, from my brief foray into college politics. He has that funny kind of half-fame. Like Gorbachev, no one cares for him now, yet there were still jokes floating around to which his name is the punch line.

As a Labour MP he had helped build the Liberal Mecca on the other side of the Thames impudently facing the Houses of Parliament and for a while children had free milk in school and free paper with crooked margins, and small black theatre groups got funding, and people renovated their local parks, and pensioners and teenage girls were granted streetlights – now it doesn't seem very much. But it must have been – it was just enough change for She Who Had To Be Obeyed to rise swiftly like a phoenix and swallow him and the rest in bright, efficient flames. Leaving a little man (he seemed literally half the size), fingering his moustache, crushed on the back seat, and written all over him was "Play with fire and you shall be burnt". People are sometimes like that – like message boards bearing dire warnings.

The Communist candidate for Brent East had tried to save some people, caught the 266 every Tuesday morning and never wore any shoes or socks. After a while, I stopped looking at him.

· · · · ·

I was twenty yards from Magid's house and right on time when I heard my name being hollered.

"Mr Pembrose! Yeah you, Pembrose! Over here!"

Out of the top right hand window of Mrs Begum's house leant an attractively long-limbed boy, about seventeen, with floppy public-school haircut which sat in pleasant contrast with his dark skin – what I'd guess you'd call roguish good-looks. He had a lot of teeth, and they were chomped round a cigarette that he was smoking menacingly. Never before have I felt so quickly and acutely that someone didn't like me. "Pembrose!"

"Yes, I'm Alex Pembrose," I said. "Who are you?"

"Mark," he said.

I tried all different ways to hide my surprise, but I could see this is a thing he does to make people uncomfortable and I was uncomfortable .

"You don't look like a Mark," I said, rising to the bait.

"No shit."

I tried a different approach.

"Is Mrs Begum in, at all?"

"Nah – Mum's out, she's in the park – she wants to talk to you."

He pointed down towards the park, and now I could just see Alsana who was at the bottom of the road at the park gate, this time all in orange, looking slightly sheepish (it was an attitude that strangely suited her) and sucking a Lemonade Sparkler. She waved, or rather beckoned, nervously.

"...I'm to go there...?"

I was careful to keep constant eye contact with Mark as it seemed to be the only way not to let him intimidate you. He wore a white vest, that revealed some impressive forearms and the fact that a pale, white, attractive female hand was curled around one of them. The rest of her (I assume there was more) was obscured by some curtain .

"Yeah...she wants to talk in private."

I wondered why the park was more private than the house.

"It's about the continuing traumas of Nerd-boy."

"Right".

"You from round here?"

"I live here, yes..."

In Willesden Green this was no kind of an answer. Within a week of moving here I worked that much out. When someone stopped you in Willesden and asked you where you were from the question had as many layers as lizard skin. The right answer involved – well I'm originally V but I was born in X but my mother's actually Y but I'm a quarter Z, I guess I *consider* myself V but I don't speak it, and then we moved to Willesden Green.

Mark frowned.

"I'm from Surrey," I said.

Mark frowned.

A father-like voice started calling in Bengali and Mark answered it fluently but quietly and quickly as if he was trying to get rid of the words as soon as possible.

"Yeah, right, well...I've got to step."

"Step?"

"Go."

"Oh, right."

"Al-laaah..."

This was more of a laugh than a word, like a sing-song and it softened him a little. There was more gruff calling and then the sound of a door opening and slamming. The female hand disappeared in a flash and the curtains swung shut to the accompaniment of raised, foreign voices.

"Meester Pembrose!"

Alsana was waving. I trudged down to the park.

We squeezed into a bench together, Alsana and I, and she pressed a thermos of PG Tips into my hands, without milk and with lemon. A way ahead of us, throwing a boomerang that stubbornly refused to come back to him, was Magid. He was long and languid like Mark, but his face was far chubbier and he wore some light blue regulation NHS specs on his nose. He didn't look much like a saviour, but he looked bright – his eyes were keener than most ten year olds – but that could be a trick of the glasses. It was a beautiful November day – crisp, bright, like the world had been remade with fresh cotton sheets.

"Is there no lesson today Mrs Begum?"

"I don't know, I don't know…I just don't know…Of course I'll pay you whatever, but I just don't know about today."

She knotted her fingers together and looked mournfully at Magid, who had just been whiplashed by the returning boomerang as he ran to meet it on its skewing path to the left.

"What's the problem, exactly?"

She poured us both another large cup of tea, and brought some savoury dough-like balls out of cling-film which we nibbled at.

"Something about monkeys, Mr Pembrose. I can't claim to understand it. My degree was in Biology, but this is far more of a *mathematical* problem, you see…I don't know what is to be said to him."

"A monkey?"

"*Infinite* monkeys, Mr Pembrose, an infinite number."

Magid tripped over the boomerang, and into some leaves, but was unnerved by the laughter of a gang of black girls who whizzed by on Chopper-bikes.

"Magid! Get your head out of the grass and come and tell Mr Pembrose about the monkeys."

Magid looked quizzically at me, but then picked up the boomerang and slouched towards us.

"Magid, this is Mr Pembrose. Mr Pembrose, this is Magid."

It was the first time we had looked at each other face to face. Because I was sat and he was standing, I did indeed feel like I was looking into the face of a man. A little man.

"Where are you from?" he asked.

"Surrey"

"Yerrus"

"Pardon?"

"Nodrap? "

"Backwards," explained Alsana. "He does that sometimes when he doesn't know a person well. Tell Mr Pembrose about the monkeys, Magid (It's upset him and he said he can't study today because of it, you see)."

"Uncle Rafi said –"

"That's his uncle," Alsana interrupted.

"Uncle Rafi said if you had a great amount of monkeys, and each had a typewriter and they were to write for an infinite amount of time, in the end they would write the Koran"

That set Alsana off into a flurry of tea-making activity and dough-ball eating.

"Well, that's about probability. You could say something similar about a die, which, if you roll it enough times will land on six."

Magid looked at me darkly, and Alsana appeared to be holding her breath.

"I mean, you could question why more time makes something more probable," I said in a tutor-prompting type of a way.

Magid fingered the edge of his boomerang and looked towards Gladstone Hill where some kids had lit a bonfire. He flung the boomerang in their direction.

"It seems," he said, as if the world rested upon it, "that it is just a problem with our ideas of infinity."

"The word of the Creator…" muttered Alsana, "how could a monkey write that?"

"Clever monkey, Yeknom Revelc," said Magid just seconds before the boomerang came careering back, caught him on the temple and knocked him out.

· · · · ·

The blow on the head combined with Alsana's claustrophobic fondness for her second born kept Magid in bed for a week and a half. The house closed ranks like a court around a mad king. Alsana kept his curtains permanently drawn and "Mark", Geeni and Mr Begum were relegated to the TV room where they watched re-runs of Columbo quietly and guiltily when Magid was trying to get some sleep. The first few days I'd come and try to teach, but Magid, as much as his mother assured me he was a maths prodigy, showed absolutely no interest in numbers. Magid loved words:

" Right. Algebra."

"Yes, yes…" said Magid, eyes to the ceiling, "but I wonder if it matters?"

"If what matters?"

"How can 'what' matter?"

"What?"

"It does matter. 'What' matters. Like, '*what* are you?' "

"Yes, Magid. Now where were we…"

Magid clapped his hands together delighted.

"Where! But *where* matters much more… it's *where* that matters."

Or:

"Right. Graphs."

"Are the little babies of Elephants and giraffes."

In the end I was re-hired as a kind of baby-sitter .

"What if you just come every other day, Mr Pembrose – just sit with him, read the papers, teach if he wants, he'd like that," said Alsana as she put the curried lamb in a gigantic pot to marinate over night.

"What papers?" said Alison irritably, as she rifled through the shelves of the coffee table, with her bottom in the air, looking for yesterday's news, "he's ten years old for God's sake!"

 "She said he likes the papers"

She passed me a handful: The *Guardian*, The *Willesden and Brent Chronicle* and The *Socialist Worker*.

"Tell him to leave the crosswords."

On the bus to Magid's, The Communist candidate for Brent East was being harassed by a group of women under a banner that was crushed against the roof of the bus, and whose left-hand corner kept dangerously obscuring Marcus' (the driver's) rear view. The Banner read:

The Asian Women's Community Action Group
Uniting the Muslim, Hindu, Buddhist and Sikh
peoples of Brent

"Bit long-winded that, eh?" said the old white guy who smelt of oxo-cubes and was sitting on the corner of my jacket.

"We are making this protest," shouted the attractive middle-aged spokes-woman, "in condemnation of the council's decision to refuse to acknowledge our repeated requests for the old bingo-hall to be made into a meeting place for the Asian community –"

"When there is already places for the Irish and the Jews and for people of Caribbean descent!" interrupted a youngish looking girl in dungarees.

"– and to ask the Communist candidate for Brent East to please join us in this action, and to speak for us at council meetings when it seems no one else will, not even the Labour councillors we voted for!"

There was limited cheering, and someone passed round some delicious long pastry things stuffed with spinach.

"I'm afraid the council have made their decision," said the Communist candidate for Brent East shuffling his feet.

He was quoted as saying exactly the same thing on the front page of the *Willesden and Brent Chronicle*, and I read it out to Magid as he sat cross legged in bed and the smell of lunch wafted up from downstairs.

"What a weak man'" said Magid .

"I suppose so."

"My Uncle Rafi says a weak man is worse than a monkey because at least a monkey is not conscious of its weakness."

"Your uncle seems full of insight about monkeys."

"What's 'insight'?" asked Magid. It was the first time he had ever asked me anything.

"Understanding, seeing things sharply."

"Oh yes, he has lots of insight. Could you open the curtains a little, please?"

The autumn light streamed in and Magid smiled gleefully like a child.

"You're not ill at all, are you?"

Magid looked at me wryly.

"What shall we learn today, Mr Pembrose?"

"I was thinking of a little physics, just to see how much you know."

He furrowed his brow like a pair of old tights.

"Or, we could do something else…"

I was mindful of the close visceral connection between my rent, my next meal and keeping-Magid-happy.

"Poetry." said Magid, "I read today something by Mr William Blake about eternity in an hour."

He spoke in a clipped, matter-of-fact way, like you learn in Teacher Training.

"Heaven in a flower. Eternity in an hour. Such a big thing in such a small thing. Do you think that's possible?"

"Do I think what is possible?"

"That big things can issue from small, like an elephant from an egg. Do elephants come from eggs?"

"No".

"My mother thinks I should do big, great things but I like very small things. Uncle Rafi says it is better to be the ringleader of a very good troupe of monkeys than the leader of a very bad country."

"Does he."

"This is a very bad country."

He said this as if he were talking about a flavour of ice cream.

"It's yours, isn't it?"

"Well, not –"

"Do you love it even though it's bad?"

"Well I –"

"Oh, you *should.*"

I wiped some sweat from my bottom lip. Magid, had, as a child (and did later, as a man) the unnerving ability of being so familiar with strangers (his eyes, his touches) that you felt you'd missed something. That he knew something about you that you didn't. Prophets have this.

He smiled craftily.

"When I'm ill I can do small things and no one minds."

Magid pulled a bright green jersey over his head and began to put on some yellow trousers (like all smart kids he had absolutely no sense of style).

"Let's go out. This man is talking outside the library today."

"Your mother wants you to stay in bed."

(I should have said "I want". All the time I was losing any claim to authority.)

"Anyway, which man?"

Magid's little finger pressed the front page urgently.

"That little man."

He pointed to the Communist candidate for Brent East.

"It's such a small thing that they want."

"Who want?"

"My people," he said.

Downstairs, in the kitchen, we met with obstruction:

"Magi-id," said Alsana.

"Mam-aa…" said Magid.

Mr Begum looked dolefully into his soup as if waiting for a thunderstorm to break.

Alsana shouted something in Bengali.

Magid shouted back.

Mark shouted at Magid.

Geeni appeared to defend Magid but still be angry at Alsana.

My name weaved in out of a beautiful tongue like misstitches in quilt.

Alsana threw a plate and two glasses at the far wall. Mr Begum stood up and all went quiet.

Mark murmured something and Alsana murmured something back.

"Take Mark with you," said Alsana and the three of us left the house.

"Got a tab?"

"I don't smoke."

"Typical."

Mark discovered one in his shirt pocket anyway, and lodged it between his lips in his vicious manner which seemed somewhat practised.

"Mr Pembrose does not smoke," said Magid, "because he and the rest of the world understand the link between tobacco and deadness."

"Shut up fuck-face," said Mark.

Magid just squeezed my left hand tighter and turned the dry leaves over with his heels.

"We still have not yet had a proper lesson, Mr Pembrose," said Magid quietly, craning his neck so as to look.

I can't quite explain the affection in his voice when he said this, and there is not space here to unravel the ease with which he held my hand nor justify how close I felt to him, how much I felt I knew him, and how there was this funny equality, (I am not good at this), all despite the fact, or maybe because, as he so rightly pointed out, we had not yet had a proper lesson.

"But this is like a school trip, so maybe that's OK," said Magid and I said yes, maybe it is.

Mark walked ahead. He had an angry young man walk. Every muscle in his body was angry. And as a white man looking on I admit I saw a panther in him – right or wrong – I saw an angry cat biting back. To every inch of Magid's Buddha-like serenity, there was quite the opposite in Mark. There was a revolution in him.

In the multicultural "niceness" of Willesden Green, at the beginning of a new optimistic decade when the last burning car had died down and all the shop windows replaced, Mark was an Angry Eighties anachronism. But unlike the Communist candidate for Brent East (who we could now see, on a disaffected podium with a complacent megaphone and a disillusioned crowd) who was the very opposite of angry, anti-angry, Mark with his tight-lipped, menacing scowl, slouching towards Willesden Green Library like the Second Coming was resolutely (can we still, this late in the day, speak honestly?) the white liberal nightmare.

The Tory, the Liberal, the Labour councillor and the Communist candidate for Brent East stood round the podium, taking turns, and there were red, blue and yellow banners and ties, and they held on to their scarves, as a blustery wind whipped round the octagon old post office and up their shirt sleeves.

An old lady ruffled Magid's hair, gave him a humbug, and talked about her heating. On the other side of the square were young men with fledgling beards and big trousers giving out leaflets which said: *Khalifah. Learn about the ideal Islamic State.* There was a mime artist leading some children around a telephone box. The Asian Women's Community Action group turned up, and heckled, which brought more people, until there was quite a hefty crowd and Magid was squeezed between me and a fat lady.

The Liberal said something about the rainbow borough of Brent. A Rastawoman with her front teeth missing sucked the rest of them in contempt. "Where's the colour in the council?" she said, and the crowd laughed. The red, yellow and blue men, pushed their pink fingertips deeper into their gloves and began again. Megaphone, drone, drone, cough, conclusion.

Mark wandered off in the direction of the big trousers. I saw how he put his cigarette out before he reached them, how his walk changed, how they clapped hands with each other like men.

The sky was a dark purple, and heavy over our heads. There was a commotion starting as the Communist candidate once again took the stand. It started in a kind of listless boredom, then some more heckling from the women, then shouts from the trousers and worried muttering from the white parents with kids in pushchairs. I turned round to make sure Magid was still behind me.

Let me remember this right.

I pushed through the crowd, mistaking him again and again for little Asian kids, or for yellow scarves, or green jumpers; I looked over to Mark, but he was locked in eager conversation with the Trousers, and the humbug lady said no, she had not seen him, and from then it was quite a few moments before I realised that the droning had ceased and that that was Magid's voice I could hear floating over the crowds and meeting with a respectful hush; quiet from those who understood him (he spoke Bengali) and bemusement from the few who didn't.

I guess he spoke for about ten minutes during which, though I could not understand a word, I saw a great crowd manipulator at work. First he made them laugh, then it became sombre, then a few of the women got a little tearful, then it became spirited again, then incredibly noisy, (throughout this, each councillor was desperately trying to get it translated for them by the Bengali

200

businessmen who filled the party coffers and followed them around as a public relations exercise) and it ended in a half frenzy where Magid had to be rescued from the attentions of the crowds and ushered through the electric doors of the library until things calmed down. The only people who were silent, the only ones not fervently arguing with their neighbours or sweeping tears from the corners of their eyes were Mark and the Trousers. They were still.

Finally, the councillors got the gist of the speech translated, debated amongst themselves quickly, and the Communist candidate for Brent East got up on the podium, reshuffled his papers and looked out on to the crowd, the biggest he had spoken to, I would guess, for quite a while:

"In the light of this very…very peculiar turn in events, my colleagues and I will be re-considering the decision as regards the renovation of the Bingo Hall."

A kind of carnival broke out and after much hassle I was told I could collect Magid from the Lost Children's Meeting Point.

· · · · ·

The next morning, Magid, in *Willesden and Brent Chronicle* terms, was big news.

Alison picked up the paper from the doormat in disbelief.

"You are joking me…"

TEN YEAR OLD BOY WOWS WILLESDEN

"You are bloody *joking* me."

I folded up the paper and put it in my coat pocket to take to Magid. Alison put some trousers on.

"I have *got* to meet this kid."

We got the bus together.

You couldn't get near the house for people and flash-bulbs. Geeni stuck her head out of the upstairs window.

"Mummy says come round the back way."

She threw down her key, and we squeezed round the crowd, through the back garden and opened the ground floor kitchen door. Alsana was making hot Ribena for journalists and the Communist candidate for Brent East.

"Mr Pembrose! I'm glad you came. Here, drink this." she thrust a hot mug into my hands, "Gentlemen, Mr Pembrose, Mr Pembrose, Gentlemen. This is Magid's private tutor. It's so bloody cold outside. And one for you –"

"Alison"

"Alison. Are you Press young lady?"

"She's with me." I said. "Where's Magid?"

"And this is Brian." she continued, pointing to the Communist candidate.

"Hullo." said Brian, standing up and offering me a podgy palm.

"Brian is a Communist," said Alsana, "but he's a very nice man all the same."

"Can I meet Magid?" asked Alison.

"Alsana, where's Magid?"

At which point Mark walked in.

"Well, surprise, surprise, look who's bought this Ghandi bullshit with everybody else."

Alsana snapped at Mark in Bengali, but he ignored her and turned to me.

"Mark, where is Magid?"

He turned his palms over and over each other like Uriah Heep and assumed a thick "Indian" accent;

"Well, sir, if you are wanting to see our wise little emperor sir, you'll be needing to go upstairs, kneel three times and enter his sacred chamber, sir, oh yes, oh yes."

"He's in his room," said Alsana, "but he's meant to be resting. He's had a lot of visitors today."

I assured her I wouldn't worry him, pushed past Mark and went upstairs.

I found him looking cautiously through the net curtains and onto the street below. There was such a heavy melancholy in the room it was almost tangible.

"Hi."

"Hi."

"How's things?"

"Peculiar." said Magid, and closed the curtains.

"I met Brian." I said.

"Yes," said Magid, "he came up to see me this morning. He's nice, really."

"So they're building the thing?"

"Oh yes. All the women came yesterday and gave me all kinds of leaflets and some really, really nice food. Alsana said I was spoilt rotten."

On the desk was a pile of leaflets in the shape of paper airplanes.

"Magid, what did you say to those people yesterday?"

No paper had so far accurately translated it, one woman saying it was not so much words as *feelings*.

Magid looked into space.

"I just said...you know, that people should love and stuff...we should all mix together, Hindu, Muslim...I said everything could be so much *nicer*...the usual."

"*That's* what you said?"

Magid shrugged his shoulders.

"It was really quite small." he said.

"Well, everyone seemed to like it."

"No," he said, holding my hands, "my brother didn't. He thinks I do things the wrong way."

There was a knock and a young woman with a shock of red hair popped her head round the door.

"Hi, right – Hi…" she looked down on to a piece of paper she was holding," Magid? We're from *Lifestyle Magazine*, we were wondering if we could talk to you briefly about the more *personal* aspects of this whole…thing?"

"You should probably go," said Magid quietly.

"Yes, right." I said and left the room.

As I walked downstairs, the contents of the kitchen had spilled out into the hallway and joined the steady stream of visitors who were making the journey to Magid's room. In the lounge Alison and Alsana were discussing possible universities for Magid. I walked past into the kitchen where I found Mark alone, looking out onto the garden.

"Seen your Guru?"

"I saw Magid, yes."

"Great."

In the garden was the rarely sighted Mr Begum. The garden was the reason why he was rarely sighted. Whenever he wasn't at work he was in that garden, attempting to make something, anything grow. But the garden was small, overshadowed by a sticky leafed tree, and filled, because they lived on a corner, with the detritus that everyone threw over the fence. Nappies, old toys, cigarette butts, road-signs, even sofas. All the rubbish, and there is so much of it, of modern life.

"Someone threw a bag of dog-shit over our fence yesterday evening," said Mark utterly deadpan, dragging his fingers through his hair, "Not for any reason, you get me, just because they couldn't find, or couldn't be fucked to find a bin. That's what my father's doing out there. He's picking up shit. Someone should get one of those journalists down here to photograph the shit. I'll give a little speech. Everybody around here is free, right? Freedom of speech, freedom of assembly, and all of that crap, and freedom to throw shit on my father's land."

I saw Mr Begum's pink marigold gloves, and the black bag in his hand, and like Mark, all of a sudden I couldn't take my eyes off them.

"You know my father's a land owner."

I looked at the ten feet by six scrap of grey-green.

"That out there was four acres of farmland, under a hot sun, worked on everyday by the servants with their oxen, who are paid well, and they eat from it as well, and it's beautiful man…it's fucking *beautiful* – and then some bastard went and threw shit in it and now it's a little piece of shit the council taxes us for and which you can't grow shit on. He was, I should of said he was, a land owner. Then someone threw shit on him."

He put his palms on the window and the heat from them sent up ghost smoke around the fingers.

"What does your father do Pembrose? Because mine, mine's a waiter. Fifteen years."

"I think your mother hopes you and Magid will have more opportunities."
I said weakly.

" It's not enough…," he said quietly. "It's not enough. Someone's got to pay
it back. It's not negotiable. It's too big. It's enormous. It's been going on too
long."

A few more journalists passed by Mr Begum and into the house, trying to
avoid the wet mud.

"Take a good fucking look, Pembrose, take a good look because something
is fucked-up here, you get me? We've got Radio India, we've got Mr Patel goes
to Market, we've got Zeinab Badawi, we always win the cricket and even Rosie
the fucking clown is Pakistani, and now, thanks to my little brother we've got
a hall to drink coffee in, but why the *fuck* is my father still picking up shit?"

You tread carefully in such conversations because lack of knowledge makes
the ground dangerous. You step into landmines. You circle around other
people's experience because you can't know it and the ice is thin. You get wet.
You don't dance with the devil in case you tread on his toes. You don't know
what it's like down there.

"You have no *idea* what this is like," he said.

These are the forms and those were the moments, when after so many
years of being certain, sure of where I stood on English ground, I felt like a
stranger. But it was momentary. This is my only story: it's just of a moment
when I didn't know what and I wasn't sure where and I needed a Guru.

● ● ● ● ●

The official opening of the Asian Women's Centre was an enjoyable affair
though the building was painted a bright orange that nobody could understand.
It was the kind of thing where you say a "good time was had by all", meaning
all the people who had the good time made all the noise. Alsana and Alison
wore matching red saris, and Alison insisted on wearing a fake bindi spot on her
forehead much to my excruciating embarrassment. Magid and I both wore all
white, and were told we looked like a bad cabaret act more than once.

The main room was awash with colour, decorations, tablecloths, (I will not
even attempt to describe the food), music, some hesitant dancing. Mrs Shastri
asked Mrs Begum to try her potato and aubergine aloo. Mrs Begum compli-
mented it, though maybe the aubergine were not entirely fresh, and insisted that
she should try her sweets that were entirely fresh with no desiccated coconut she
could be assured.

Nobody drank, but everybody celebrated and towards the end of the
evening Alison pushed me into a corner, kissed me, and told me how happy she
was that we lived here and how 'colourful' it was after those little, grey univer-
sity towns.

And Magid spoke once more, very briefly, and this time in English; but
they were dull words, and straight-jacketed, written for him by the council.
And he struggled over the words and they sat uncomfortably on his tongue just

like a ten-year-old, and everyone was a little confused and disappointed but put it down to nerves and the officialness of the occasion.

Everyone was waiting for the guru.

After the speech Magid came over to me.

"I let them down," he said.

"You were fine."

"But it wasn't enough."

"How could it be?"

"But 'it' is."

I knew this one well enough by now.

"'it' exists, yes – in that it's built, it's 'be-ing", 'it' is here." I put his little hand against the wall to feel it.

"So that should be enough?" he asked. It was the second question he'd ever asked me.

"It's what they wanted." I said.

That's all I can remember for the moment and about all than can be re-told effectively. I cannot tell the bits I do not know. It was much, much later that night that we heard about the smashed windows, and I wasn't alone at about 2am on Gladstone Hill , when we heard about a "gang of youths", when you could still see the burning because the light from it was as orange as a street lamp, and that was the last night I saw the Begums all together because when Mark finally came home at four am, and left his cricket bat by the door calm as anything, the house closed ranks once again, and it didn't really ever re-open.

Communication breakdown.

I met Magid again. I taught him years later in his secondary school at A level when he was preparing for University. Like most prodigies (if he ever was one and I am far from sure of that) he had slowed down considerably, and was just a very bright kid, but it no longer looked out of place now he was five feet ten. He still always looked for the reasonable solution, even though it was a tough school, and he got his fair share of punches. He had changed his name to Matthew; Matt, everyone called him. We were affectionate with each other, but I don't think we knew why. I wonder how much he remembered. The sum of our mutual experience – it was so small. His work was always neatly presented, I wrote him a very good reference. I think he became a lawyer.

205

The Faculty of Divinity
J M Tyree

This hand is not a miracle,
          says the Very Reverend Rowan –
                    musing, gowned, in the faculty

of Divinity. Nor is your trembling at the sound
          of your lover's voice – nor this patch of sky
                    we are allowed to see. Or the peace

of warming winds that sunlight weaves
          within the light-tongued leaves. If
                    leisure and the season of your pace

grace you with the sight, a leaf may
          topple in the turning flow of falling air,
                    and if the sun conjoins its creases to

your drifting thoughts, you may sense
          how the seed is sown in just this now
                    for you – you become aware of delicate

embroideries of light, soundless tapestries of wind
          bursting audibly into the flame of red-veined leaves,
                    the endless webs of interfused visions which

form the fabric of these days – But this is not miraculous –
          unless the more miraculous, your being unaware
                    of how it was arranged – I say arranged because

I know no other way to speak. For you become aware
          of such a fruitful, branching chaos cured
                    of any need to say –

                Who caused it?

Plain Useless
Kit Whitfield

When she was sixteen, my mother saw a freak show for the first time. She wandered the dust paths in sandalled feet with toenails painted Cardinal Red, gazing at the coloured bulbs, a few of them broken, the squashy-faced clowns and sharp-nosed jugglers, and flames and coloured scarves and pipe-organ music were in the air all around her. Then she found the freak tent, striped green and yellow, sagging under the guy ropes. She liked green and yellow, so she lifted the flap and stepped into the darkness. Her feet made a little rustle on the sawdust, and the smell of it mingled with old cigar-smoke and sweat; she breathed it in. Eyes wide, one hand playing with the end of her long yellow braid, she tiptoed from spotlight to spotlight.

The first sign declared, 'The World's Tiniest Man and Woman'. They stood, faces and bodies together, turning in a slow, stiff-backed waltz; it reminded her of her musical box at home, with a ballerina in it turning on a pivot while the little engine picked out music. There was a dip in the sawdust under their turning feet, and no footprints around it. She imagined them standing there, turning all evening. After a while, her eye was drawn to the next spotlight, where the 'Strongest Man In The World' stood, smothered in shifting muscles as he lifted his bar bell. His leopard-spotted loincloth left his chest and legs bare; they were shaven as smooth as her own.

The she stepped nine steps to another spotlight, past the formaldehyde jar containing the 'Six-Legged Spider Frog', and saw the contortionist. That was it for her. She stood alone in the tent and watched him for two hours without ever sitting down. People came and went, sometimes clustering around her to watch him, and, if she held her breath long enough, wandering on to look at something else. She stood, her braid in her mouth, and watched the thin young man winding his limbs around each other as if they were paper. After an hour, he walked over to the piano in the corner of the spotlight with a pace as upright and light as a marionette, and laid himself on the stool, chest down, bending his legs over his shoulders so he could play with both hands and feet. He played a funeral march which she half recognised, but with a chiming dissonance she couldn't place, until she looked and saw that each playing limb had six fingers or toes. Her hair in her mouth tasted faintly of bitter shampoo, and her lips had never felt warmer.

After two hours, a midget brought him a battered thermos and he sat down in the sawdust, his legs folded up to his chest like a spider, sipping. Then he looked up at her and held out the cup. As he smiled, lines wrinkled around his eyes, lines twistier than his whole body could create, and she walked forward on buckling legs to take the cup. His voice when he started talking to her was clear and soft, and her own took on an intonation that she didn't recognise. She sipped the cup, a mixture of tea and some burning spirit, which almost made her gag but also set wings fluttering in her head that her few swigs of cheap whisky on too-loud Friday nights had never touched. He didn't laugh at her as she choked. They talked without suspicion, and when he reached out and touched her cheek with his six-fingered hand, she dropped the cup, and hot tea and gin soaked into the sawdust.

Later that evening, she knocked at the caravan of the circus owner and asked for a job.

"Can you juggle?"

"No."

"Lift heavy equipment?"

"No."

"Clown?"

"No."

"Dance?"

"Well, not really."

"Trapeze? Tame animals? Work a carousel?"

"No."

"Any deformities, can you pass as a freak?"

"No."

"Go on home to your mother, girlie," he said, and shut the door. She banged on it, and his hoarse voice roared from within, "Be off with you, before I put you out!" She heard a soft mutter within; it sounded like the word "useless".

Tears in her eyes blurring the bright lights, she stumbled away. She went to hide in the first marquee she came to, and ducked inside, to find herself in the clown tent. She sat huddled on the floor, shrinking down at every roar of laughter. As the clowns slapped each other, she thought about going home, going back to church and embroidery on Sunday, to rows of clean desks at schools, to rides in parents' cars with boys who thought getting drunk an achievement. She huddled lower, and bit hard on her fingernails to keep from sobbing out loud. The clowns were playing tricks on one another now. The one who had sat down on a custard pie whipped a pen out of his pocket, and squirted it into the face of the other. The inked clown shook his head and rubbed his eyes, smearing blue all over his face and hands. My mother watched and somewhere in her head, an idea came that made her shiver, and she slipped out of the tent and made for the road, skipping all the way.

The second car that passed noticed her shiny hair and outstretched thumb. The driver talked a lot about pretty hair and pretty skin and how he'd love to properly christen his car, but she stared out of the window all the way, and when they got into town, she opened the door and hopped out with a "Thank you", which was as much conversation as he had out of her.

The tattooist's was still open. She'd stared at it before with her girlfriends, all of them covering their mouths and giggling, but the windows were full of posters showing the pictures you could get on your body, and beyond them, closed Venetian blinds, so she'd never seen the inside. Now she pushed open the door, which had a bell at the top which jingled like a jeweller's, and tiptoed in.

There were a few easy chairs, all empty, and a counter, behind which a man with half-moon glasses and grey stubble came out of a back room. "What can I do for you, Missy?" he asked.

She emptied her purse on the counter, containing all the money she had. "What will you do on me for this?"

"Well, that'll buy you a pretty little something. Here, have a look at these, see what you like." He took out a thick book like a photograph album, with pictures of hearts and roses and butterflies, none of them bigger than two inches across.

"Is that all?"

"How much were you thinking of?"

"All of me."

"Excuse me?"

"I want to be tattooed all over me."

"On that pretty skin? Are you sure?"

She nodded. "I'll pay you, I promise. Only I'd have to pay you in instell – instalments. I'd give you my address and everything."

His eyes took in her white summer blouse and gingham skirt and ankle bracelet. "I don't know, Missy."

"I'll pay you double." He sighed and frowned. "Triple. I'll pay you triple. With interest, you can name it. Here, look, this is my address, the Gerry Capaldi Travelling Circus. I'll post you money every month, I promise."

"You got any proof you're from there?"

She felt in her pockets and took out a flier, the same one that had brought her to the circus and the coloured lights and the tea and gin soaking into the sawdust. On the back were the next few months' worth of venues, which the contortionist had scribbled down. "Please?"

He looked at her a moment, then gave a little laugh. "You're under age aren't you? Don't answer that one, I don't want to know. Triple, you say?"

"I promise."

"Well, business is slow tonight. You come on in, Missy, we'll fix you up."

It took several sessions to cover her, months. In the days between, she swept and cleaned and cooked, and slept in one of the easy chairs in the waiting room, and sat tapping her feet in his office, looking at the calendar. She sent a postcard to her parents to tell them that she had not been kidnapped but would not be coming home for some time, and a long letter to the contortionist with a return address.

The needle buzzed and stung, tracing slow patterns into the night. My mother lay on the couch with shut teeth, and thought of swarms of bees and scratching cats' claws, and sawdust, and twelve supple fingers. She made a resolution not to look at herself until it was done; so when he was working on her, in between other clients, she lay there, gritting her teeth to stop herself twitching with impatience. Time went by slowly under the needle, but more and more patterns were burned into her. She came to know the room very well: the ceiling cracks got fixed in her memory from hours of lying on her back, staring hard to keep herself from flinching, the red, scuffed linoleum she learned by heart while he did her back. The dark corners were her favourite; when she stared at them, the shadows seemed soft and welcoming, something else to think about. The room smelled of antiseptic cleaning fluid from when she had got sick, the first session. She never complained, but only pressed him to keep going. They didn't talk during the sessions; he leaned over her and focused on one inch of fair, fine-grained skin at a time; stretching it with one hand as she bit her lips and clenched her fists, and repeated in her head the phrases from the letters the contortionist sent her.

The final session was completed in the small hours at the end of a long day. There was a little window, high up in the corner of the room, and grey light was seeping through it before he finally set down his needles. He rubbed his eyes; the room was cold in the early morning. "You can look at yourself now. It's finished," he said, his fingers pinching the bridge of his nose, and jerked his head towards a mirror.

She slid off the couch. She was naked in the cold dawn. Her chest, the last area he'd done, was stinging like frostbite and seeping blood along the faultlines, and she clutched her arms round herself, wishing he'd turn away. But once she saw herself in the mirror, she thought she'd never feel naked again. From neck to ankles, there was no more bare pale skin but a burst of flowers – irises, roses, daisies, speedwell – with snakes entwining in their stems beside butterflies and watching eyes. It was crudely done, of course – she'd hurried him to finish so much that he'd left gaps between the flowers and given few details; she looked like a child's drawing, but she was covered and bold and colourful, and the simple designs pleased her eyes. Her hands and feet were bare of colour; at each ankle and wrist was a bracelet of interlocking ivy leaves, with a choker of the same pattern around the neck. Her eyes had hollows under them; the skin on her face was dull and her hair was limp, but a sprig of ivy twined up her neck with a spray of roses that blossomed on her cheek and dimpled into three dimensions when she smiled. She was smiling now, and her lips were still pink, and she rose on tiptoes and spun around on her bare feet, laughing. Her chest hurt with the movement, but she kept spinning, light-heeled, and couldn't stop.

"One last touch, Missy," said the old man's voice, making her jump. She stopped twirling; the world wheeled for a moment and she sat down on the couch with a bump. The room was still spinning as he took hold of her left ear-lobe, and buzzed on a pattern. Then he passed her a small hand mirror, and she turned her head to one side to see.

210

"A gold coin," she said, smiling.

"That's a reminder for you. Here's what you owe me," he said, and wrote down some numbers on a piece of paper. She swallowed when she read it, and looked up at him. "You pay me every month now, you understand?"

"I'll pay you," she said.

"Right, now, let's get you bandaged." He wrapped her chest in white, leaving her thick and stiff-armed like a corpse. "You remember the drill. Leave those bandages on for twenty-four hours and keep dry till the scab comes off, then you can do what you like." She nodded; it was hard to breathe with her chest wrapped so tightly. He taped a bandage over her ear, anchoring it on her unpainted cheek. "That's all. Now off you go."

Blinking with tiredness and feeling sick, she walked out of the shop. The lift she hitched back made no comments about her pretty hair, but saw the bandages and kept a respectful silence. As she watched him, she breathed deeply and her sickness began to fade. She smiled, wrinkling the dressing on her cheek.

She slept all day at a friend's house. The friend cried when she said she was running away, and scolded her over the tattoos, but she lent her her bed. My mother stayed in bed for the day, hiding under the covers and imagining the ink soaking deeper and deeper into her flesh, the flowers taking root under the scabs. On the twenty-fifth hour she rose, peeled off the bandages and slipped her short-sleeved blouse and knee-length skirt over her new multi-coloured body. She took out her earrings and left them with the ankle bracelet for her friend; she didn't need them any more. She went home and packed a small case, showed herself to her parents to give them the opportunity to throw her out rather than miss her as a runaway, then hitched a lift. The circus had moved on, but the letters had told her the right venue. It was early morning, and there were few cars on the road, but she got a lift from a woman who cast nearly as many glances at her arms as at the road, and my mother leaned back, awarding herself a penny for every glance. By the time she reached the circus, her fortune was made.

On her way to the manager's caravan, she met the contortionist again – met my father, that is. He ran over to her, smiling, and stopped short when he saw the green arms and legs. "I'm joining you," she told him. He looked at her, a little wide-eyed. His look went up and down her patterned limbs, over the same blouse and skirt she'd worn when they met, a little dirty now, a little worn; over her hands clutching each other, and back to her face. She swallowed, and gave him her best smile. He looked at her an instant more, and then burst out laughing.

"Come on," he said, and took her hand. "Have you asked Gerry for the job yet?" She shook her head. "I'll come with you. I can't wait to see his face."

She stopped, and pulled on his hand to stop him too. "Have I done right? Do you like it?" she said, and tightened her hand on his.

He looked at her watchful face, and touched the flowered cheek. His fingers dabbed at her skin, testing the green and red pattern. She almost flinched

– the memory of the needles was still close – but instead she leaned towards him and turned her face against the curious fingers, and he looked a little surprised to find that her skin was as warm and smooth as when they'd first met. "You look beautiful," he told her. "Now come along, and let's see if Gerry has a heart attack."

Hand-in-hand, they made their way to Gerry Capaldi's caravan. "Gerry!" my father called. Gerry stumped to the door and opened it, his hair half-slicked with gel and half still in juicy black tangles, with a comb in his hand.

"Gerry, this young lady would like a job," my father told him. Gerry gave a grunt, and turned to look at her. She stood in the dust, and slipped off her blouse and lifted her skirt, giving a slow twirl.

He put his comb down. "Weren't you the one here the other night?"

"Will I do now?" she asked.

"Huh. Tattooed lady, eh?"

"A pretty sight," my father put in, cradling a patterned forearm in his hands. Gerry cast him a suspicious look. "Like that, is it? Eh, well. Wait there and I'll get you a contract." The two of them smiled, and caught each other's hands again. "But you'd better marry the girl, you hear? I don't want you making a habit of this." And he shuffled into the depths of his caravan, leaving my parents standing outside, looking at each other in mild shock in the dawn.

I was born about nine months after that – in the first aid tent behind the marquee, with Simon, the circus's resident medic in attendance. The flowers on my mother's stomach stretched as I grew inside her, turning them into species unknown in the Western hemisphere. My earliest memories involve her doing sit-ups on our caravan floor, trying to pull them back out of the Amazon into a temperate zone. "This is a daisy," she'd point, "and this is ivy, and this is a snake lost in the jungle."

"Does she ever get home?"

"No, she doesn't. But she doesn't want to. She likes being lost, she's happier in the jungle."

"What about the eyes, Mummy?"

"Ah, the eyes. They're magic eyes. They make sure that nobody looks at you in a bad way. People can only give you good looks, lucky looks. They keep you safe from bad eyes."

There was no room for a crib, so I slept in a drawer lined with a tea-towel, lying with my feet under my chin like any other bendy baby and sucking my left hand – the one with six fingers, not just five. It was only when I started to walk that they realised I was actually quite stiff, and started to make me lie on the ground while they stretched my legs this way and that to limber me up. My mother thought I should get tattooed down my five-fingered, five-toed right side, and learn to twist my six-digitted left, so we could do a triple act, but that could wait till I was older. It had to wait, actually, since payments on her own tattoos were still far from settled. I was earning my keep by dancing with the midgets and letting Mick the strong-man lift me on his dumb-bell – which I loved, it was as good as the rides Eddie the carousel man, who used to give me toffees behind my mother's back, would let me have. I'd dress in a green and yellow checked clown suit too, and ride on the two-headed goat when we paraded through the towns, and I was trying to learn to juggle, though I was far from good at it. Jackie-of-all-trades, everyone called me, and I've been Jackie ever since.

That brought some money in. My mother insisted that Gerry pay me for my hard work, though I always thought of it as playing, and she'd add my little monthly wage to about half of hers, and post off a cheque to the tattooist. This wasn't much. The circus was never quite on the ropes, but always close to them; Gerry paid insurance fees and site rentals and taxes and things with long names I never took in, so no one got paid a lot. There were points where we had to live off porridge. That's another early memory of mine – my father saying "Porridge again? Why in hell did you agree to pay him triple?"

"I wasn't much of a haggler back then," my mother told him, with the closest to an apologetic face I've ever seen on her, and my father gave a resigned sigh.

"Well, you like porridge, don't you pet?" he said to me, and poked a spoon at my face.

I did. Eddie would always be good for a few toffees, and there was always plenty of porridge to go around; to my mind, this made up a staple diet. "Sweets are bad for your teeth," my mother would tell me when she caught me eating them. "They'll all fall out."

"We could make her hair grey if she did," remarked my father. "No teeth, lines on her face – The World's Smallest Old Woman?"

"I don't want to," I told him. He laughed, and pulled one of my plaits, but my mother sighed. I was seven by then, and still only doing odd-jobs. I was getting too big to ride on goats, and I couldn't balance on Mick's dumbbell, and for all the stretching exercises, I'd never be as supple as my father.

There was an old man from Quebec
Who wrapped both his legs round his neck,
But then he forgot
How to undo the knot,
And now he's an absolute wreck.

That was me. My mother told me limericks, along with fairy stories and tales about lucky eyes, and that one felt like my epitaph. The one time I'd managed to get my feet behind my head, I'd stuck like that, and cried and cried for half an hour before my father could finally unbend me. I'd been trying to juggle since I could walk, but I still dropped balls. The two-headed goat had died, and sat stuffed in the freak tent, and no live replacement could be found for love or money, even if I had been little enough to ride it. Even if there had, animals tended to get stubborn or nervous when I tried to manage them. Six fingers and toes on one side didn't qualify me as a freak, and I was too young to be tattooed. I had no mechanical sense and couldn't remember the simplest lighting or sound procedure. Worst of all, I was afraid of heights. In a circus, I was just plain useless.

It was Gerry, bless him, who finally pointed this out. One morning when I was about eight, he knocked on our caravan door.

"Got your mail," he said, handing a letter to my mother.

"Hello Gerry," I said, looking up from my juggling balls. I'd been on the verge of giving up and going back to picking at my stickers of cats and rainbows on the yellow-glass window by the bed, but seeing that he was watching me I threw them back into the air again. One I caught, just – I had to lean way over and grab at it – one bounced off the wall behind me, and one hit Gerry.

"For God's sake, child!" he roared.

"Sorry, sorry," I whispered, and crawled under the shelf-bed, pulling the blanket down to hide myself.

"Not much of a juggler, is she?" he said to my mother.

"Not much," she said.

"Well, what can she do?"

"Oh, this and that," my father put in.

"Like? Time she started working at one thing if she wants to get good."

"She hasn't quite made her mind up yet," my father said, sitting on the bed above me and feeling under it with one bare foot to find me.

"Don't sit there and lie. She can't do much, can she?"

"She's willing enough."

"She's plain useless. You know I like the girl, but she's got to earn her keep. We can't afford wages to a kid who isn't working."

"Gerry!" said my mother. "She's a good girl. She tries hard."

Gerry grunted. "Try she may do, but she still can't juggle worth a damn."

"Gerry, we need the money," my father said, his voice quiet.

Gerry sighed. "Don't we all." Nobody said anything. "Look, let her start doing odd jobs, tidying up and that. And for God's sake, find something she does well." With that, he left, leaving the door to bang back open behind him. I could hear my mother going over to shut it, and muttering something about fixing the latch.

I whimpered, and my father reached under the bed, located me, dragged me out and set me on his lap. My mother sat down beside him and opened the letter. I cuddled up to him and sniffed, and she passed me a pack of tissues, not taking her eyes off the letter. She glanced through it for a moment more, then gave an angry, hissing sigh and slapped the page with the back of her hand.

"What's up?" my father asked.

"Listen to this. Dear Madam, we deeply regret to inform you of the death of Mr Isaiah Gow. 'We understand that you still have a debt outstanding to him; since this is a business and not a personal debt, there can be no remittal

214

of the same. In future, kindly make out cheques to his successor, Mr Caleb Gow. Thank you for your cooperation, yours sincerely.' Oh, I wish they'd let up."

"How much longer is it going to take us to pay it off?" my father asked over the top of my head.

"At this rate, years. It's down to a couple of thousand, but we just don't have it. It could be years."

"God," he sighed, and put me down. He put an arm around her, fingering her left earlobe, the one with the gold coin on it. "Are you sorry?" she asked, not looking at him but into her lap.

"For what?"

"That I did it. That I landed myself on you with this debt."

He brushed a strand of hair off her face. "No. Are you?"

"I – never regretted it. I just feel bad for you sometimes, you and Jackie."

"We'll manage," he said. "And you'll find something you like doing soon, won't you love?" he added to me.

"I'll try," I said.

"Don't worry about it," he told me. "Gerry's bark is worse than his bite, anyway. There's no hurry."

I watched them for a moment, the smooth curve of his back, my mother's green arms. He leaned over and kissed her. The rose on her cheek shifted as her mouth pulled out of line. She drew away and turned to me. "Go and play with Eddie, will you love?" she said. I went out of the caravan and stood in the dust outside. I leaned against the van wall for a while, chewing my sixth fingernail and listening, my eyes welling up again, but it was very quiet.

In the end, I sniffed and went to find Eddie. He was tinkering with the carousel engine when I found him, his grey-and-brown hair in his eyes, his slightly hunched back looking more crooked than usual as he leaned over it. "Hello Eddie," I said.

"Hello you," he said, without looking up.

"Will you give me a ride?"

"Can't, sorry Jackie, the engine's on the blink. Here, have an apple. You sound a bit down."

"Thank you," I said, taking the apple; fruit was a rare treat in my family. The apple was a big green one with a sharp juicy inside; I sank my teeth in.

"Damn," he muttered; a little bit of metal flicked out of his fingers. I picked it up and handed it to him. "Thanks."

"'S'all right."

"You're a bit quiet today. What's wrong?"

I gripped the apple with both hands; drops of juice gleamed at the bitten edges. "Gerry says I'm useless."

"Good old Gerry, never was very tactful. And why are you so useless?"

"I can't do anything."

"Like what?"

215

"Tricks and stuff. Mummy can't either, but she's got tattoos, and I'm too young. And I can't do any of the stuff Dad can…" I drowned my sorrows in another mouthful of apple.

"Doesn't make you useless. You can always use a pretty face. Let's see, what can you do? Pass the spanner, will you?"

I passed it. "Nothing really."

"Well, you could be a ringmaster, they don't do tricks."

"I'm a girl."

"So?"

"Anyway, my voice isn't loud enough."

"An usher, front-of-house stuff?"

"Gerry says you have to be able to juggle to do that."

"Oh dear. I know, what about a disembodied head?"

"What?"

"Easiest thing in the world. You build a box, with three sides and glass at the front, paint the sides, and put two mirrors in. One of them goes down the side, the other's at forty-five degrees to it – like that –" he sketched a V in the air – "so they reflect each other and it looks like an empty box. Then you stand behind the back one and they can't see your body, it looks like a head by itself. You just stand there and look like a head. It could go in the sideshow." Eddie grinned. "How about that?"

"We don't have a box," I said in a little voice.

"Then we make one, Miss Doom. Shouldn't cost too much, just mirrors and wood, and there's always paint kicking around here somewhere. How's that sound?"

"Well…easy." I smiled at him and crossed my fingers for luck. It sounded good, but also like the kind of thing I could still be fired from and replaced, not something that was part of me. Still, it was better than nothing, enough to cheer me up.

"That should do it," said Eddie, nodding at the engine. "I'll test it this afternoon. Let's go suggest it to Gerry, shall we?"

Gerry liked the idea – that is, he gave a nod and said "Guess it might work." My mother came looking for me while we were sitting by the carousel, Eddie sketching plans of how the box should work, and we explained the idea. "Eddie, you're a genius," she said, and kissed the top of his head. "You like the idea, Jackie?"

"Yes Mummy."

"Think, you'll be just a head. It'll be like my lucky eyes, you can be a lucky head." I smiled, and traced a flower on her leg.

By the time we moved on again, the box was finished. Eddie had built it to flat-pack, and it stowed easily in our great vans. We marched through the new town, handing out leaflets to the sound of the pipe organ. I always loved this part; the chance to see the enormous houses with so many windows and several stories, the people all upright and curious with their little cars like toys, the shiny shop windows and pavements and postboxes, fantastical towns with everything either too big or too little. I bowed and smiled and handed out leaflets while my father and some others drove the vans and caravans to the site quietly, round the back. Once we got to work putting tents up, I got out of the way, and stayed in our caravan making cups of tea for people and practising faces in my father's shaving mirror, ready to go into the box. I did my homework – imposed by my mother, who was teaching me herself; there was always a stack of books, history, geography, maths, science, in the corner of our caravan. I always did my homework quickly – it was boringly easy. I had it long finished, and was beginning to be bored, when my father came into the caravan and said, "Come on Jackie, let's get you made up."

I giggled, and he tossed me a box of foundation. I tried to catch it one-handed, missed it and laughed again. I picked it up and layered on thick, pale smudges, covering my face. My father tilted my chin up and applied other touches – lipstick, eye shadow, some little stars at the corners of my eyes to match the ones painted on the box. "That should be enough," he said. "Better not overdo it if they're only going to be looking at your face – you can leave your dungarees on, pet, nobody'll see them." He started to make up his own face. "Now off you go. You're in the green and yellow tent – Eddie's waiting for you to help you with the box."

I skipped out of the caravan. It was a warm afternoon, and I tried not to run – I'd get all sweaty and smear my face – but I still trotted all the way to the tent. Eddie was there, hunched over the box. "There you are," he said. "Right, step inside." He folded mirrors in front of me, then others at an angle to them; they were in three sections, one lot hiding my torso, one hiding my hips and thighs and one hiding my legs. The neck-hole was sanded smooth; I leaned against it. "Now, you can open the box yourself from the inside – you just press here," he explained. "Only don't, not when people are around, or they'll see you've got a body. Okay?"

"Yes," I said, and shuffled my feet, doing a little dance.

"Don't do that, either, they'll hear it. Now I'd better get going, we open any minute. Good luck."

"You too." I called as he hurried out. I hummed a little tune to myself, waiting. Mick the strong man was in the next spotlight, I saw. "Are you ready, Mick?" I called.

"Yeah," he said, glancing to and fro. "Don't talk to me, though, kiddo, it looks bad. Just ignore everyone."

I sighed, and stood in the box, leaning back a little. Then I glanced up – some people were wandering into the tent. I smiled a little, and opened my eyes wide, using a baby-face I'd practised earlier. I could hear Mick lifting his bar-bell, and music in the background, but I didn't turn my head. They wandered in front of me, two couples, I saw now. One of the women laughed a little, and said, "How do they do that?"

"Mirrors," her partner told her.

"Cute," she said, and took his hand, pulling him to another spotlight. I bit my lip, and stiffened my feet, trying not to stamp them. Some more people wandered by, glancing at me. Two elderly men stopped in front of me. "They do that with mirrors, you know," the smaller one said to the taller. I smiled and batted my eyes and clenched my teeth.

I stood there for an hour, watching people drift past. Almost everyone who stopped said "They do that with mirrors". My back and legs were numb from standing still for so long, and I had a crick in my neck which stabbed every time I flinched. In a quiet patch when the tent was empty, I started to whimper, soft little squeaks.

Mick noticed. "Take a break, Jack, you must be tired," he said, and waved at Dominic, the lighting man, to cut out my spotlight. I pushed the box open and jumped down, my legs almost folding under me as I landed in the sawdust. I stumbled around the tent, looking for one or other of my parents. I came to my mother first, standing on her pedestal.

"Is it going well?" she asked.

I shook my head. "Everyone who stops just says, they do it with mirrors." I put my littlest finger, the sixth one, into my mouth, and sucked hard.

"That's not so bad, is it?" she said. "After all, everyone knows how I'm tattooed, it doesn't mean they don't like looking at me. It's the same for you." I shook my head again and stamped my foot. My mother glanced up – more people were coming into the tent. "Take a break, Jackie," she said. "Go wander around for a bit, you'd better not talk to me now."

My legs were half-asleep and my feet hurt. I staggered out of the tent. The sun had gone down outside, but it was still light. The sky was faded blue and yellow at the horizon, and even though this site was on grass, the air felt dusty. There was a wind coming up, flapping the tents like sails. The jugglers and fire-eaters were in full swing, the flames fluttering in the wind with a noise like billowing cloth; the clowns were dancing; everyone was plying their trades. A few people glanced at my starred and painted face, but I didn't stop walking. I made straight for Eddie's carousel, and tapped him on the shoulder.

"Eddie, it was no good. Everyone *knew* it was mirrors, they all said so." I could hear the engine of the carousel scraping as I talked.

"A town of cynics. Next one will be better, you'll see."

"No it won't."

"Don't be a misery. Anyway, I'm working, I need to keep an eye on the machine." The scraping got louder, and Eddie looked towards it and frowned. "Do you hear that?"

"Yes," I muttered.

"Doesn't sound good. I'd better shut down after this ride."

"I can crawl under and see if it's wobbling."

"No you can't, Miss – oh God, what now?" There was a squeak from the crowd. Something white blew past me – a lady's hat. The wind tumbled it under the carousel. Eddie grimaced.

"I'll get it!" I shouted, and dived after it.

"Jackie come back, the engine's on!"

"Don't shout at me," I called back, crawling after the hat. The draught kept moving it along, and I wasn't quite quick enough to catch it.

"Jackie, it's not safe, get out of there!"

"I can *do* it! I can *do* it!" I yelled. The engine was right beside me; I could feel the heat as I stretched for the hat. I could almost reach it.

Then the world exploded from the knees down. Machinery ground and scraped and there was a flurry of cries overhead, and I lay pinned, my fingers plucking at the grass, screaming. I struggled and thrashed, but my legs were being torn apart. My throat hurt from screaming, the high shrieks turned into dry, hoarse cries, burning my throat. The engine growled and clattered, grinding me to pieces. I thought I could smell the blood – but later someone told me this wasn't from my legs. I gave myself a bloody nose, beating my head against the ground, again and again and again.

I remember people running and tugging at the metal and my father crawling under the machine and stretching out an arm, gripping my hand until they got me out. I couldn't see, but I could hear his voice, hoarse, saying "It's all right Jackie, it's all right darling," over and over. I remember a flashing blue light and siren, and lying on a hard ambulance cot with a loose sheet, with people flurrying around me. I remember the noise of the siren pulsing in my head and me crying "Daddy make them turn it off," and him saying "They're doing their best Jackie," and me crying again because the noise wouldn't stop. I remember struggling again as someone came towards me to stick a needle in my arm.

I don't remember everything.

I was only eight.

The hospital room was big and white, it was on the third floor, with a bed right in the middle of it that went on wheels but didn't fold away. It was such a waste of space. It smelled clean and like disinfectant, and the nice doctor held both my hands in his when he explained why they'd had to cut off both my legs. My parents were there. My father slumped in a chair in the corner, his head down and his shoulders shaking, and I looked away, hot and ashamed - he shouldn't ever cry in front of me. My mother sat straight-backed, her hands clenched in her lap, giving me a tight, dry-eyed smile. I lay there, and when the nice doctor asked me if there was anything I'd like I asked for a biro. He brought me paper too, but I didn't touch it. I lay in bed, tracing on my arm a row of lucky eyes.

"Lucky we're insured," Gerry told my parents. "Thank God I paid it this year. I was starting to think it was a waste of money."

"It may take a year or two," the lawyer explained, "to settle the damages. You should be prepared for that, but I think we can handle it with minimum distress to the child. Since we understand you are in some financial difficulties, Mr Capaldi has agreed to advance you a sum against future damages – I think that would be useful?"

"Very," my mother told them.

She made out two cheques right away. One was to the company that sold wheelchairs, for a chair that would fold up small and fit easily into a caravan. The other was to the tattooist, Caleb Gow. The money lifted us clear out of debt, and porridge began to be less frequent. She made me lift weights and practise getting myself out of the chair. Between us, my father and I figured out ways to pull myself on my hands, and my mother made me practise them. Without my stiff, heavy legs, my body became easier to swing about. After a while, I could even get up steps using only my hands.

Sometimes at night I woke up, crying, both hands clutching for where my legs used to be and only grasping sheets. In court, I put on a brave smile and stuck up for Eddie. The carousel is scrap metal now, and Eddie works on lighting, but people felt sorry for me and the insurance realised this and paid without a murmur. When I asked her to, my mother took a little of the money and went to a tattooist, a different one, a young man with clean red hair and a chipped front tooth, and an art school diploma on his wall.

She hadn't said much about the idea, except that it should really be my money, but I told her things wouldn't be tidy until she had this done, and she didn't ask me what I meant. He sketched pictures in a notebook until they found a design they both liked, a new picture to cover up the gold coin on her ear. I sat in my wheelchair in the clean, bright room and watched her bite her lips and rub her fists together and refuse to hold the hand I offered her, as the new picture took shape. A delicate picture, with clear lines and pretty colours and different shades and highlights. Another flower – this one with star-shaped petals.

This is my mother's story, and mine. It could be different. I sometimes think of how different it could be, with less blood and more flowers, and fewer eyes. I could have run away and joined the hospital, or studied for law or insurance. But I'm not running anywhere now. I'm staying in the circus. My mother came here for the first time when she was sixteen, close to how old I am now, and that's all. I'm staying. It's useless to look any further.

You'll see me any evening in the circus. I am in my mirror-box, a smiling blonde head. People stop to look at my pretty face. I keep my eyes wide open and stare at them; I only blink when they look away. This makes them uncomfortable. They shift and fidget, and usually they whisper - "They do it with mirrors." And when they do, I unlatch the lower section they think is hiding my legs with all eleven fingers, and it swings open as if by magic.

And I watch their faces change.

220

The Descent of Dr Campbell

Laura James

Pick a theologian, any theologian.

If, at 3.05pm on Wednesday the 8th of October, 1997, you had asked your chosen scholar to name the world's greatest living expert on comparative religion, he or she would not have hesitated.

"Anthony Campbell!" the unanimous acclamation would have rung out. "MA, DPhil, Fellow of Magdalen College, Oxford. Author of such learned tomes as *The Twain Shall Meet: Links Between Eastern and Western Beliefs, Apollo Conquers Dionysius: The Religious Legacy of Ancient Greece* and *Some Comments on the Ritual Archetypes of Native American Tribes.* That's the man!"

Nevertheless, your informant would have been mistaken.

Since 3.02pm that same afternoon, Dr Campbell had been the world's greatest *dead* expert on comparative religion.

He had just performed an elegant swallow-dive from the top of Magdalen Tower.

At three o'clock, Campbell stood poised on the carved parapet, swaying gently in the breeze. He heard the hour strike beneath him, and gazed for the last time on the world he was leaving behind. Out of habit, he had carefully wrapped his glasses in a handkerchief and placed them in his pocket before ascending, so that all he could see was a blur of russet and gold, green and grey. It reminded him vaguely of a piece of Modern Art he had seen on his last visit to the Tate. He couldn't remember the name of the painter.

Not without grace, he launched himself into the soft air and fell.

The sixty-year-old don was not in a state of spiritual despair. He was certainly not high, except in the literal sense. He had not even had his head turned by an excess of religion and decided that the prophecy "He shall give his angels charge concerning thee: and in their hands they shall bear thee up, lest at any time thou dash thy foot against a stone" applied to him personally. If we must seek out some deep psychological explanation for his suicide – and he himself would not have acknowledged that any such existed – it would perhaps be most accurate to say that he was a thwarted scientist.

Dr Campbell knew what the various Christian sects thought happened after death. He was intimately acquainted with the Muslim Paradise. He understood the principles and practice of reincarnation, even unto the precise gradations of birds and beasts. The Elysian Fields could hold no mysteries for him, nor

Hades, nor the various realms of ancestor spirits. He was also well aware how many people believed in total extinction, and why.

He knew more than any other of those who study the beliefs of their fellow men, and enough for all of them put together. But, for A A Campbell, it was *not* enough. With a fiercely burning academic passion, he wanted to answer the final question. He had neatly framed the various hypotheses which the human race had come up with over so many millennia. Now it only remained to test them. With scientific scrupulousness, he believed none, considered – or tried to consider – all.

He might be snuffed out like a candle flame. He might be reborn. (He had calculated that he was probably worthy of a small chimpanzee or marmoset.) He might be forced to inhabit any one of hundreds of ghostly half-existences or uncomfortable Hells. Browning's

"Twenty-nine distinct damnations,
One sure if another fails"

were as nothing when compared to *his* prospects. For that, of course, was the one certainty. Salvation was not an option. To believe fervently in any one particular hypothesis might prejudice the experiment. He was in a state of perfect agnosticism, worthy of the scientist he might have been.

Or almost perfect.

There was once a very obscure tribe of American Indians with an anthropologically fascinating theory about the afterlife. They believed that only a few fortunates would be saved. The elect were to be that happy band of men and women who had been marked out as divine by their possession of the ability to waggle their ears.

It was their great tragedy that, over the last few centuries, no recorded member of the tribe had ever inherited or acquired such an enviable skill. Dr Campbell's account of their desperate attempts at ear exercise, as old age hastened on, and death drew near, was one of the most moving and admired passages of his *Comments.*

By a strange coincidence, Campbell's own ears were agile in this special way. Thus, his conviction that salvation was not for him shows that one religion, at least, he had rejected outright. We should not lay too much emphasis upon this single flaw in an otherwise blameless researcher. It was, after all, a remarkably silly idea.

It would be tasteless to dwell upon this great man's inevitable and untidy conjunction with the pavement.

The soul of Anthony Ambrose Campbell opened its eyes, noting automatically that it appeared to have retained them. Noticing its noting, it noted that it still had its notebook and trusty old yellow fieldwork pencil. A spot of introspection informed it that, so far as it could tell, its identity appeared to be in place as well. These fundamentals having been established, Dr Campbell unwrapped his spectacles, polished them up, hooked them on, and looked about him with stern interest.

He was standing amid tall, golden grass. It rippled as breezes ran through it, stretching – he turned around and checked carefully – as far as the eye could see in all directions. This was not, admittedly, very far, as the grass was about six feet high, and Campbell had not been an imposing man. The sky was deep blue and cloudless; the sun, although bright, was not excessively hot.

The professor sat down cross-legged and recorded all these details. Then he thought about them. It was something of a blow not to have been transported directly to whoever was in charge, but it seemed to be received wisdom that some authoritative figure would turn up eventually. Had he been reincarnated, it was hardly likely that he would have retained his old brown suit. Unless something nasty was waiting around the corner, this was none of the seventy-two hells he had catalogued so exhaustively.

Dr Campbell allowed himself a small, satisfied smile. Insofar as he had been unable to avoid a preference, it had certainly been for some kind of neutral territory. Eternal torture sounded painfully monotonous. Indeed, when he considered what might have been, he felt rather sprightly. He parted the grasses ahead of him with enthusiasm, and trotted away to find out what was happening.

For a long time, nothing appeared to be happening. For a *subjectively* long time, he corrected himself. It was a little early to be drawing conclusions about the temporal aspects of eternity, so long the subject of such fierce academic controversy. (He had contributed his own mite to the debate in his day.) The sun was motionless. He was not hungry or tired, and had a suspicion that he could never be either again. Then he heard a voice. It was a deep, rolling, masculine voice.

"*Hearts*," it said, in tones no man would dare contradict.

The sound had come from straight ahead, and Campbell pressed on, seized by scholarly excitement. Was he about to meet God?

If so, God had an Australian accent.

"Are you a blind dog?" it demanded.

Campbell, wondering vaguely whether it was Judgement Day, and what he was supposed to reply, scribbled the words down in his notebook and hurried even faster. He thrust aside a final handful of grass and found himself in a small clearing. Three men and one woman, who had been sitting on the ground in a tight circle, turned around to stare at him. He stopped, panting and trying to catch his breath.

The woman rose. She was wearing a long purple tunic, Grecian in style, and her rather brassy golden hair was piled atop her head. (Surely *not* the Elysian Fields, he thought.) Her face and figure were middle-aged, but attractive.

"Do you play whist?" she enquired.

A man who has been a university lecturer for thirty years is used to answering difficult questions on his feet. But, on this occasion, Campbell was quite unable to speak. He goggled. The three men were also standing now, and he could see a number of ancient playing cards scattered on the ground behind them. The youngest spoke, but not to him. He had long blond hair, sulky eyes, an elegant short tunic and reminded the don of a particularly recalcitrant student.

"For the gods' sakes, Helen!" he snapped. "No more whist!"

She gave him a cold glance, and the greying man in bronze armour scowled. "You talk too much, Paris. You always did. Can *you* think of anything else to do?"

The lad looked mutinous, and the fourth member of the party stepped forward quickly. He was a mild, elderly man wearing a sparse tonsure, a baggy black habit, and over-large sandals. His was the voice which bore such a remarkable resemblance to that of God. Except, of course, Campbell hoped, for the Australian accent.

"Now Paris, Menelaus," he said soothingly, patting each of them on the head. "Let's remember what we agreed about forgiving each other's trespasses."

There was a fraught pause, and the distracted professor suddenly found his voice. "Excuse me, madam," he addressed the lady, with a dated little bow, "but are you, by any chance, Helen of Troy?"

This turned out to be an unfortunate *faux pas*. The warrior rounded upon him viciously. "Sparta!" he hissed.

"Troy," muttered the young man, although without much conviction.

The woman looked supremely uninterested, and the monk sighed. "Why don't we say, Helen of the Aegean?" he suggested patiently. "Or would it be the Adriatic? I always mix them up."

Campbell was spluttering by now. "Then we *are* in the Elysian Fields?" he demanded.

"Oh no," said the monk. "I don't think so." He beckoned the don over to the far side of the clearing, while the other three sat down again. Menelaus shuffled the deck. "I'm afraid poor Paris wouldn't really qualify for Elysium," he whispered. "He's not exactly a hero, you see. Nor am I, of course."

"But this *is* the afterlife?" Campbell tried.

The monk looked perplexed. "Well, we're certainly all dead," he admitted. "But I wouldn't like to think that this was all there is. The Scripture clearly states –"

The professor's researcher's soul took over. He waved his pencil authoritatively. "May I have your name, please?"

"Brother Francis," said the monk.

"Now, Brother Francis, I want you to tell me, in your own words, precisely who you are, how you got here, and what you have experienced since your arrival."

A medium-size chunk of subjective time later, Dr Campbell sat down and flicked through his notebook. He had discovered the following facts:

1) There were a number of individuals and groups settled here and there in the grass, whiling away the time as best they could.
2) The monk could think of no common factor linking them.
3) The plain appeared to go on forever.
4) The environment remained constant, including position of sun, colour of grass, etc.
5) A resident arrived with everything he had been wearing at the moment of his death. (Paris claimed not to be able to remember where he had left his armour. Brother Francis had suffered a heart attack from the shock of finding a deck of playing cards in a fellow monk's cell in his small but strict religious community in Canberra in 1907, and inadvertently brought them with him.)

Campbell had known so much about so many things for so long that he found it oddly refreshing to rediscover the sensation of complete ignorance. He had no idea what to conclude from all of this. There were some interestingly primitive features...

A shadow covered his notes, and he looked up. The monk was standing over him, looking diffident.

"Well, well, what is it?" he asked, testily.

"I'm very sorry to disturb you," apologised Brother Francis, "but I wondered whether – that is, we wondered whether you knew – you see, I was 17 when I found my vocation, and I never approved of gambling – that is –"

"*What* is?" demanded Campbell, not, he felt, unreasonably.

"Do you know any card games?"

It was when Helen won the fifty-third game of *vingt-et-un* that the doctor decided it was time to leave.

"After all," he pointed out to Brother Francis, with some severity, "I did *not* commit suicide in that spectacular but intensely painful manner, merely in order to sit around playing cards."

The monk apologised at once for inadvertently giving the impression that it had occurred to him to believe anything of the sort. "What *will* you do?" he enquired humbly, eager to make amends.

"Ahem," Dr Campbell began. "It seems to me that the first priority is to ascertain whether the locality is finite or infinite. Therefore, I intend to walk in a straight line towards the sun, questioning, as a second priority, any indigenous personnel I may encounter."

"How long will you do that for?" asked Brother Francis, in some awe.

"For as long as it takes," the professor returned grimly. His determined expression hinted that the afterlife had jolly well better co-operate if it knew what was good for it.

Paris, who had been lounging in the long grass, stood up abruptly. "I'll come with you," he announced, eyeing the deck of cards with intense malevolence.

No one could think of any reason why he should not, so he did. Brother Francis waved goodbye to them in an amiable fashion, and Helen inclined her head. Menelaus was playing Patience, and pretended not to notice their departure.

The two men walked in silence for some time. Paris had never given the impression of being precisely conversational, and Campbell was writing down everything that had happened so far. When he had finished, he waited in vain for a remark from his companion. Finally, he searched his own repertoire of small talk.

"I've always been particularly interested in the darker manifestations of the cult of the Mother in Ancient Asia Minor – Ilium in particular," he tried, hopefully.

No response.

"How do *you* feel about the theory that the Trojan War was in fact an inevitable clash between earth-worship and sky-worship, with your abduction of Helen a subsequent invention by several poets calling themselves Homer?"

An expression of ineffable scorn crossed the young man's perfect face.

They walked on. Then Campbell had a thought. Anything was possible, he supposed. "Did you *really* meet Aphrodite?"

Paris spat. "The bitch got me killed, and for what?"

The world's foremost expert in comparative religion copied down his words reverently.

After that, the Trojan prince began to unbend enough to produce titbits of information concerning religion in Troy, Bronze Age life in general, and the internal politics of Olympus, about which he appeared to know an amazing amount. Campbell, who was already planning a sensational monograph (provisionally entitled *Homer Got It Right*), tried to reciprocate with a few little *bons mots* on the subject of various members of Magdalen Senior Common Room, but his companion didn't seem very interested.

They passed an Elizabethan gentlewoman and a Masai warrior at a distance, but neither came close enough to say hello, so they trudged on. Paris said that he had met the lady before, that her name was Katherine, and that she amused herself by weaving the grass into golden mats. He rather thought he had lent her his dagger with which to tidy up the edges.

"How kind of you," remarked the professor, feeling called upon to comment.

"That's what Brother Francis said," Paris responded, moodily. Then, suddenly, he stopped. He lifted his head and pricked up his ears, listening.

"They're coming," he said.

"What? Who?" squeaked Campbell, adjusting his glasses. He looked around nervously. Then he heard it: a low, heavy humming that seemed to fill the clear air. It came from somewhere over to the left, but it was getting louder by the moment. The sound became a drumming, then a thunder, and the ground began to shake. The don wondered whether he was finally going to get to meet some supernatural entities.

A herd of buffalo galloped past at full speed, flattening the prairie grass in a broad swathe. Silently, the two men watched the massive animals disappear into the distance.

Campbell was cast down. "Why buffalo?" he asked miserably.

Paris shrugged. "They just turn up occasionally." His ears moved again as he strained to hear the receding roll of the herd's retreat.

Moving ears.

Buffalo.

An endless prairie, for God's sake.

Campbell suddenly realised where he had to be. The plain shattered into pieces around him as he closed his eyes.

When he reopened them, he found himself in a drab, grey corridor. It stretched out endlessly in both directions and a cold wind blew through it. In front of him was a white door, adorned by a neat sign. It said, "Customer Services Department". Dr Campbell's hand twitched to take out his yellow pencil, but, angrily, he stilled it. Turning the brass handle, he walked through the door.

A man bearing a remarkable facial resemblance to the President of the United States was sitting at a small desk, writing. This threw the professor for a fleeting instant. Then he noticed something was missing.

"Where's Paris?" he asked.

The man looked up. He blinked, smiled rather apologetically, then began to leaf through a pile of papers. "I think it was the Elysian Fields," he muttered. "No, here we are. The Isles of the Blest." He put down his pen. "Same place, more or less," he added.

"But he wasn't a hero," said Campbell, blankly.

"I expect *he* thought he was. People often do, I believe. Why do you ask about him?" The man looked around vaguely, then he noticed a little yellow post-it stuck to his filing cabinet. "Ah, yes. Anthony Ambrose Campbell. You met a version of the poor chap in an Amerindian paradise, didn't you?"

Campbell sank down into a chair. "Is that all there is?" he asked pleadingly. "People who can wiggle their ears live forever, on a wide, golden prairie dreamed up by some shaman? No reason, no logic? No God?"

"Oh, there's certainly a God!" said the little man reprovingly, as if Campbell had suggested something in rather bad taste. "You can pop in to see him in a minute, if you like. And it's all most reasonable, I assure you. Every human being lives forever in perfect, eternal bliss." He beamed across the desk.

The professor frowned. "So why, may I ask, did I end up playing poker in North America?"

The Customer Services Manager sat forward eagerly. It was obvious that he had really been looking forward to this question. "You," he said, wagging a stern finger at Campbell, "were a very difficult case. Perfect bliss, you understand, is hardly perfect if one was anticipating something else entirely. The saints of Heaven would be quite upset to find themselves in Valhalla all of a sudden. And vice versa, of course. Most human beings have their own idea of Paradise. (A few people in the Middle Ages insisted on Purgatory, though I tried to keep it as brief as possible.) The atheists I put somewhere congenial on grounds of ignorance, last-minute repentance, that sort of thing. But one could hardly say that *you* were ignorant of religion, could one?" He chuckled.

"You knew about all the possibilities, and you knew that you were ineligible for most of them. The prairie was the best I could manage on such short notice. Plenty of room for research, which was what you really wanted, wasn't it?"

A peculiar thought struck Campbell. "Are you God?" he asked.

The little man blushed. And transformed into a figure at once awesome and inevitably *right*, as the office dissolved away into a starry sky.

"I am, as a matter of fact," He boomed, and His Voice was the voice of an identical twin of Brother Francis, who had happened to train as a BBC newsreader. "Was there anything else you wanted to know?"

The don thought about it. Then he asked, a little proudly, "Am I the first person to – ahem – see through the facade?"

"Yes indeed. Nobody else has ever visualised the afterlife primarily as a research opportunity. You are the first client for whom we have had to set up this particular scenario."

Campbell registered this. And winced. "Are you saying that *all* of my discoveries were planned to suit me?"

"That's right, yes."

"Up to and including this conversation?"

"Of course."

There was a very long silence. Eventually, Dr Campbell sighed. "So what happens now?"

Golden infinity with a wise, white beard smiled at him. "What would you like?"

'A lupine sky'
Robin French

A lupine sky glues herself to the edges of my sightline
A great black tree grasps fingers at its scribbled outline
I balance bellyfirst on the magic carpet of a Motown bassline

In the softly spoken attic at the top of the third staircase
I lie drunk with Green and Gaye, Flack, Womack,
                          Jackson, Brown and Isaac Hayes
I try to roll a joint upon the speaker of the wonderbass

Give up and let my limbs drop in the whispered water of the tide
Just think about a mind, it must be very like a mouth inside
I lap out like a wolfcub at the memory of you by my side

Rocketman

Meg Vandermerwe

(Summer 1969)

Moon walking

My brother is in the back yard doing his impression of the astronauts walking on the moon: "That's one small step for man, one giant leap for mankind." He repeats this over and over: *one small step for man one giant leap for mankind one small step for man one giant leap for mankind.* As he talks he jumps from one foot to the other, slowly slowly. Like he really is walking on the moon. Like he's one of those rocket men on TV, kicking up moon dust and talking to the President from a telephone in outer space. The night they landed my father came home early, and we all watched it live in the living room. Everybody sat still and quiet, even Minnie, and I saw Robin was thinking hard as he leaned forward into the blue flickering light.

the eagle has landed the eagle has landed the eagle has landed I drop my doll and start jumping around with him. There hasn't been any rain all summer and the yellow brown grass pricks my feet. *the eagle has landed the eagle has landed the eagle has landed* Just then the back door opens and my mother comes out. She has been cooking and there are stains on her apron. Robin doesn't notice she's standing there looking at us, until she yells at him to stop. *Robin! Robin, get your sister in here!* Robin stops pretending and turns right around to look at her. *Mission Control we have a problem.*

Cake

Our house is by the highway. Sometimes when I can't sleep I kneel by my bedroom window and count the cars that go driving by: big, shiny trucks going up and down, fathers on their way home after their late shift at work, sweethearts out for a drive. Next door there is a motel with a pool, and in the summer time, when it gets really hot, our mother takes us there. Because today is Robin's birthday she took him and some of the kids from his grade and the neighborhood.

For his birthday, my parents gave Robin a new football. I know he really wanted one of those space ship models they sell at Simmers in town, but my father says it's time Robin started acting like other boys his age. He says that come the Fall he's sending Robin to the George Washington Military Academy. *Fourteen. You're not a baby anymore*

• • • • •

Everybody is back from the pool and hanging around the yard, waiting for the barbecue. My father is by the grill, getting the coals just right. He pokes at them with a stick until sparks leap up like fireflies, and the coals burn red red hot. He isn't wearing his cap and I can see the wetness on the part of his head where his hair is going. He says it is because we kids drive him so crazy that he is losing his hair. I am standing at the table with all the food on it. It's my job to make sure that Minnie doesn't jump up and lick the food the way she does sometimes when we are having dinner in the kitchen; and to give the grown ups plates and knives and forks if they ask. My mother tells me I must smile and act like a lady. She says if I don't learn to be a lady, no man's ever going to want to marry me. I tell her I don't want to get married. But my mother says I will. She is laughing with the other mothers as they set up bottles of soda that hiss when you pop them open. She is wearing her red cotton dress and red lipstick and I watch as she lets out a laugh you can hear from the other side of the yard. When she laughs her lips part wide and her brown hair falls away from her face and she looks very pretty.

I'm waiting for her to notice that Robin's missing. He's been missing since they got back from the pool because he hates parties and being with kids who aren't even his friends. He hasn't got many friends, just me and Ed White. Ed White's a rocket man who died when his space ship blew up, but Robin says Ed still talks to him all the time.

My mother has gone inside to fetch the cake. It is chocolate with white frosting and Robin's name written on it in blue curly letters. When she is out of sight my father comes up next to me and stands close. *Where the hell's your brother. Go and find him before your mother gets back.* Over the fence I can hear the sound of the traffic as it speeds by.

Planetarium

Our father is taking our mother to the hospital to see her aunt who is sick. It is dark outside and Robin says the hospital called to say Aunt G is dying, and that's why they are going out this late. When the car has pulled down and out of the driveway, and we can't see the red of its taillights anymore, we climb up on to the roof of the garage. If it's a clear night Robin likes to sit up there and watch the sky, and sometimes I go with him. We climb up and lie on our backs with the dirt and the dead butterflies and look at the stars shining back at us like a thousand fairy lights strung up across the black. If Robin feels like it he tells me about them. Like how they've all got special names: the Big Dipper, the North Star, the Seven Sisters, the Bear. Or how in the old days sailors read them to find their way back home from the ocean. Robin knows historical stuff like that; he keeps it all in his head like a library. If you ask him he'll explain all about the Russians sending the first satellite into space, and how many dogs died before we managed to get one man on the moon.

Tonight though, all he wants to talk about are his dreams about being a rocket man. How when he grows up he's going to be one of those men at

NASA and ride a rocket deep into space. *What does NASA stand for?* When he gets there he says he's going straight to the moon. Robin's just crazy about the moon, he's got pictures of it all over his bedroom walls which he gets from magazines he buys, and which the planetarium gave him that time he went for his science project. I ask him what he'll do when he gets there and he says he's got big plans. My brother's full of big plans. He tells everybody that he won't have to stay in this crummy town forever because when he gets to the moon he's building a city. A city on the moon. I try to imagine it white and shining. Whenever Robin talks about the moon, I look him straight in the eyes so he knows I'm listening, but my father's different. He says Robin's nuts. He says no fool is ever going to let Robin near his rocket, and even if some fool did, nothing can survive on the moon. Rock and ash that's all it is. *rock and ash rock and ash rock and ash.* Robin doesn't say anything when our father goes stepping on his dreams like that. He stays real quiet and writes in his notebook.

Ball

It's hot and sunny and I'm lying on the deck chair that's lost its cover. I'm wearing my yellow bathing suit and my legs and shoulders have started to tingle and turn pink. My father is in the yard with Robin. He's trying to teach him to play football but Robin isn't very good. I listen to my father's voice as he gives Robin orders: *Come on, not like that, like this.* He pretend catches the ball to show Robin how to jump so he won't miss a high pass. *Got that?* My father asks. Robin doesn't say anything. He just rubs between his fingers, the way he does when he's feeling the butterflies.

When my father throws the ball he makes a little sound and I watch it spin through the air like a brown bullet until it hits Robin hard. Robin catches it but doesn't hold on. The ball slips from his fingers and bounces and rocks along the ground until it hits the fence and stops. *Fuuuummmmble* my father says like he's one of those sports reporters on the radio. Minnie comes over and jumps onto my lap. I put my hand on her soft fur and close my eyes and listen to the sound of kids splashing in the pool next door. They are laughing and screaming and I imagine I am one of them, holding my breath under the clear water. *You're gonna have to learn to play football if you're going to Fort Washington. They don't like pansies.*

· · · · ·

It has cooled. The yard is getting full of shadows and soon the crickets will be out singing their scratchy song. When the hairs on my arms start to stand up, I push Minnie off, and get ready to go inside. With my fingertips I feel the bumps on the back of my legs that match the pattern on the chair. My father is still practicing football with Robin. Robin's face is red with trying and he has hurt his knee. Later, when Robin and my father can't see to play anymore, my father will let Robin go inside too. From my room I will hear the sound of Robin's sneakers coming up the stairs, and then his door softly snapping shut.

Riding

Robin doesn't feel like talking. He's got what my mother calls the 'mean reds', so I leave him alone thinking, and take my bike round to Ruby Glakey's house. Mr Glakey is a truck driver so most of the time he's on the road. My father says that it is probably Mrs Glakey who keeps him driving because she's always crying or hugging people. 'A real piece of work' he calls her. My mother says nobody in the family has been the same since Ruby's brother went missing in Vietnam.

When I get to Ruby's house Mrs Glakey is outside digging up her flowerbeds. She is wearing a dress with orange patterns all over it and a straw hat and no shoes. When I come through the gate she looks up at me "Well, hi there Caroline, what a nice surprise. Come over here and give me a kiss" She puts her arms around me and squeezes so tight I think my heart's going to stop. "Ruby's upstairs. She'll be glad to see you"

Inside I find Ruby in her bedroom dancing to her sister's Chubby Checker records. When she sees me she stops what she's doing and shows me the new stuff her father has sent her from the road. Mr Glakey is always sending Ruby and her sister stuff from the places he's been to. She's got caps and T-shirts and pins and stuffed bears with things like, 'The Big Apple,' and 'The Home of the Sweet Potato' written on them. This time Ruby shows me a T-shirt. It's light green with a big yellow sun on it, and at the bottom its got written: 'California, America's Sunshine State!" in black, cartoon letters. Ruby puts the T-shirt over what she's wearing. It comes right down to her knees and if you look quickly you think she's wearing the T-shirt and nothing else.

Ruby and me decide we'll go watch the cars on the highway so Mrs Glakey makes us sandwiches and puts them in paper bags with some cookies. We take our bikes and go sit on the walkway that runs over the top of the highway, and look at the cars as they drive past underneath. Whilst we are talking Ruby drops bits of chocolate chip onto the cars that zip under. She tells me about how her father says he's coming home for a few days and when he does he's going to take her to the new movie house that's opened up. Then she asks me if I want to come. I say sure and bite into my sandwich. Jelly oozes out of the sides and drops onto my shorts.

After we've watched the cars for a while and made up stories about whose driving them, Ruby stands up and starts to dance. She says she's going to be a famous dancer when she grows up and I tell her how I'm going to make dresses for rich ladies. Then Ruby says: "This is how my sister dances with her boyfriend." She turns her back to me and starts rubbing her hands up and down her sides. She looks like two people kissing and we laugh until our eyes get wet and our stomachs hurt.

Pool

My brother is playing dead. He lets his body float up and just hang in the water, head down, everything real still. Sometimes when our mother takes us to the pool, Robin lets me swim through his legs and make-believe I'm a dolphin, but not today. Today he wants to play dead so I let him. I let him until he doesn't move at all, not even a tiny bit. Until I can't see those bubbles floating up around his head. Until I think he might really be dead. And then I get scared. I get scared and feel the way I did that time I got lost at the grocery store. When I get that feeling I start to kick the water. I kick and kick and kick as hard as I can, until Robin stops playing dead and tells me to quit it.

Dressing Up
My mother likes to dress up. She says she used to get dressed up all the time when she and my father first started dating because he would take her to all kinds of fancy places, even though he couldn't afford it. She says he would do it just to impress her because he thought she was classy and he wanted her to be his girl. She says he took her dancing or to the movies, and they would stay out late and grandpa would get mad. My mother and father never go out together anymore. My father says that he's too busy making ends meet. He says that when Robin and I get into the real world we'll understand what he's talking about. My mother still likes to dress up though. Sometimes if my father isn't coming home until real late, my mother clicks on the radio and gets dressed to go out. First she puts on her face, then her clothes. When she's looking all neat and pretty she takes herself to the movies. She likes the old ones. The ones with singing and dancing and beautiful women with perfect hair, and handsome men who always pull out chairs and open doors. When she's taking herself to the movies she drops Robin and me over at Ruby's, and Mrs Glakey gives us popcorn and lets us stay up as late as we want.

Snake
From my window I see Minnie arching her back at something in the yard so I go down to take a look. Lying there in the sunshine I see it, gold and black. At first I thinks it's a prank snake, like the ones the boys leave in the girls' locker room at school. Then after I've watched it for a long while I see it move. It rubs its belly in the dirt, just a little from side to side like it's getting comfortable. When I've seen it move I run to tell my mother that there's a snake in the yard, and she calls my father at work and tells him to come home right away. I don't think my father gonna come because my mother starts to cry and says she can't just leave a snake in the yard when there's children to think about. When my father's car pulls up I can tell he's mad about having to come home in the day. He takes off his jacket and walks up to the shed at the back of the house without saying a word to me or my mother. He comes out holding the shovel he uses for digging and walks slowly up to the snake. It's still lying in the sunshine where I saw it and it doesn't move even when my father is close enough for his shadow to touch its body. Maybe its dead now I say. No he tells me, its just sleeping. Then he lifts the shovel up high and brings it down, quick on the snake's head. The snake leaps around in the dirt and my father brings the shovel down again

and again until it stops leaping. When my father's sure the snake's dead, he picks it up with the shovel and throws it over the fence into the highway. Later, when my mother has gone inside, and my father is back at work, I go look at the blood patch on the ground. It's the color of crushed black berries and with my foot I kick dirt over it until you can't see it anymore.

Going Away
On the morning Robin is going away, I wake up early and go downstairs in my pajamas to say goodbye. My father is driving him and he says he wants to hit the road before the traffic gets heavy. Robin's got a far away look in his eyes as he stands with his suitcase, waiting for my father to unlock the trunk of the car. He is wearing his new blue and white uniform and his brown hair is cut short. Last night my mother helped him pack up the things he needed, and this morning she made him a baloney sandwich that she put in a bag with a quart of milk so he doesn't get hungry on his first day. She gives it to him as he stands in the driveway. Suddenly my throat gets all achy, like something's got stuck in it, and I start to cry. My mother comes over and puts her arms around me and tells me not to cry because Robin will soon be home for the holidays. She is wearing her robe wrapped tight around her and I put my hand in the pocket. When my father has finished putting Robin's things in the car he says they should go if they are to make it to where they're going by lunchtime. Robin doesn't take a look back as he's driving away, even though I'm waving like crazy.

After I can't see Robin or the car anymore I go to Robin's room. All his pictures are still there and his moon stuff because my father says Robin isn't allowed that kind of junk at his new school. Robin says if I break anything, he'll kick my butt when he comes home, so I don't touch anything. I just take a real good look and then leave, closing the door behind me.

Epilogue: the moon – a rocket man's guide to
The moon is dry and dusty and bare. There is no air to breathe. It is very hot when the sun shines and very cold when it does not. Nothing lives there. Notable physical features include: Aristoteles Arzachel Atlas Autolycus Azoph Bally Ball Barrow Beaumont Bessarion Besel Biot But Blancarius Blanchinus Bond (w c) Bonpland Boscovich Brayley Bulliardus

The Sea of Tranquility: Latitude 0.6875 N
Longitude 23.43 E

Full moon occurs at the instant during the month when the earth is most nearly in line between the sun and the moon. At the instant of a full moon, a man on the moon and at the center of the moon's visible disk, would cast no shadow. In those months when the moon is closely enough in line north and south, an eclipse occurs. In astronomy the word eclipse means the obscuration of light of one celestial body by another. The two most familiar types of eclipse involve the sun, the earth and the moon , but equally well, one component of a double star may eclipse the other if their orbit are properly orientated relative to the earth R D Baldwin The University of Chicago. 1966

Dear Sir I am a boy of twelve years and would like to become a rocket man. How should I go about it? Robin Richards. M I Ohio

NASA or the National Aeronautics and Space Administration has a strict program for selecting its lunar astronauts. The initial measurable qualities demanded of candidates for astronaut training, by NASA's Manned Spacecraft Center in Houston are as follows: he must be a citizen of the United States of America; he must be an experienced test pilot with 1,000 hours in jets, having attained experimental test flights in industry, NASA, or the military; he must be under thirty five years of age; he must be under six feet in height; he must not mind: small spaces, darkness, isolation, the heat, the cold, silence, death.

Travelling time from planet Earth to the lunar surface: approximately 41 hrs. Cost of sending one man to the moon: approximately 4 billion dollars.

Facts: 1958 American government initiates plans to land a manned craft on the moon. April 12, 1962 VOSTOK I Soviet pilot Yuri Gagarin becomes first man to fly in space, orbiting the Earth once at 17,000 mph, 200 miles up, for 89 minutes. June 3–7 1965, GEMINI 4, Jim McDivitt and Edward H White Jr orbit Earth for three days. During orbit Edward White becomes America's first space walker. January 27,1967 APOLLO I, Virgil I Grisson, Roger B Chaffee and Edward H White II killed by fire during routine pre-launch test. July 19, 1969 APOLLO XI 9.32am EDT KSL Florida Complex 39-A Neil Armstrong Michael Collins and Edwin Aldrin Jr lift off for lunar surface. July 20, 1969, 4.18pm EDT Armstrong and Aldrin Jr successfully land spacecraft in Sea of Tranquility. July 21, 1969 1.54 EDT lift off lunar surface for return flight. July 24, 1969 12.50pm EDT crew splashdown in Pacific Ocean. Total duration of space expedition: 8 days, 3hrs 18 minutes. In that time an APOLLO XI astronaut will have: spent 21 hours 36 minutes on lunar surface; collected 15.9 pounds of samples; consumed 91.72 pounds of food; slept 32 hrs; grown 2 inches; prayed twice.

• • • • •

See the rocket it is white it is bright. Come inside, hold on tight 10 9 8 7 6 5 4 3 2 1 Go. The rocket goes Up Up Up You go Up Up Up. Soon you will reach the moon and then this is what you will do. You will take a ride in a moon car, you will climb a moon mountain, you will live in a moon house. But first put on your space suit. Without it you can not live in the hot hot days. You can not live in the cold cold nights. You can not breathe the grey grey dust. So put on your space suit. Climb a moon mountain. Ride a moon car. Live in a moon house. Be a rocket man.

Miss Bankhead's Invitation to Dinner
Emily Haworth-Booth

I had seduced everyone from here to Times Square
and further. Well, everyone except for her.

So I prepared dinner for two, raw fish and candlelight.
I told her directions, I told her Tuesday night.

If Oppenheim was the Garbo of Montparnasse, then what was she?
Late. I expected her for two hours, gave up at three.

Then after ten, a chinese girl's shown in. Red lips, black wig.
I look at her out of the corner of my eye. Like this.

Miss Garbo could no come but send me, Miss.
So we sit down. I watch her silver fingers mince the fish.

Then she bends over the oysters towards me.
The seams of my stockings. The edge of my seat.

And when it's over it's her own voice that says
(like butter) *Pleased to have met you Miss.*

When You Break It
Robert McGill

The afternoon that I heard the news I went to my mother's house, the house of my boyhood, the house of balances. No one answered my knocking, but the door was open so I went in. I found her in the living room, small and quiet in the closing light of the sun. She had it out again, had laid it in the middle of the floor and spread it as best she could across the worn green carpet until its edges touched each wall of the room. But still much of its area was folded and wrinkled and overlapping so that it seemed impossibly huge, as though it had billowed from a chasm in the floor and flowed over slippers, stacks of magazines, furniture, threatening to engulf the entire house. She lay at its centre, her head resting on a bunch in the fabric, her breath softly buzzing as she slept.

· · · · ·

My father begins his dying in a transport plane above Brussels in 1944. It is a nasty, vibrating old beast, the giant metal belly full of nervous young paratroopers, many of whom are swearing even before they cross the Channel that an engine must have been hit, the machine labours and lists so badly. Half of them fall over when they try to stand. They move towards the open door in single file, wide-eyed, hesitant, taking the steps of children barefoot on a shingle beach. You could not possibly convince them at this moment that the plane will return safely to England and half of them will be dead when they hit the earth. My father is eighteen.

Many of them have scrambled to be the first out, motivated by a hybrid of impatient anguish and hunger for honour. My father is among them. He has jumped before, from a two-seater into Grey County pastures dotted with stone piles, even hounded the pilot to let him try just once with a hunting rifle in his hands. The pilot was a good friend but refused to allow it. In this meagre experience my father is at an advantage over his fellows, none of them more than twenty-one and all enlisted in the last two months. (Each has a different story to explain his lateness in coming to this war. Some are just now old enough to pass for eighteen. Some had a duty to the business, or the farm, or the church. No story mentions taunting and shame. No one, it seems, was afraid.) There were two weeks of combat training at Val Cartier, horrible not for the physical rigour but because their instructor's broken English was virtually incomprehensible to this group of boys from places like Elora and Tiverton, and then a day of instruction in jumping at Bournemouth, on the ground. Which of them

238

can remember all of it now? Beneath the roar of the propellers they are each murmuring: Jump clear. Count three. Pull the chord.

It is my father's turn. He steps ahead and catches the toe of his boot on the coaming of the door. He falls forward, hands reaching for the plane, missing. Towards the spinning earth he plummets, head-first, limbs flailing. The careful litany of procedure is gone, replaced by the howling of the air in his ears, the shocking helplessness in this wide, empty sky. He is completely upside down when he feels something go by him on his left, and he realizes he has rocketed past Sterling, the man who jumped before him, perhaps even by Hughes, the first soldier out, who is now drifting safely downward. When he manages to find the cord, he pulls so hard that his mind outpaces the mechanism and tells him he has broken it. Then comes the jolt as the pack vomits out its silk parcel and latches on to air. He is floating. He is alive.

There is little sky left to fall through, and he is already rolling up his parachute when he hears the first gunshots. He looks up, and the air above him is blossoming with paratroopers, but there is a rigidity in their bodies unexplained even by their inexperience. They are being fired upon. This was unexpected. Hughes lands heavily a hundred metres away and does not move. Fitzpatrick is clutching a thigh and cries out when he hits the ground. My father looks about frantically and sees the flash of the discharges from a nearby wood. He does what he must do. He falls to the ground with the parachute in his hands and waits, lays his head in the mud and watches the endless bodies fall beside him. And someone is talking, whispering all the while to him that if he had fallen more slowly he would be crying out, too.

Three nights later after dinner he finds himself urinating every ten minutes. He begins to feel horribly ill. The next day he is out of the war and in the hospital. One of the nurses tells him the fighting is practically over, anyway. He isn't missing much.

· · · · ·

There is to be no medal for my father, no ceremony, only an honourable discharge because he does not have a body suitable for soldiering. They send him back overseas to Toronto for tests.

"We find sometimes that an intense period of stress can be the catalyst for the onset of the disease, they say. But it was going to happen sooner or later. It's hereditary. Anybody with it in your family?"

"One grandfather," he replies.

"Well, it's not so bad," they tell him. "You just take your shots and eat right and everything else will be fine. You won't be missing out on much."

My mother takes a train from Owen Sound, stays the night at a cousin's house before going to him the next day at the hospital. She is not yet my mother, not anybody's mother, and at sixteen cannot yet possibly imagine herself as one. She has been to the city only once before, a childhood trip to the National Exhibition. At the reception desk she feels dozens of eyes upon her.

Her hands fidget, turning over and over as though shaking an egg-timer.

"Are you the wife?" each person asks as she follows the chain of secretaries and nurses.

"No," she says hesitantly. "Not the wife. But soon." They nod, understanding when five years ago the hesitation would have troubled them, perhaps understanding in a way that she herself does not. A doctor leads her down a hallway, covertly watching her face, her stride, assessing how she will handle it, not the weight of the news, but the long drain of the after. He takes her to a room with an empty examining table and two metal chairs. Then he begins to explain.

He tells her it is a problem of regulation. Insulin takes sugar from the blood and puts it in the muscles. No insulin means the sugar stays in the blood, makes you tired, makes you have to go to the toilet all the time. And, of course, there are complications later on. So you cut down on sugary foods, give him insulin injections to balance things. But too much insulin makes him shaky, makes him a bit queer, like he's drunk. So then you give him sugar.

She quickly learns which foods are safe and which ones aren't. Then comes the careful matter of determining which of the permissible ones he will actually eat. He has always been finicky. The list of foods that he both can and will consume is insufferably short. Tuna salad and green beans become staples. She spends hours flipping through recipe books, consulting with his mother as to what he might like. In the months ahead she will watch as he pushes plate after plate away. Once, he takes a pot of casserole she spent an afternoon preparing and scrapes it mercilessly into the trash. She will plead with him not to buy ice cream cones downtown, not to drink with the other men. When he finally takes over the dime store from his father and begins his relentless work there, avoiding his meals and his new bride, she is almost grateful.

• • • • •

On her wedding day my mother wears a dress made of my father's parachute. Her own mother has made the alterations. Parts that had to be cut away have been saved and changed into sashes and puffs for the sleeves. The cord has been salvaged and transformed into a lace trim. My grandmother has chosen not to make a train, but rather has left the marvellous circular shape intact, so that my mother occupies the centre of her dress like the pistil of a flower. The effect is so spectacular that no one comments upon the white of the silk even with the rushed engagement, nor even when Will is born seven months later. When I am young my mother occasionally presents her wedding album and shows us the photographs of her in it. Will grunts his disinterest when she opens it, but sits down as he is told. The front page has a splendid eight-by-ten of her with my father at her side, discreetly bunching the dress in his left hand so that he can stand near her. Gene and Ruth, October 12, 1945, it says below. But the one that always fascinates me is the one on the opposite page, a wallet-sized photograph of my mother by herself. It is dwarfed by the other photographs in the album, clearly an oddity that no one wished to dupli-cate yet no one bothered to discard. The picture is overexposed so the dress blends with the background and my mother's features come drifting starkly out of whiteness. It is the one picture in which she is not smiling.

Sometimes at school our class goes into the gymnasium and plays with a multi-coloured parachute. We hold it by the edges and shake it about and send balls popping across the surface, or throw it flying up and then pull it down around us, creating our own serene, slowly collapsing dome. I can almost see my mother fitting neatly at the centre of the parachute, magically suspended above us, only her legs dangling in view. And somewhere below us my father, plummeting towards a bomb-battered field in Belgium, praying that he will make it home to his new fiancée.

· · · · ·

Housed within the early memory of my father's dime store are the large glass jars, dozens of them, each brimming and beckoning with its particular confection. There are licorice sticks, gobstoppers, cinnamon hearts, *Tootsie rolls.* Some days when our mother takes us shopping downtown we all go in, and if he is in a good mood he gives us each a brown paper bag from behind the counter and sends us to fill it. Choose them carefully, he tells us sternly. They're for the children of my most important customer. Will and I run to the bins with delight, Will's eagerness exposing the child within the body that is almost a man's. We agonize over each bag-bulging choice, not needing to see the wink at our mother to know that we are filling the bags for ourselves. When we finish, my father weighs them on the scale behind the counter to make sure one is not heavier than the other. Will always makes a terrible fuss over this part of the ritual. I'm bigger, he complains. I need more. But the protest is just as much pretence as my father's severity, for Will's bag is always found to be the lighter of the two, and my father invariably reaches for some caramels or a package of candy cigarettes to compensate.

When this practice eventually stops, I am old enough to consider that it has perhaps grown too painful for my father to watch his children enraptured by that pleasure which he denies himself; painful not because he craves the expe-rience or would even enjoy it, but simply because the prohibition is inexorable, almost external. There are years when I am able to take this thought and the sight of him in his wheelchair and push myself to live on his behalf, to run and fight and gorge. Yet later still, when the memories are more distant, they become clearer and I realize that those moments in the store gave him a satis-faction greater than our own, for his strength was consumed by the business and the disease, and he was left with no resolve to deny us anything. It was, I am now sure, our mother who must have put an end to those times at the store, only she who could have properly weighed the temporary bliss at the candy counter against spoiled dinners and screaming trips to the dentist's.

· · · · ·

For years my father gives his complete devotion to that store, rising before dawn and working until long after closing time each night. Sometimes he will take his shot but neglect to eat afterwards. When this happens he begins to act strangely. The customers assume he's been drinking. If my mother is there he gains a frightening half-smile whenever she speaks to him. He talks more loudly, acts like a child. It is exhausting at home, humiliating and nearly impossible in public when she reddens at the stares of passers-by and he simply puts on a show as she coaxes him to sit down and eat some chocolate, have a glucose tablet. Her quiet, ingratiating voice enrages him.

"Who do you think you are?" he shouts at her. She learns that she has to be firm, order him. "Gene: Take This Now." Only then does he obey.

"There's nothing wrong with me," my father often declares as he paces around the kitchen frantically or begins to stray across the dividing line on the highway. "You're crazy," he says. Sometimes he is so insistent that she begins to believe him, begins to wonder if she is just imagining his imbalance, if perhaps this is how all husbands are. She starts to insist that Will stay at home with her when our father is there.

The doctors are of no help. Specialists can't tell her anything. Emergency wards don't know how to deal with him. Once, waiting outside yet another examining room, she is met by the attending physician, who tells her that her husband is perfectly fine. They open the door and there is Gene, jumping up and down on his bed.

"Whoopee," he is saying. "Whoopee."

As an adult, my brother will tell me that he remembers my father's 'episodes.' He will tell me the story of one night when I am not even a year old. My father is unbalanced again, singing loudly in the kitchen.

"He dances overhead on the ceiling near my bed, in my sight, through the night." My mother has me in my nursery, holding me, singing 'Rock A Bye Baby,' a strange counter-melody to my father's crooning.

"I try to hide in vain, underneath my counterpane; there's my love, up above…" And my voice, on top of them both, wailing.

I stood there in the hallway between the two rooms, my brother will tell me. I didn't know which one of you I was supposed to save.

But if Will is the child who came too early, I am the one who came too late. I have only a fragmentary recollection of such incidents. My strongest memories are of the man in the wheelchair, quiet and balanced but ill and failing.

• • • • •

My father is nominally the disciplinarian of the family, but I come to understand very early that it is my mother who makes the rules. She is strict and unfaltering in her punishments. Occasionally we will appeal to our father, but his deference to our mother on such issues inevitably overrides his empathy, and his sad smile saps our resistance. They are a hard, irresistible combination. Neither of us are difficult children, but then, neither of us is

242

given any chance to be. Will begins working at the store by the time he is eleven. Even then there is an unspoken understanding that he is entering an apprenticeship.

I am more my mother's child. I was born in December so she keeps me home from school an extra year. She teaches me to read herself. There is a small poster on the front of the refrigerator that she has taken from a Good Housekeeping and uses to drill me.

HOUSE RULES
• If you open it, close it.
• If you borrow it, return it.
• If you value it, take care of it.
• If you make a mess, clean it up.
• If you take it, put it back.
• If you turn it on, turn it off.
• If you break it, fix it.
• If it belongs to someone else, get permission before using it.
• If it's none of your business, don't ask questions.
• If it will tarnish someone's reputation, keep it to yourself.

The longer words in the last few are difficult for me. In order to satisfy her I end up repeating them from memory rather than reading them. She doesn't seem to notice.

At this age I am fascinated by my father's stories of the war. He tells us that the greatest day of his life was the day he wore that parachute. To the young me this sounds like heroism. As an adult I will come to realize that it is a dare. He is daring my mother. But she never gives in to that goading, needful temptation. She never makes the mimicking reply that he wants of her. She may even believe that the words for which he is hoping would be true. Perhaps it is simply because she knows he is trying to force her hand that she refuses to acquiesce. The greatest day of her own life, insists her silence, is still to be determined.

· · · · ·

"You could get it, too," she sometimes says when my father has gone to bed and Will is still storming around the kitchen, ravaged by that thing to which she has seemingly become inured. She says: "It runs in families, you know. You could get it, too." She never says this to me, only to him, as though it were some kind of consolation, some manner of excuse for the temper and the recklessness. She must know how it goads him: to threaten her own son with a disease, and an inherited one, at that. She says it with such a tone of well-meaning that he can only acknowledge its truth. But when we find ourselves alone he seethes.

"I will never get it. I swear. Never."

"Anyone can get it," I say once. "How would you stop it?" I ask this question to show him he is wrong, proud of my own crude medical understanding, but also because I believe at some level that Will can stop it, that Will can do anything.

"I don't know," he says. But I won't. I just won't.

. . . . .

One day my mother takes me to the store to visit my father and Will. The sound of breaking glass greets us. My father is behind the candy counter, staring down vacantly at the epicentre of a pile of jelly beans and shards of the jar that held them.

"Oh dear," he says. Then he picks up another one. He drops it, too. Will comes rushing up from the back of the store.

"What's wrong?" he asks. He looks at my mother, whose hand grips mine like a vice. It connects me to the circuit of their silent anxiety.

"Nothing's wrong. These jars are worthless. Look how easily they break."

"You need to get some food," says Will cautiously. The customer he was waiting on has followed him to the front of the store.

"Baloney," says my father. Baloney". He never uses that word except when he is not well. He reaches for another glass jar.

My father is not a violent man, nor is he even a strong man, for even now the disease has begun to weaken him, draw the skin tight against the cheek bones and whittle the already-slender arms. Will is thin and gawky, but at fifteen he is already three inches taller and burgeoning with the energy of his age. Will grabs my father by the waist and carries him out of the store, my father screaming in outrage all the way. My mother follows, and she takes over once they are outside. Will comes back in, shaking, his face and arms flushed, and goes to the cash register. He tries to placate the shaken customer with a gritting smile as he makes change, but she receives her money without a word and leaves quickly.

"We'll be lucky to see her again," he says to me. His grin falters when he looks down and sees my red eyes, the fear in them. He tousles my hair, says there's no point in crying. I am six years old and he is teaching me. Make a decision, act. Be strong. Don't get maudlin. Mind the business. But he doesn't come home that night. The next morning my father is back at the store when Will comes in. My father sees him walking down the aisle and smiles cheerfully.

"Well, good morning!" he says. It's about time you got here. Will begins to stumble out an apology, but he stops when he scrutinizes the untroubled face and realizes: Gene has no memory of the incident. Later we will find out that he remembers it only when he is unbalanced. Will has to look the man in the face with the sole burden of this memory for another eight years until his father dies.

. . . . .

244

I woke my mother gently from her slumber. She opened her eyes, confused for a moment, but then the texture of it on her face, the soft whiteness of it spreading over the room reminded her and she became immediately sullen. She pulled back when I tried to help her to her feet, turned her back as if to shield something from me.

"Mom," I said softly. "Ruth."

"I can't cut it," she said after a time. "I'm too weak."

"I don't know what you mean."

"Please," she said. She turned, extended her hand to me. In it was a pair of scissors. I took them in one hand, then took an edge of it in my other, looking at my mother's face all the time, which was not looking back but was focused on the movement of my fingers. I slowly squeezed the blades until they met the resistance of the hem. Then I felt the scissors shear through the silk, and my mother screeched. I stopped. She brought her withered hands to her face.

"All right," I said. "All right."

I took her to the kitchen and put the kettle on to boil. I sat beside her and there was silence in that house until steam began to whistle from the spout. I didn't know what to say. I was so used to calling home and telling her that I'd won something. Hey Mom, they gave me more research funding. Hey Mom, I won that tennis tournament. What was I supposed to tell her now? Hey Mom. Guess what I won this time.

"Mom, I have something to tell you." Her face fell. I was being so careful, but her face told me that she was already guessing, that she had been waiting for this moment, dreading its arrival.

"It's Will, isn't it?"

"No," I said. "It's not Will. It's me."

We drank tea, hot and plain as had always been the family custom, and she began to speak. She told me she didn't want to frighten me. She said she knew that things were different now, that there were wonderful new treatments. I put out my hand, and as she began to tell me about my father she took it, examined it like a seer. Her palms were rough and wrinkled, but my fingertips were pulsing and I was sure that even she could feel them, awash as they were in caffeine and the morning's injection, foreign and electric in the blood, its new ritual mingling with the energy of memory. I clenched my tea cup in its precarious space between table and floor and looked over my mother's shoulder to where the parachute clothed the living room. It lay there like a drop-cloth ready for spills, anticipating renovation, demanding to be put away.

For Compatriots Who Want To Ride Whales

Robert McGill

It's all about the trick of learning how
to fasten on, for whales will fool you when
they can: at first impassive, dawdling, now

accelerating for the surface, then
the breach that leaves you frozen in the air
before they fall like submarines again

and when you follow them, they're waiting there
with mouths that yawn, articulate and wide,
the belly stretching underneath the stare

to take what gravity and chance provide.
Or diving deep, the ears explode and eyes
compress, your elbows digging at her side,

and maddened by the pressure of your thighs
she eagle-shrieks at frequencies above
our frail capacity. At last, she flies

along the bedrock of the sea, a shove
that scrapes your acne on the stone. So sure
her motion that you fear a whale's love,

her ambiguity in movement, her
desires, her needs, expressed according to
the rules that whales create when whales confer.

Perhaps a whale must rid itself of you
to love you, if it can. More whales have died
for love, we hope, than we can count. So too

will more before these mysteries subide.
We should be careful of the whales we ride.

Notes on Authors

Stephen Burt

Stephen Burt's book of poems, *Popular Music*, appeared in the USA in 1999, where it won the Colorado Prize. His poems have been seen on occasion in *Boston Review, Jacket, Metre, Paris Review, PN Review*, and *Poetry Review*; he writes about poets and poetry every so often for the *London Review of Books*, the *TLS*, and *Thumbscrew*, among other journals. He teaches at Macalester College in St Paul, Minnesota, USA.

Helen Cleary

Helen Cleary lives in Sloley, Norfolk, where she is writing her second novel – when she is not working for the BBC History website. She did the UEA creative writing MA and has written screenplays for film makers and animators. She is represented by Simon Trewin at PFD.

Olivia Cole

Olivia Cole is a second year reading English at Christ Church, Oxford.

Stephanie Cross

Stephanie Cross is a third-year English student at Emmanuel College, Cambridge. She would like to write a novel, but would prefer to write several.

Jennifer Donnelly

Jennifer Donnelly is a second-year English student at Newnham College, Cambridge. As well as her own writing projects, she co-runs *Alarum* an on-line writers' group. She was born in Lancashire and can't wait to return home.

Amy Flanders

Amy Flanders grew up in California and attended UC Berkeley. She is now working on her DPhil in Modern History at Oxford. She has only recently returned to writing poetry, but hopes to tear herself away from her thesis long enough to write some more.

Hannah Forbes Black

Hannah Forbes Black is only incidentally a 20-year-old English student. She means well.

Sean Forester

Sean Forester is from the San Francisco Bay Area. He has attended The Great Books Program at St John's College, USA, and is reading English at Cambridge on a Rotary Scholarship. His interest in images has also led him to painting which he studies at Cecil Studios, Florence, and the Atelier.

Stephanie Frank

When she is not running, cooking, or writing, Stephanie Frank pursues a degree in Philosophical Theology at Oxford. During her first expatriate year, she contributed to the *May Anthologies* 2000. She also enjoys travelling and everyday poignancies along the way.

Robin French

Robin French graduated in 2001, having spent a good deal of his time writing and performing for the Cambridge Footlights. He now lives in London, earning money as a script reader and a sitcom writer.

Nick Gill

Nick Gill eats almost nothing most of the time, but lives on a diet of sunlight and nectar. His heart died quite recently, and the merest illusion of his life is maintained by smoke and mirrors. He is quite tall.

Susan Gordon

S C Gordon was born in the north west of England in 1981. A Medieval English student at St Anne's, Oxford, she has written poetry for most of her life. Major influences include T S Eliot, Bernard O'Donoghue, Larkin and Garcia Lorca.

Kelly Grovier

Kelly Grovier is a postgraduate student in English at Christ Church, Oxford, and is currently writing a doctoral thesis on William Wordsworth and Samuel Taylor Coleridge.

Arnie Guha

A former Cambridge Nehru Scholar at Pembroke College, Arnab Guha now lives in Toronto where he seeks to counterbalance his day job as a management consultant by working on a long poem on Canada, drawing inspiration and strength from his wife, Zoe, his constant, Canadian muse.

Irene Hahn

Irene Hahn is an MPhil candidate in American Literature at Clare Hall, Cambridge. Originally from Conneticu, she received her BA in English and Social Anthropology from Harvard University in 2000, where she won the Edward Eager Memorial Prize for Creative Writing.

Tim Hancock

Tim Hancock was writing poems in Cambridge between 1992 and 1996, when he should have been writing a PhD. Sadly, creativity now takes second place to criticism: presently Lecturer in English at the University of Ulster.

Emily Haworth-Booth

Emily Haworth-Booth won the Young National Poetry Competition in 1998, then studied for a year at Chelsea College of Art before starting an English degree at Clare College, Cambridge.

Nicki Heinen

Nicki Heinen was born in Germany in 1977 and moved to England six years later. She is in her third year studying English at Girton College, Cambridge, and plans to work in the theatre when she graduates.

Stephen Henighan

Stephen Henighan (DPhil, 1996) teaches Spanish American literature at the University of Guelph, Ontario. Since leaving Oxford he has published: *The Places Where Names Vanish* (1998; novel), *North of Tourism* (1999; short stories), *Assuming the light* (1999; criticism), and *When Words Deny the World* (2002; criticism).

Yuriy Humber

Yuriy Humber is a finalist at Sidney Sussex College, Cambridge. Alongside family and friends he'd especially like to thank Tim Neave for intriguing him into poetry and all his help and criticism since. May we continue.

Laura James

Laura James is currently studying for an MPhil in International Relations at Magdalen College, Oxford. She was brought up in Kenya, and has since travelled widely in the vain hope of regaining some of that early glamour. Her hobby is the translation of Latin poetry. Nobody knows why.

Greg Kimura

Greg Kimura is a PhD student in Philosophy of Religion at Peterhouse, University of Cambridge. He is from Anchorage, Alaska. His short story *Moving Company* was published in last year's *May Anthologies*.

Jeff Kochan

Jeff Kochan is from Edmonton, Canada, an oil and gas city with the world's highest density of steelworkers cum sculptors. He is at Cambridge writing a PhD on the poetics off tool use.

Laura Kolb

Originally from Virginia, Laura currently reads English at Newnham College. At the moment, she is particularly interested in ideas of make-believe and the impact of drama and film on real-world individuals.

Nick Laird

Nick Laird: born 1975, Cookstown, County Tyrone; Cambridge University, First in English Literature, University Quiller-Couch Award for Creative Writing; regular *TLS* reviewer of fiction and poetry for the *TLS*; two poems in New Writing 11; runner-up in *TLS*/Blackwells Poetry Competition 2002; Commercial Litigator at magic circle law firm.

Hannah Langworth

Hannah Langworth is in her final year of an undergraduate English degree at University College, Oxford.

Josie Long

Josie Long is 20 years old. She is a second-year English student at Lady Margaret Hall, Oxford. This is the second story she has ever written. The other was much better. It had a horse in.

Robert McGill

Robert McGill was born in Wiarton, Ontario and moved to England in 1999. He is currently in the Creative Writing MA programme at the University of East Anglia.

Seamus Perry

Seamus Perry is Reader in English Literature at the University of Glasgow. He is the author of a study of Samuel Taylor Coleridge, and an editor of the journal *Essays in Criticism.*

Jane Rosenzweig

Since graduating from Oxford in 1993, Jane Rosenzweig has studied writing at the University of Iowa Writers' Workshop and worked as a magazine editor and television critic. Her fiction and non-fiction has appeared in a number of American periodicals. She currently teaches writing at Harvard and is at work on a novel.

Phil Shaw

Phil Shaw currently studies at Keble College, Oxford.

Christopher Simons

Christopher Simons is a DPhil candidate studying Roantic Poetry at Lincoln College, Oxford. He was born in Winnipeg, Canada, and received degrees from Harvard and the University of Toronto. His work is influenced by languages, travel, and the sciences.

Zadie Smith

Zadie Smith was born in north-west London in 1975, and continues to live in the area. *The Autograph Man* is her second novel. Her first book *White Teeth* was the winner of The Whitbread First Novel Award, The James Tait Black Memorial Prize for Fiction, and The Commonwealth Writers' First Book Award.

Nicholas Sparks

Nicholas Sparks left Oxford for London in 1995 and is still based there, and intermittently, New York and Amsterdam. After a period immersed in the British Art scene his current interests include Nordic American writing, Ancient Near-Eastern literature and food texts.

Matthew Sperling

Matthew Sperling (Ger, n.m., 'sparrow') was born in 1982 in Canterbury, and studies English at Keble College, Oxford. He won the Lord Alfred Douglas prize, 2001, and spent the money drinking his way round Eastern Europe. Peter is his imaginary friend.

Ben Teasdale

After graduating, Ben took an MA in Creative Writing at UEA, worked as a script editor and has just written a ten-part drama for BBC Television. He still intends to write his apocalypse-inducing first novel; maybe in English this time

Dave Thorley

What Dave Thorley lacks in stature, he compensates in hair. In 1979, his hum-drum existence began, going interrupted until 1999, when he was runner-up in the Bridport (poetry) Prize. Since, he has been recovering from the side effects of his rich poetic nature.

J M Tyree

J M Tyree currently lives in New York City, where he works as a freelance writer. He recently completed writing his first novel.

Meg Vandermerwe

Meg Vandermerwe was born in 1978. She read English at St Hilda's College Oxford, and is a graduate of the University of East Anglia's Creative Writing MA. She is currently working on her first novel, *book of light*, a Jewish epic told in four voices.

Skye Wheeler

Skye Wheeler is a third-year Philosophy student at New Hall College, Cambridge. She is essentially nomadic and hopes to remain so.

Kit Whitfield

Kit Whitfield read English at Christ's College, Cambridge from 1996–1999, during which time she appeared in three *May Anthologies* and won the T R Henn Prize for Original Composition. After graduating, she took an MA in Creative Writing at the University of East Anglia. She is currently completing a novel and working as a freelance editor.